Beautiful Norway

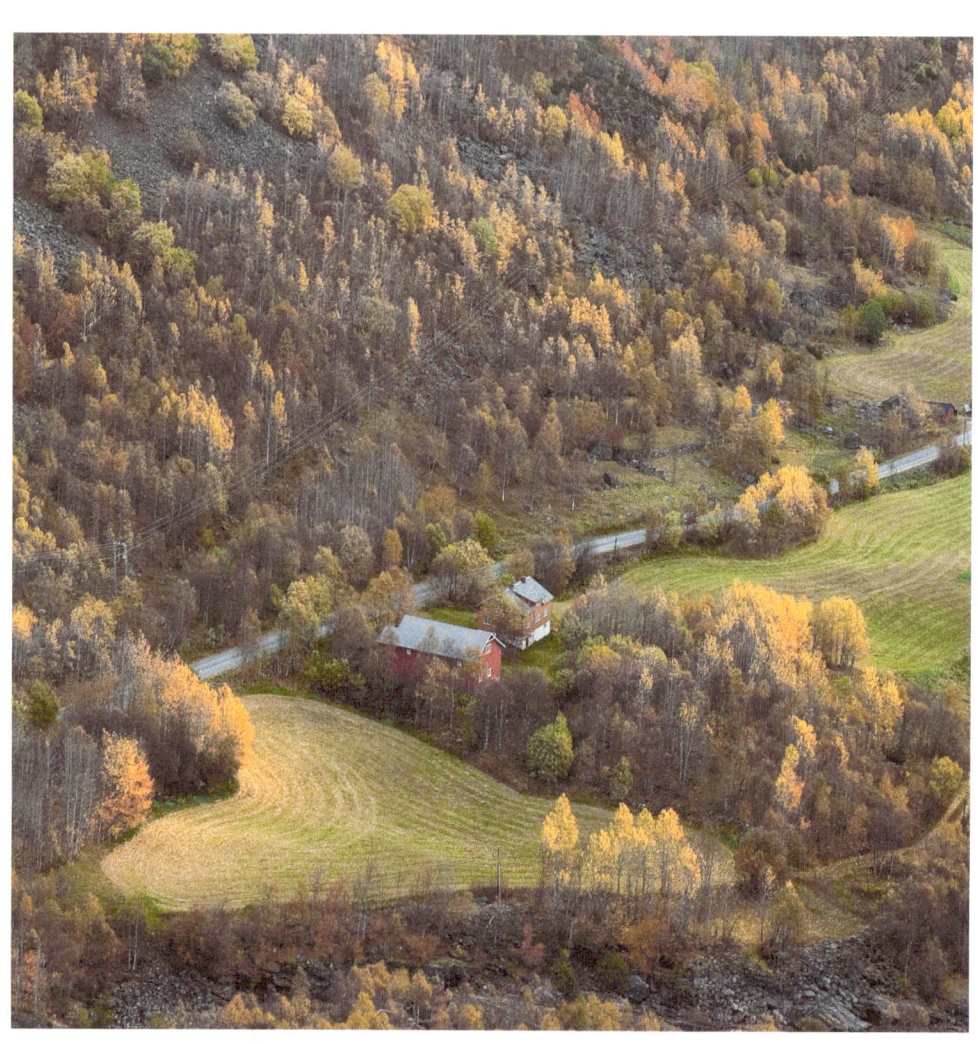

Beautiful Norway

photographs by David Lacina

Copyright (C) 2014 David Lacina
photo.lacina.net

All rights reserved.

No part of this publication may be reproduced in any manner in any
media, or transmitted by any means whatsoever, electronic or mechanical
(including photocopy, film or video recording, Internet posting, or any
other information storage and retrieval system), without the prior written
permission of the publisher.

First edition, 2014

Printed by CreateSpace

All photographs from this book are available as fine art prints. For more
information, please visit http://photo.lacina.net

ISBN: 978-82-999572-0-5

Introduction

So, there I stood at my final destination after almost a whole day travelling by bus. I looked around me, noticing the sky had cleared up and sun was now lighting up the surrounding streets. It was early March 2000 and I had just arrived from my native Czech Republic to a country as yet unknown to me. I wasn't sure what to expect, but I was full of curiosity.

Before travelling to this Scandinavian country, only one thing was certain: I was going to spend a year as an IT exchange student in a city called Sandefjord, some 120km south west of Oslo. What I did not know at that time was, even though I'd been told the locals were cold and difficult to get to know, I would, in fact, meet some of the kindest and most friendly people of my life. I didn't expect a year to turn into thirteen wonderful years spent trekking the unbelievable Norwegian mountains, sailing the fjords of North Sea and visiting remote places untouched by humans. In this book, I take you on a long journey, a journey that started that very day, when I, feeling somewhat lonely, first set my foot on Norwegian soil. To some, the loneliness might sound negative; for me, it was salvation. As I had plenty of time on my own, I decided to buy my first camera. The idea behind this was simple; I wanted to send home some photos of this new place. I bought a used fully manual SLR camera and my first roll of colour film. The camera became my new companion on my frequent trips out in nature. I haven't left home without my photo bag since then and my trips took on a new meaning. I am now trying to share both the beautiful scenery I saw and the feelings I experienced. I will let you judge how successful I was. The photo journey will take you all over Norway: from the South with its characteristic farmscapes, through central Norway where you find the country's highest mountains and to the North, beyond the polar circle, where you find the Lofoten archipelago with its incredible jagged mountains unlike any other part of Norway. I also take you to the famous Norwegian fjords and together we will discover some islands accessible only by private boat. Over the last years I've visited most of these places several times to capture the different moods of the spot. Many of the photographed places are remote and far from tourist crowds; I hope you will enjoy them as I did.

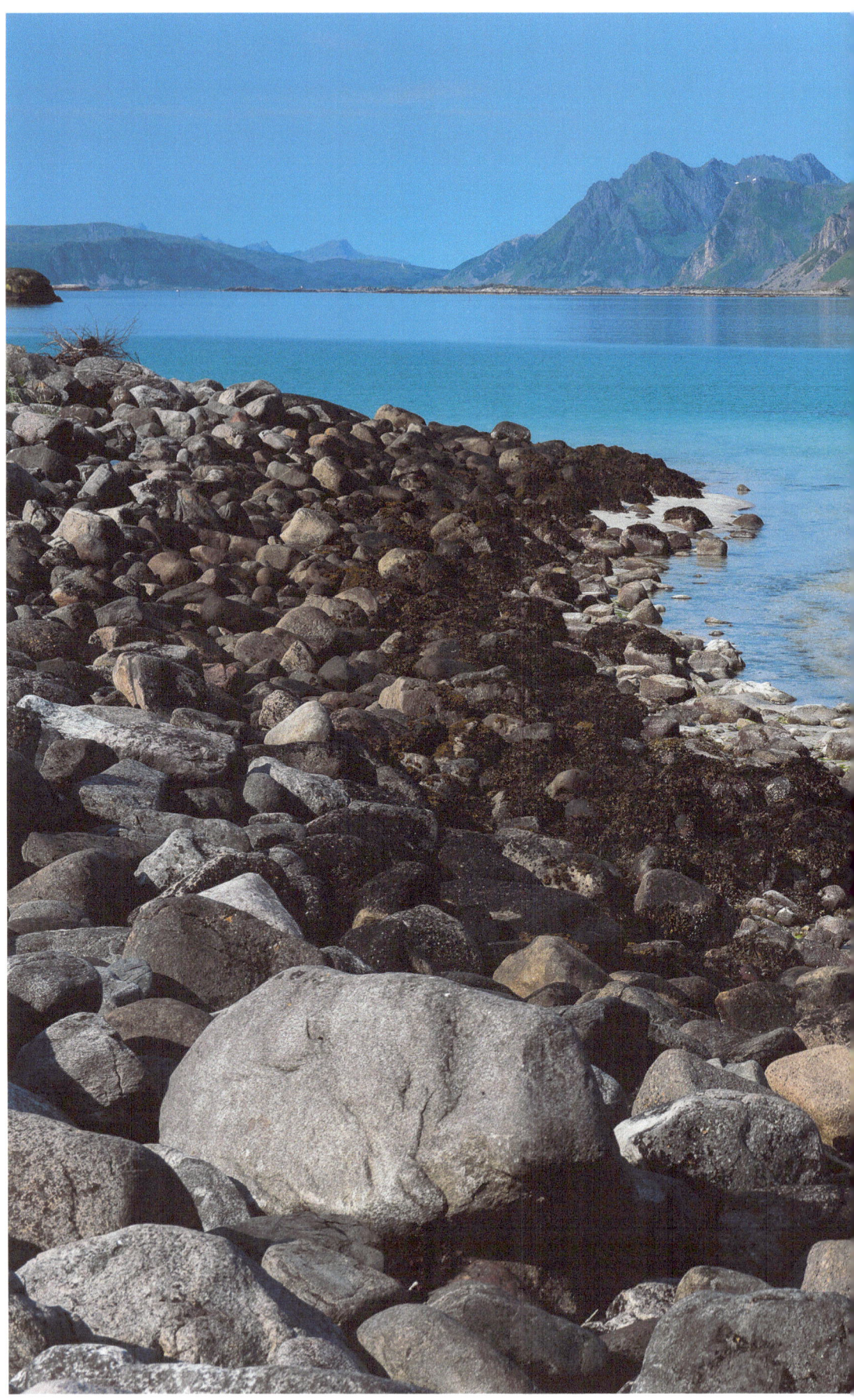

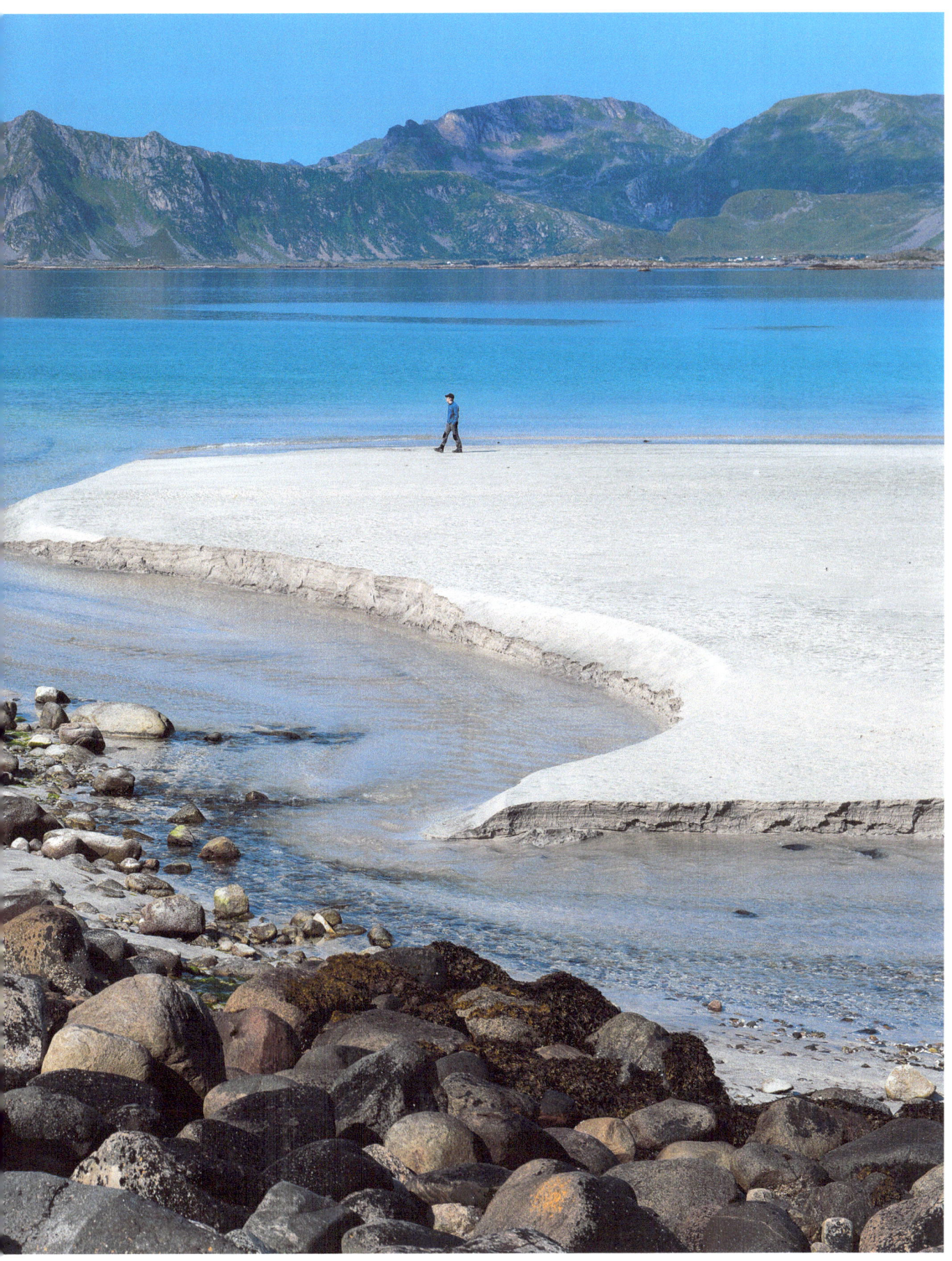

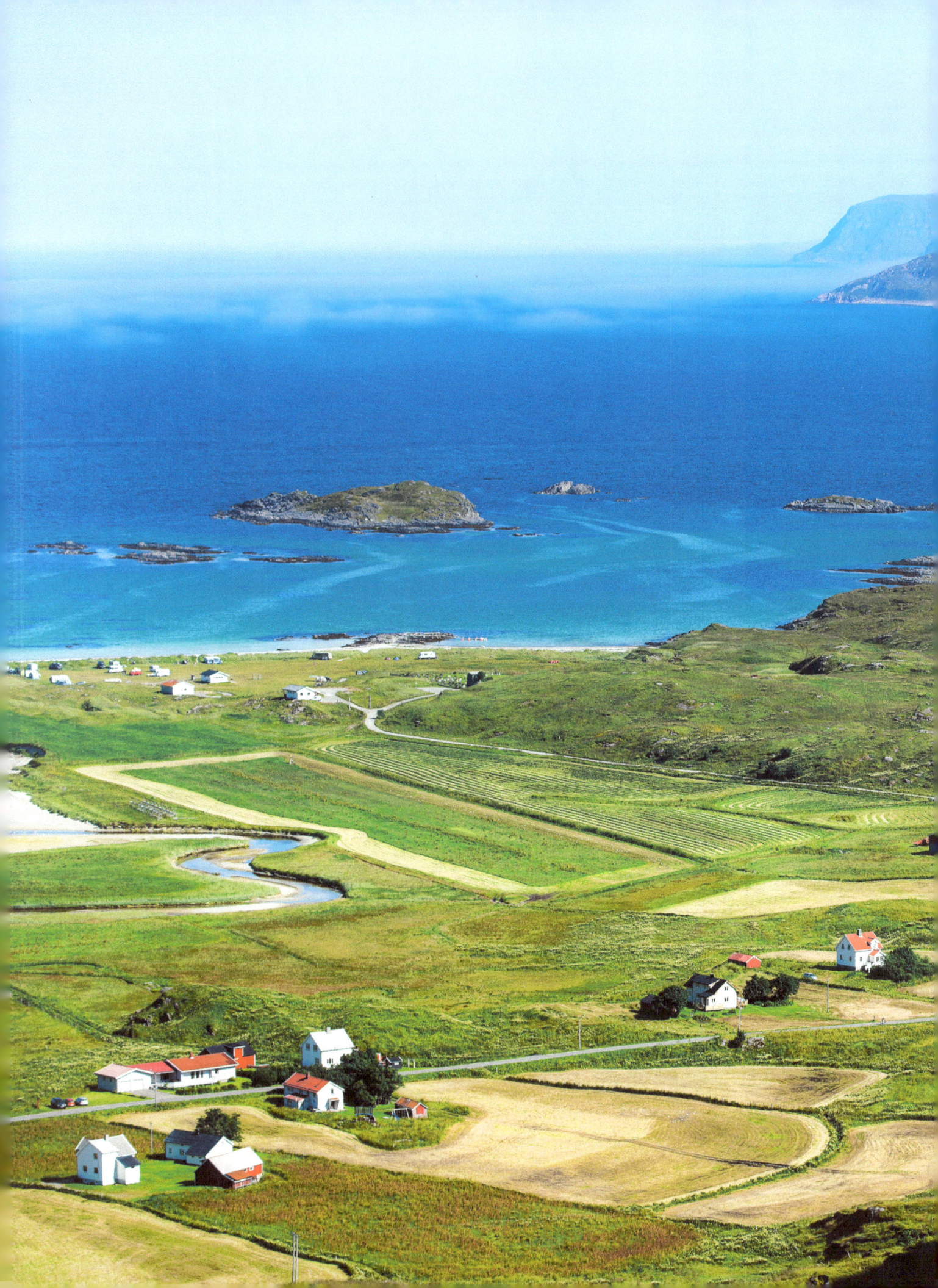

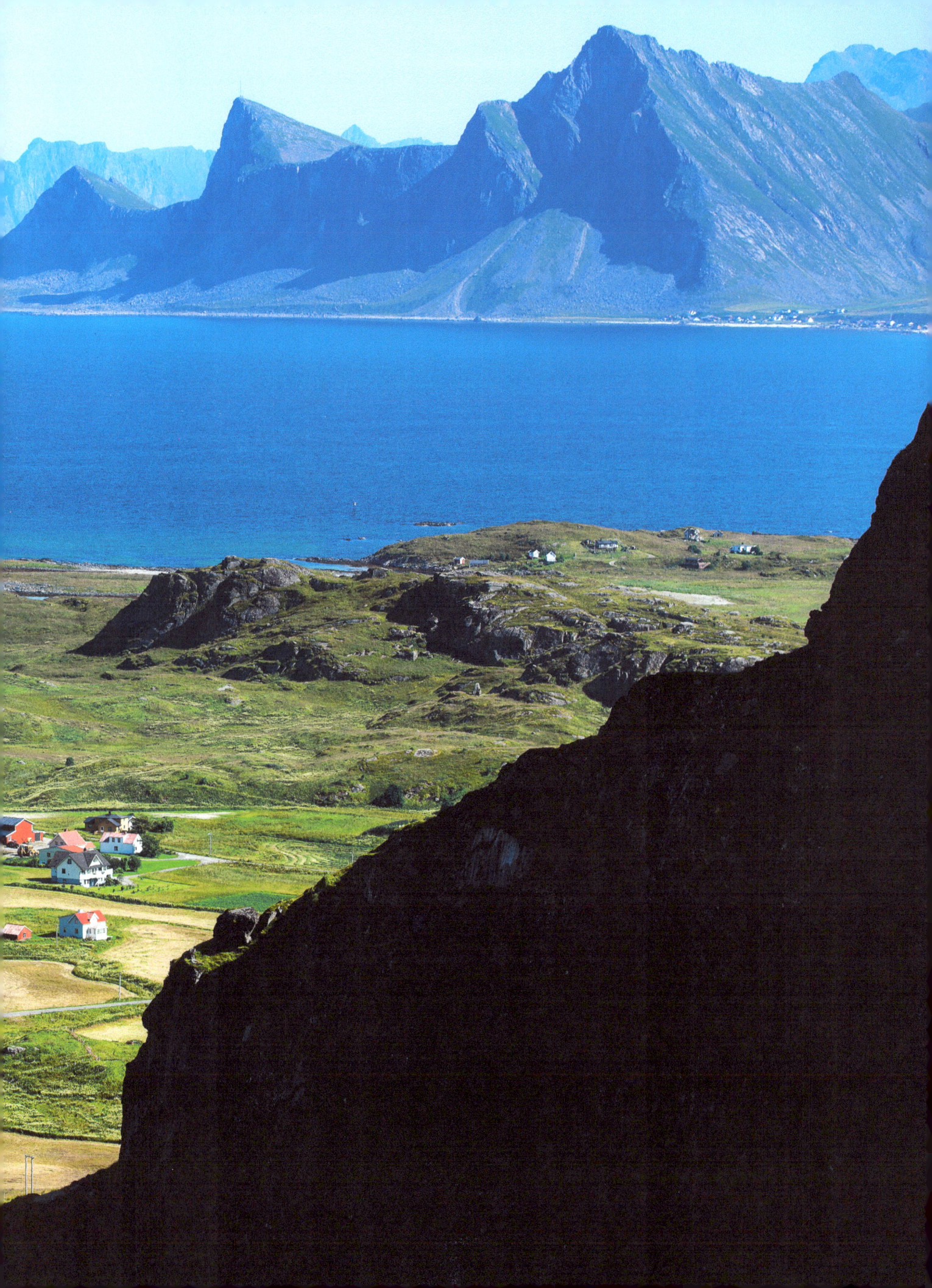

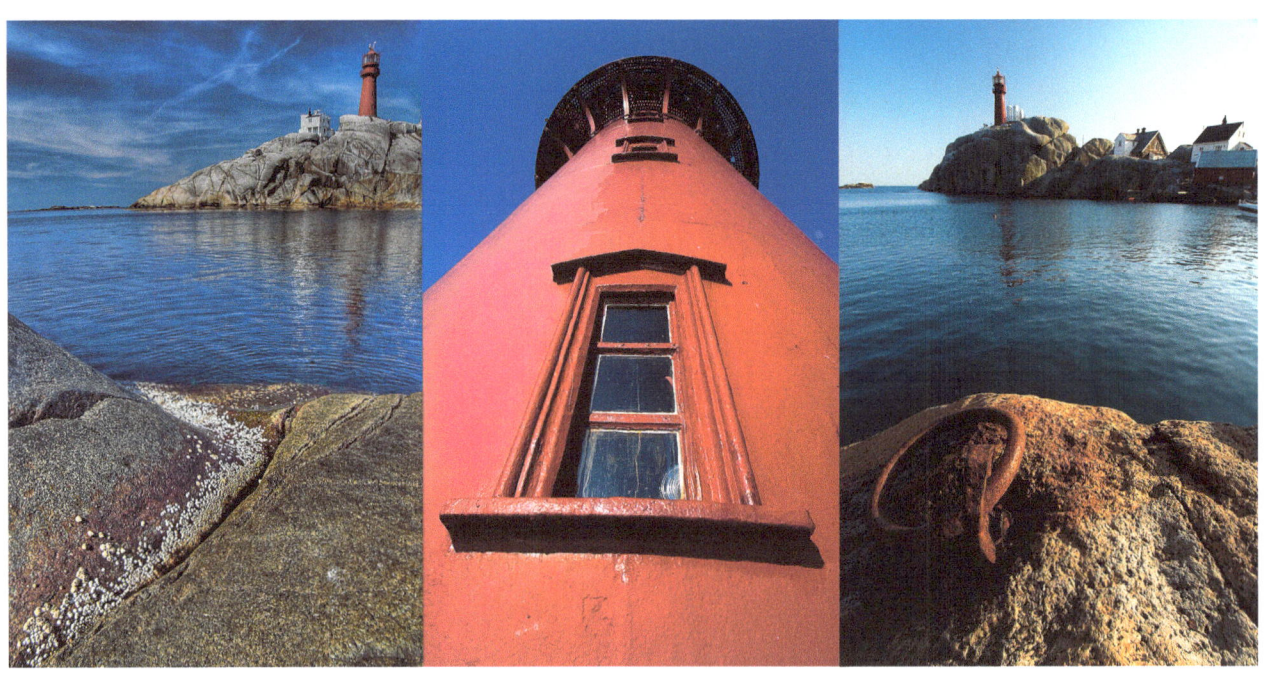

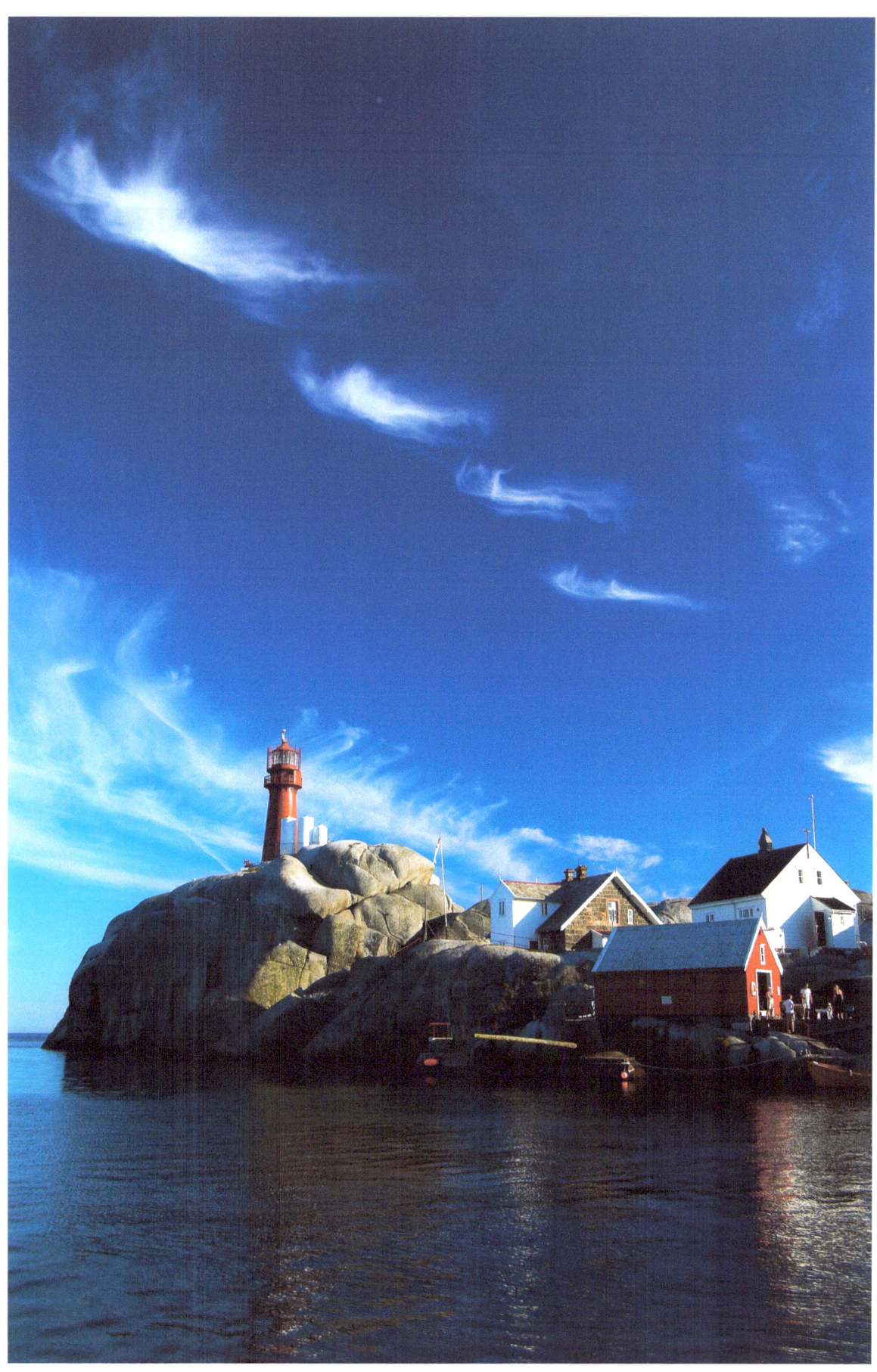

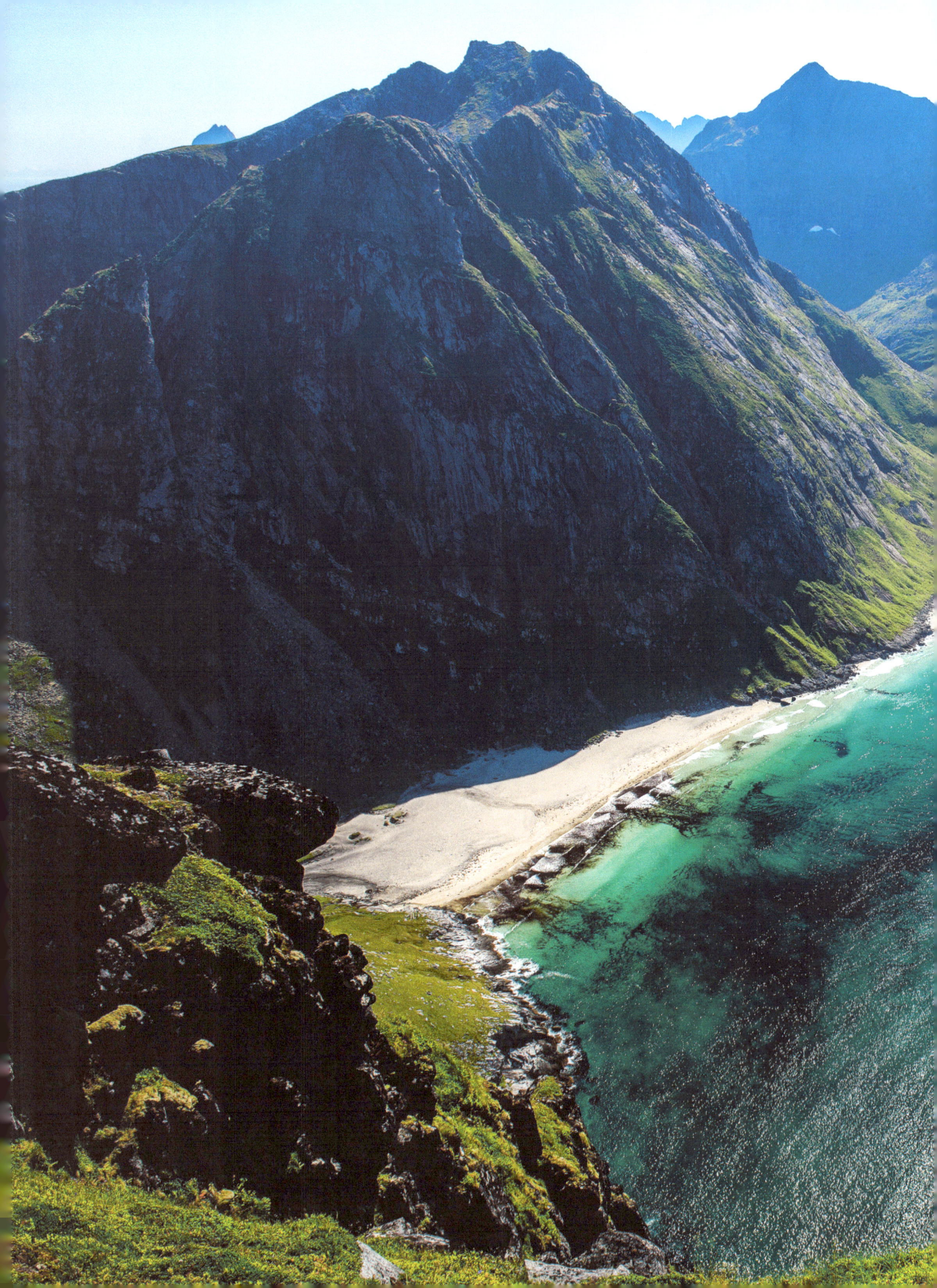

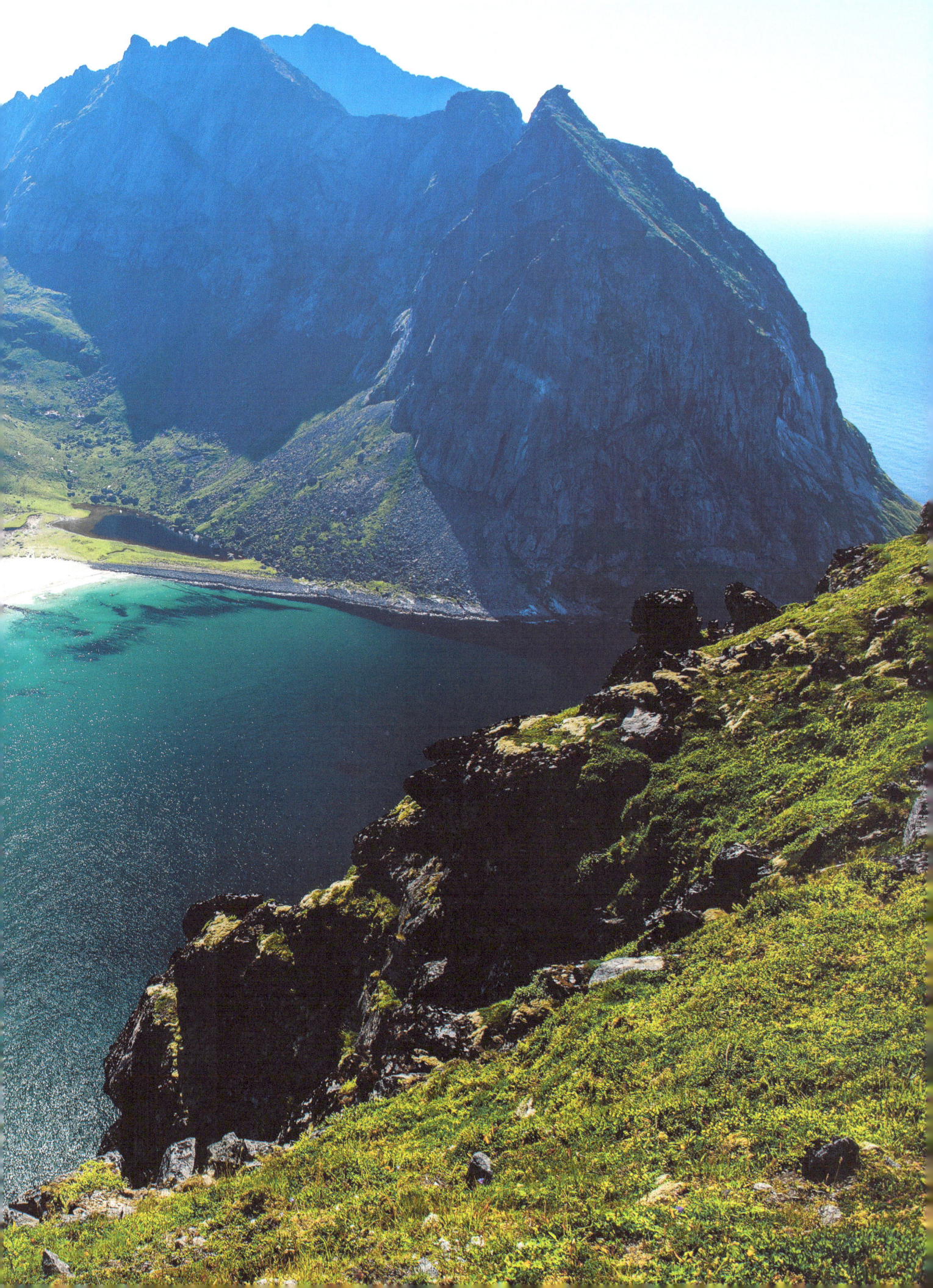

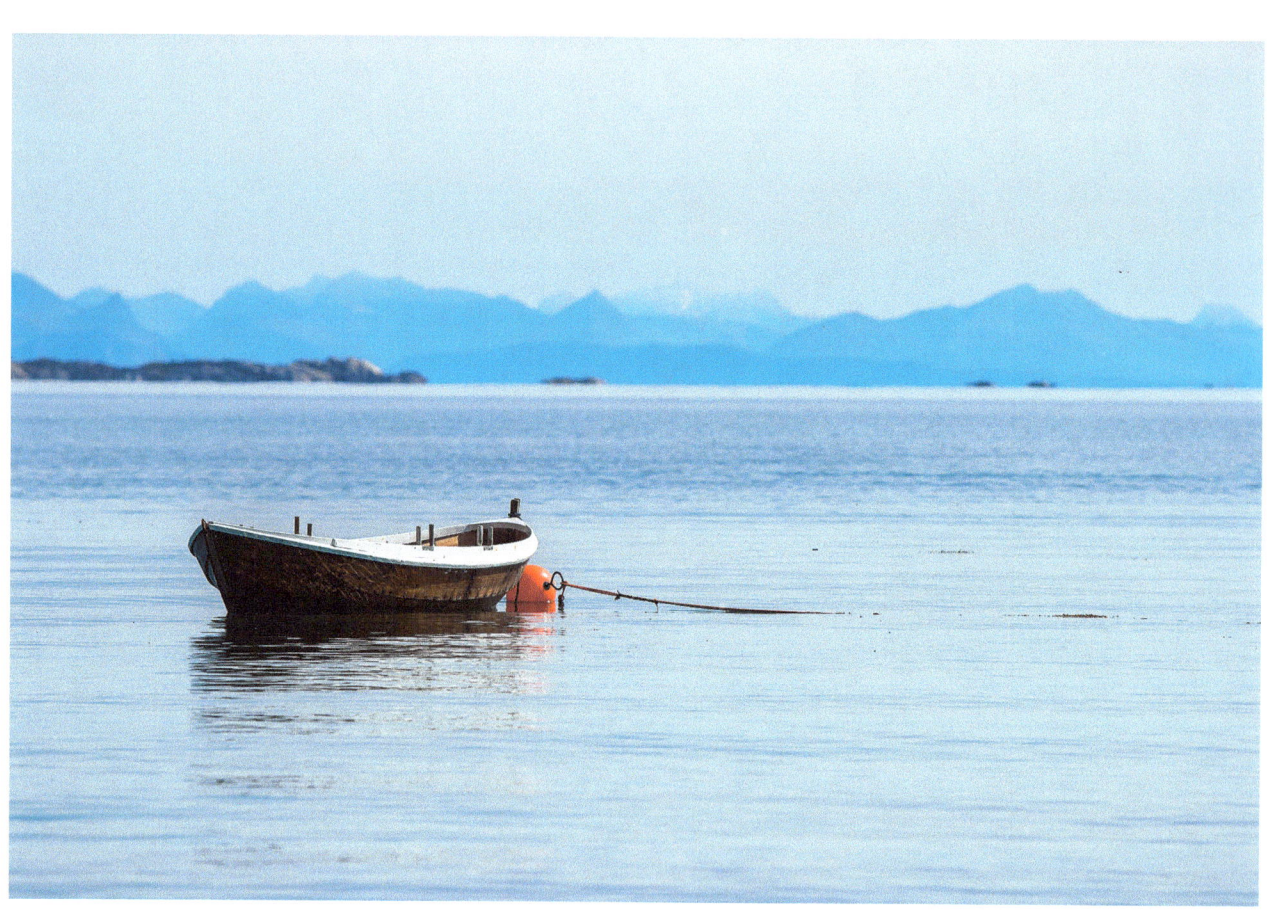

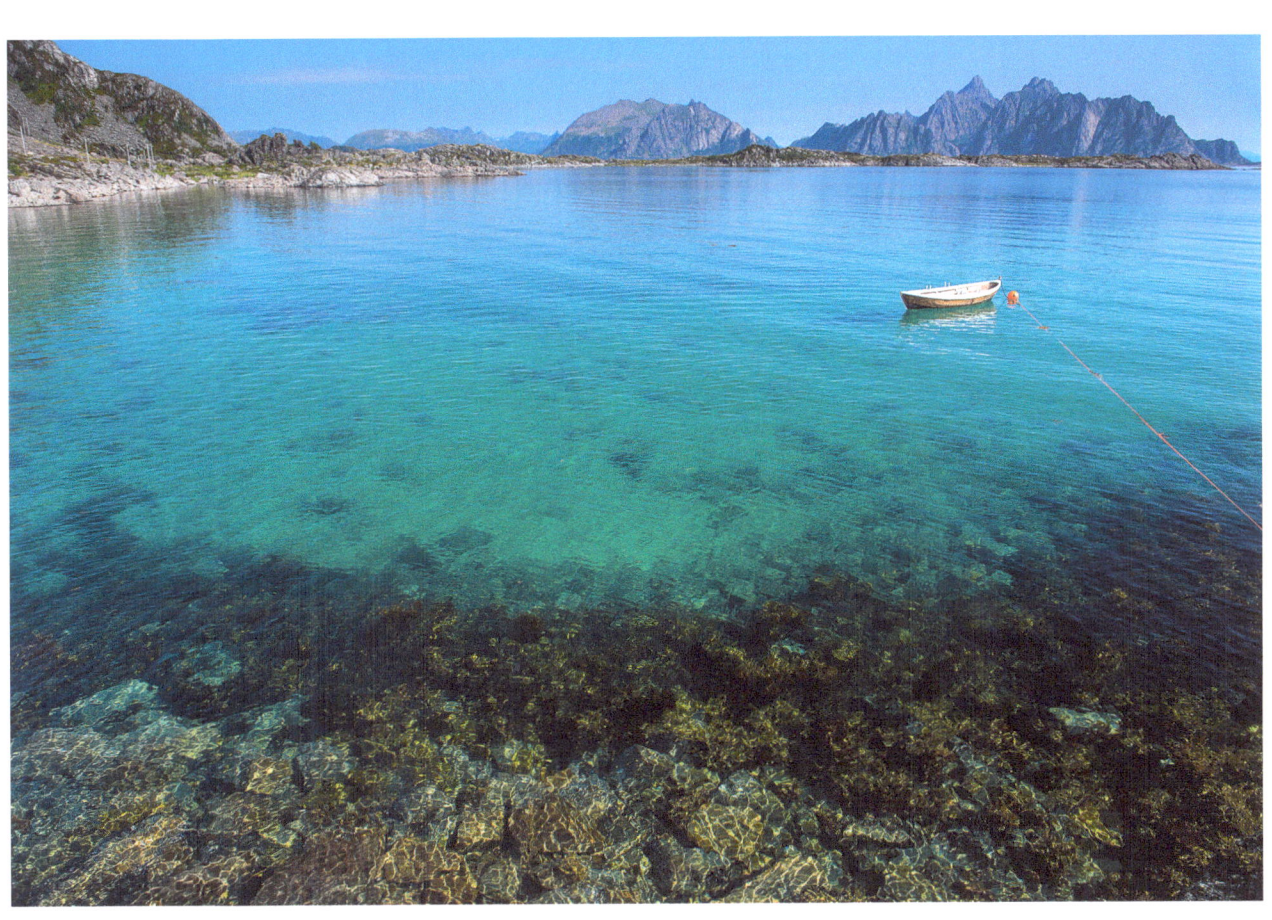

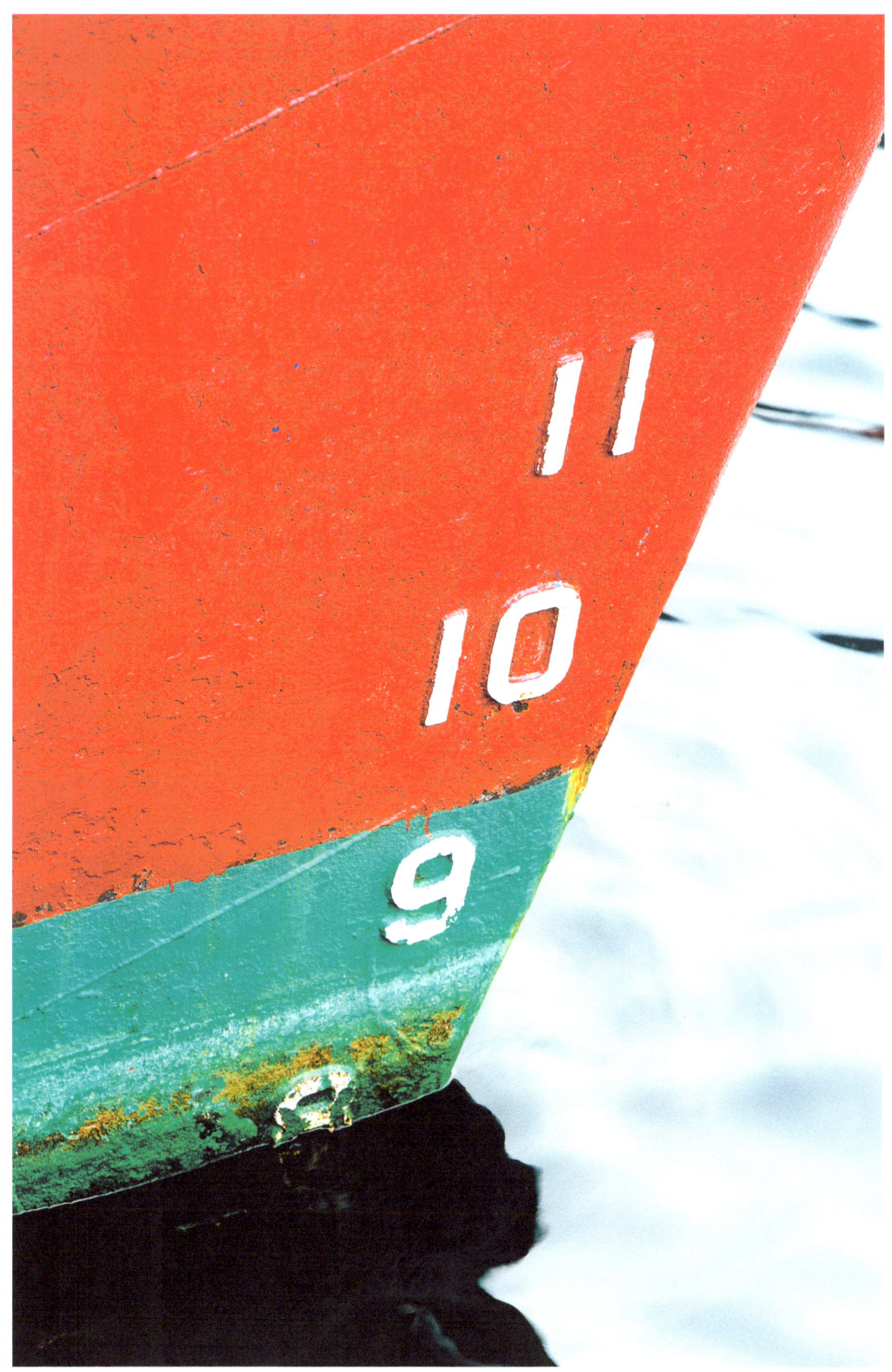

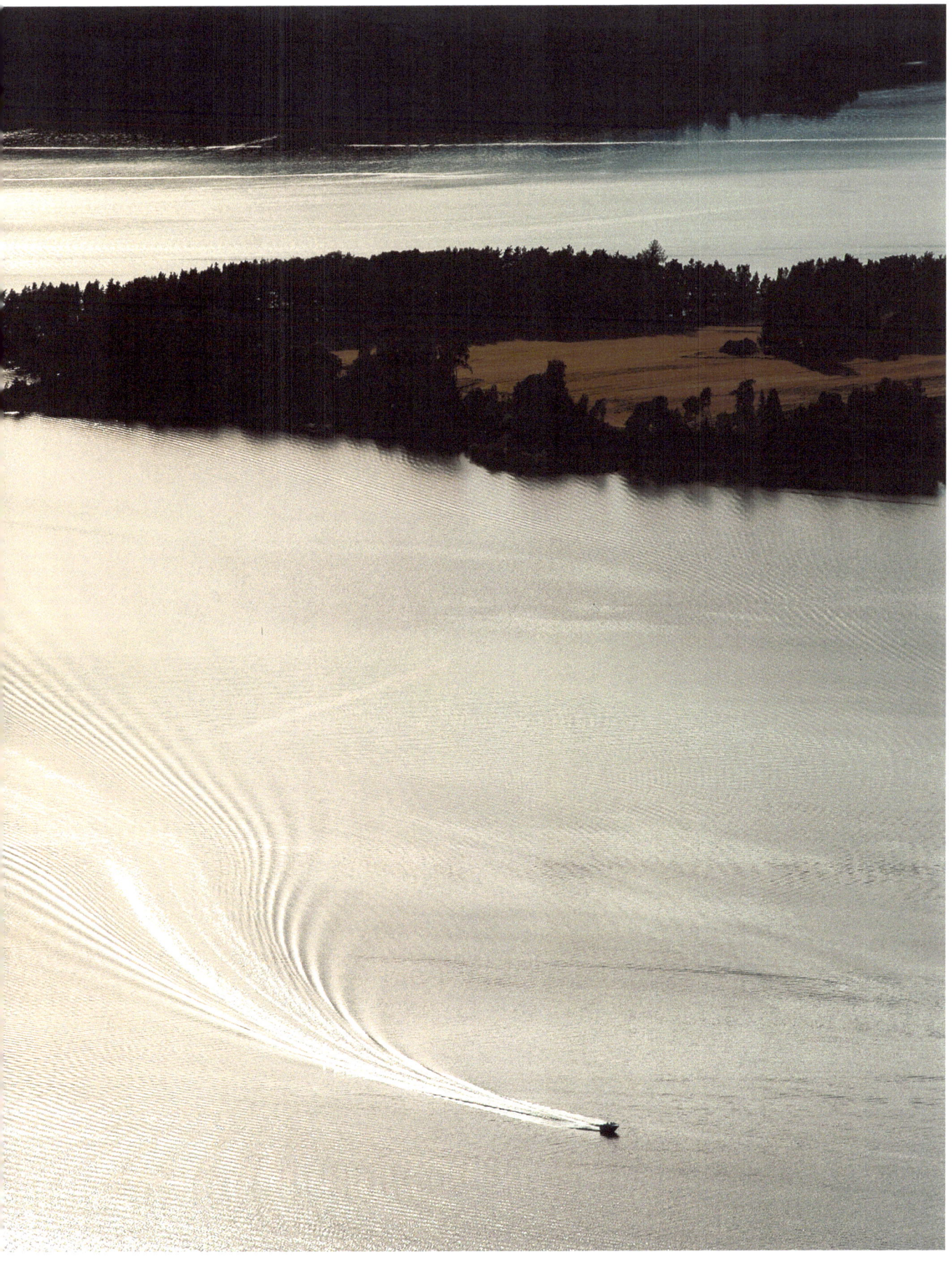

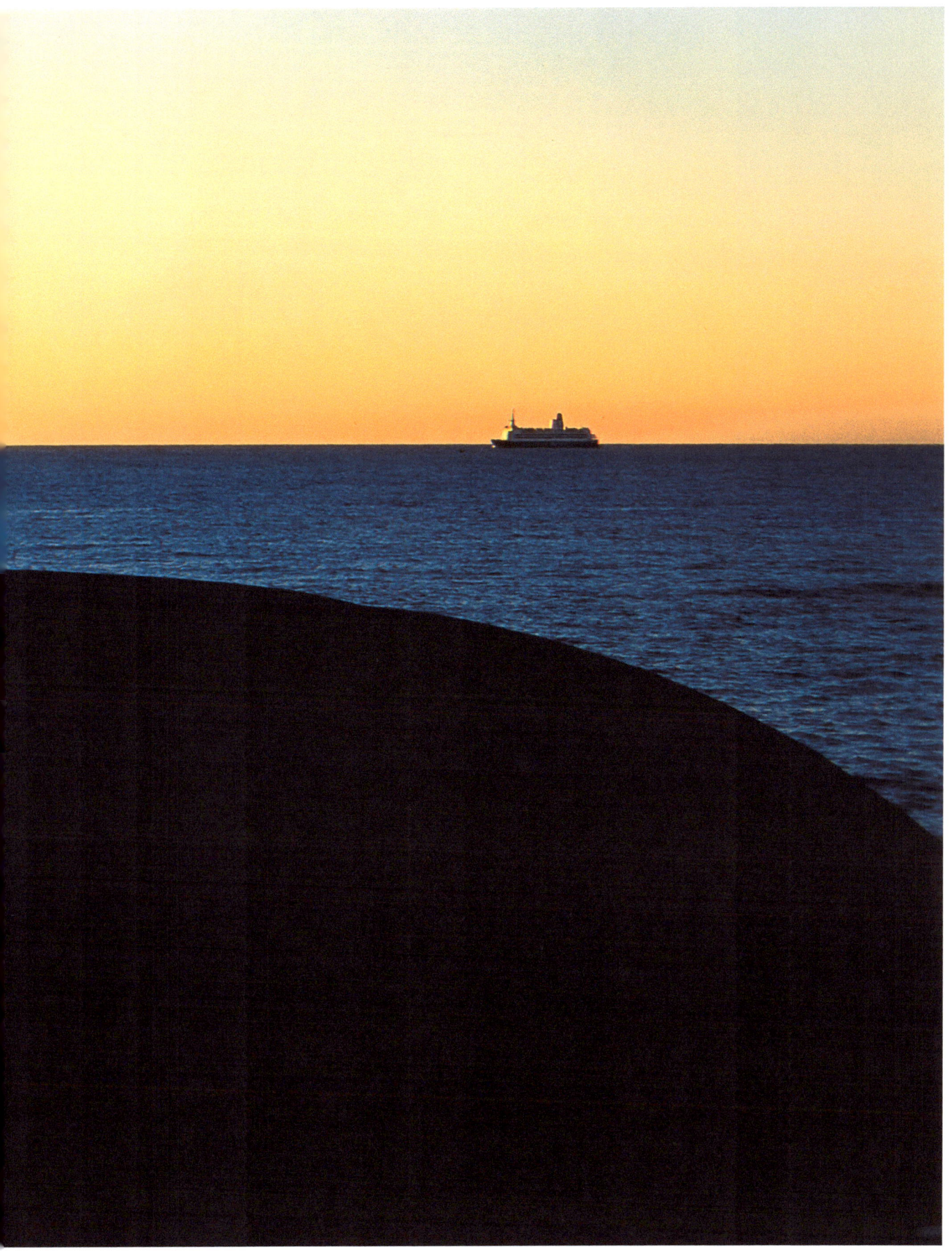

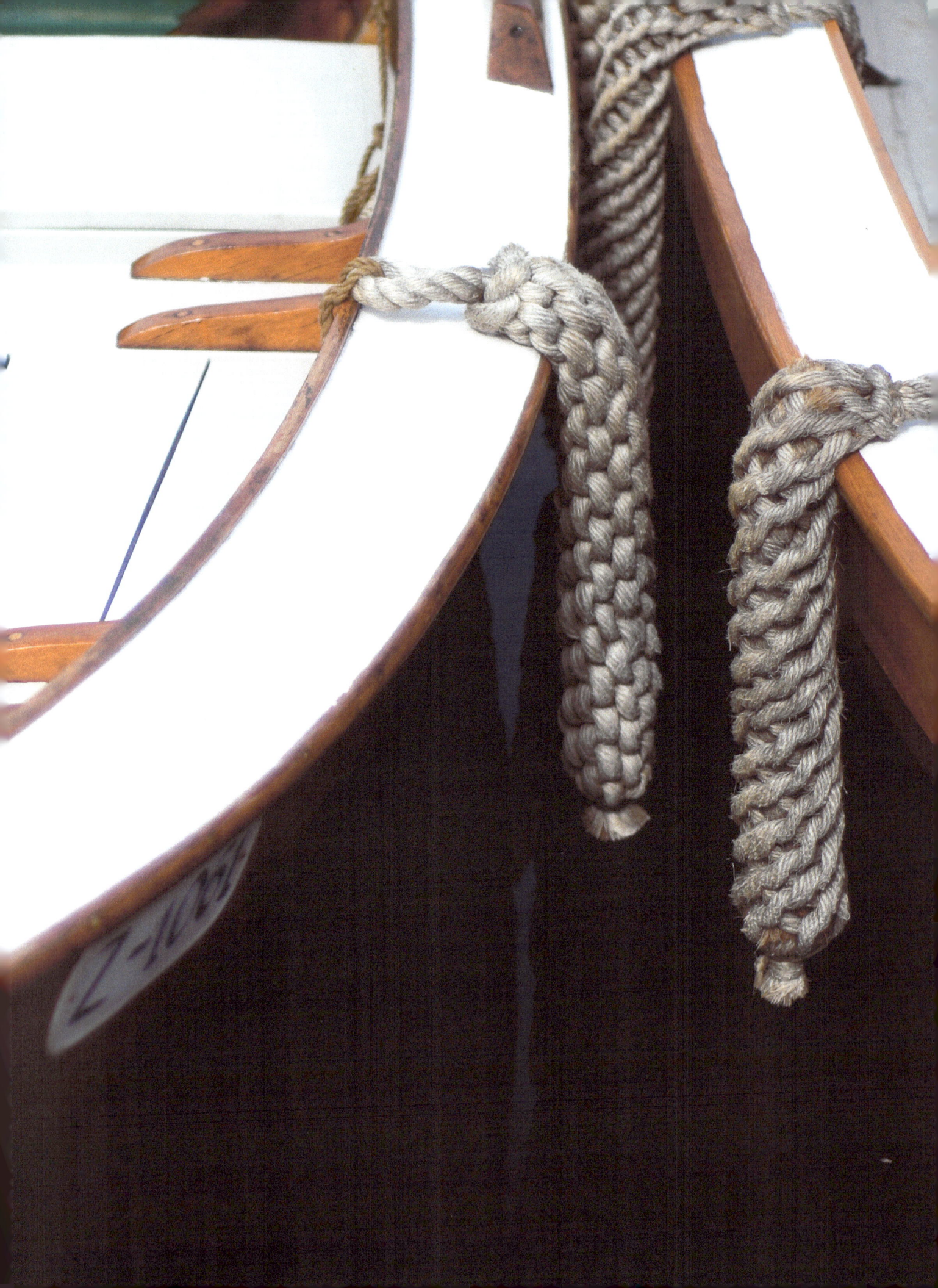

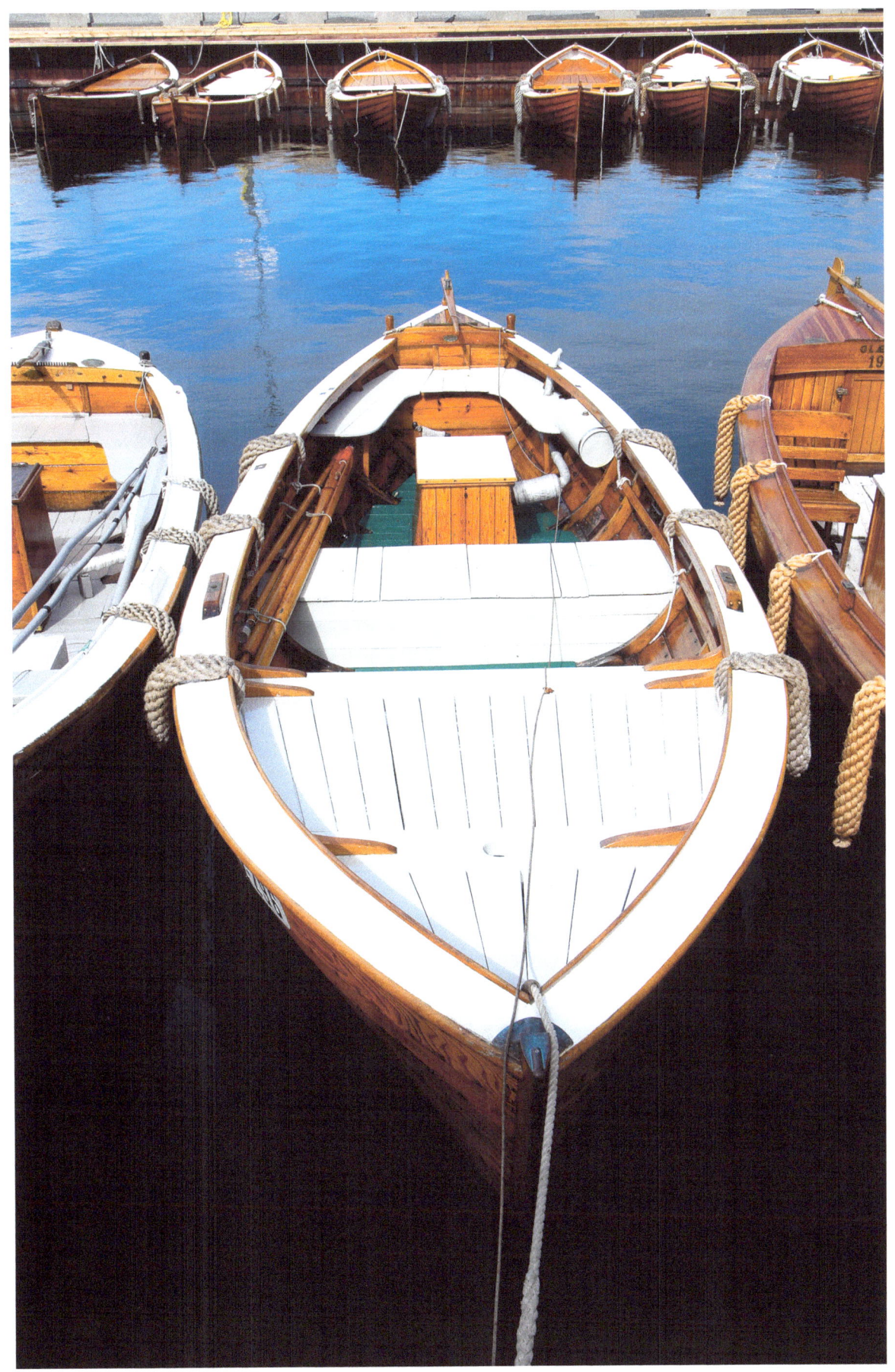

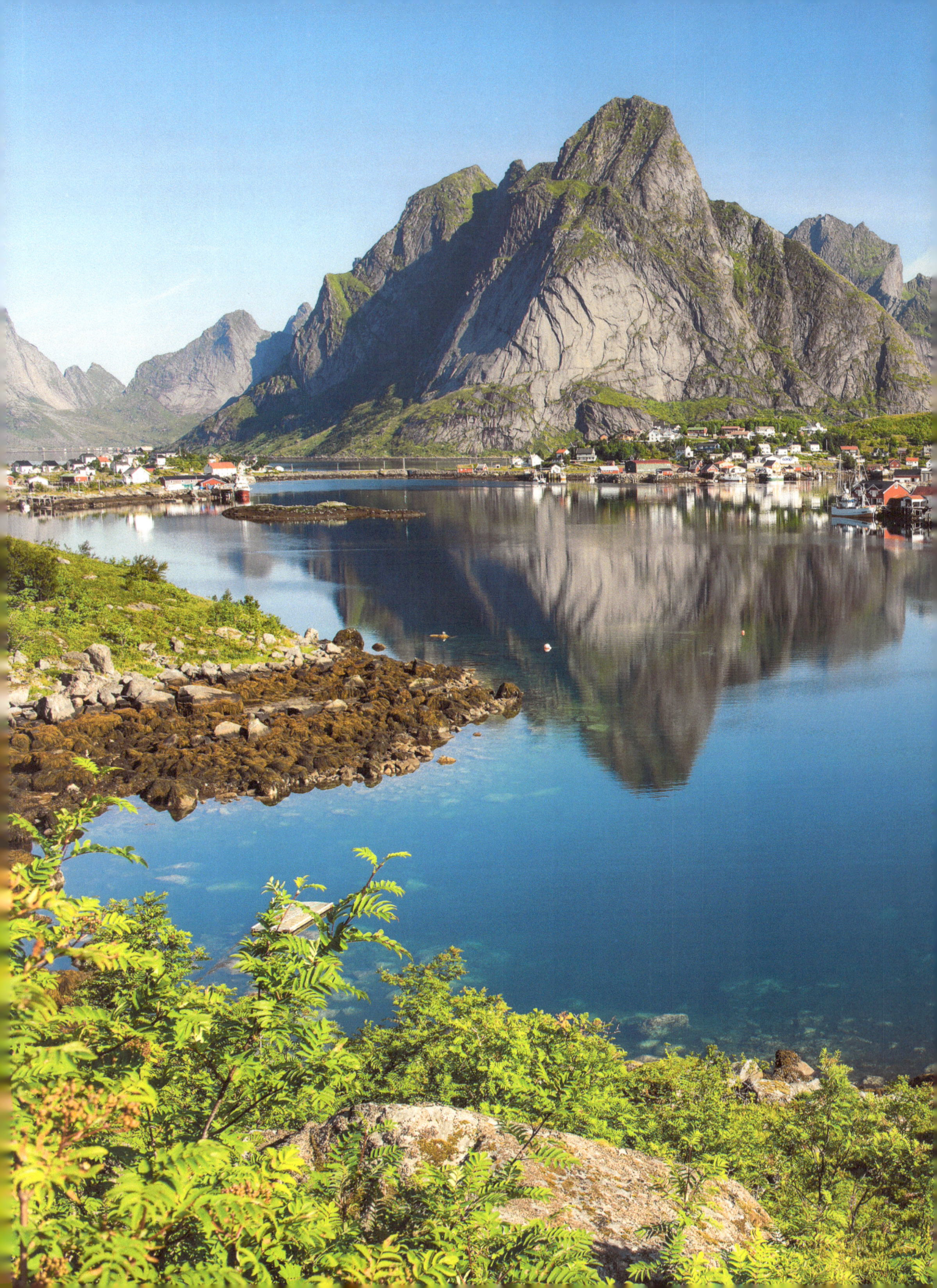

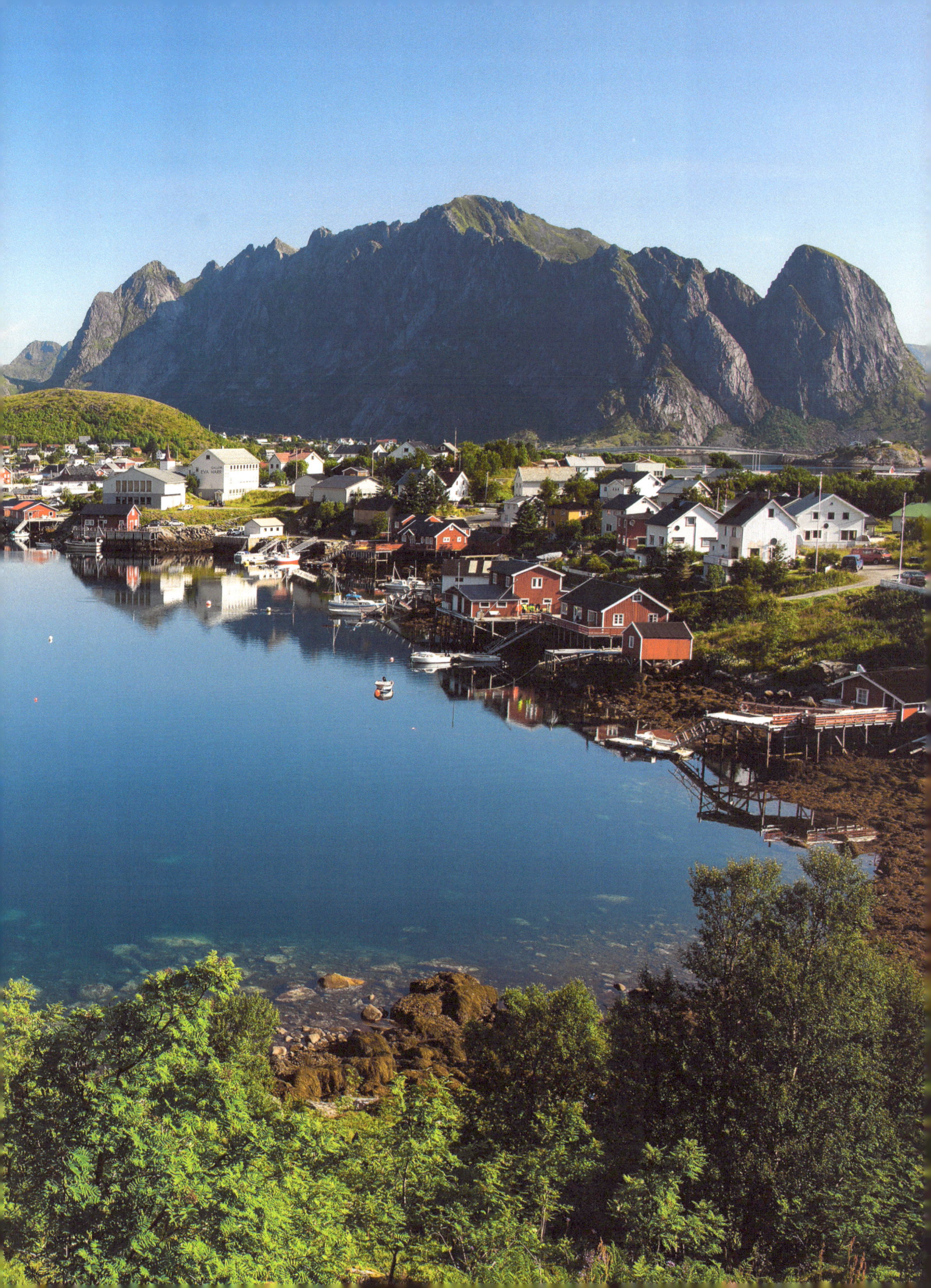

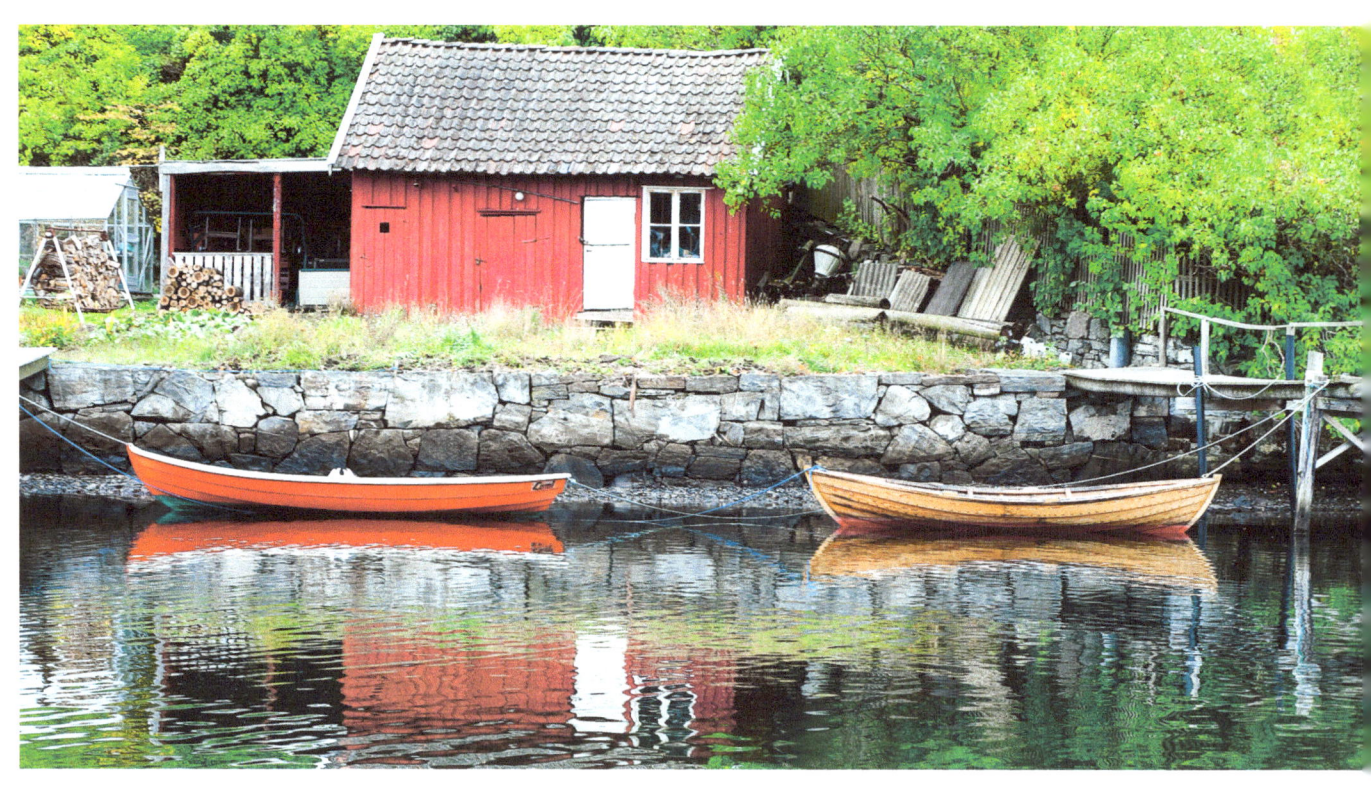

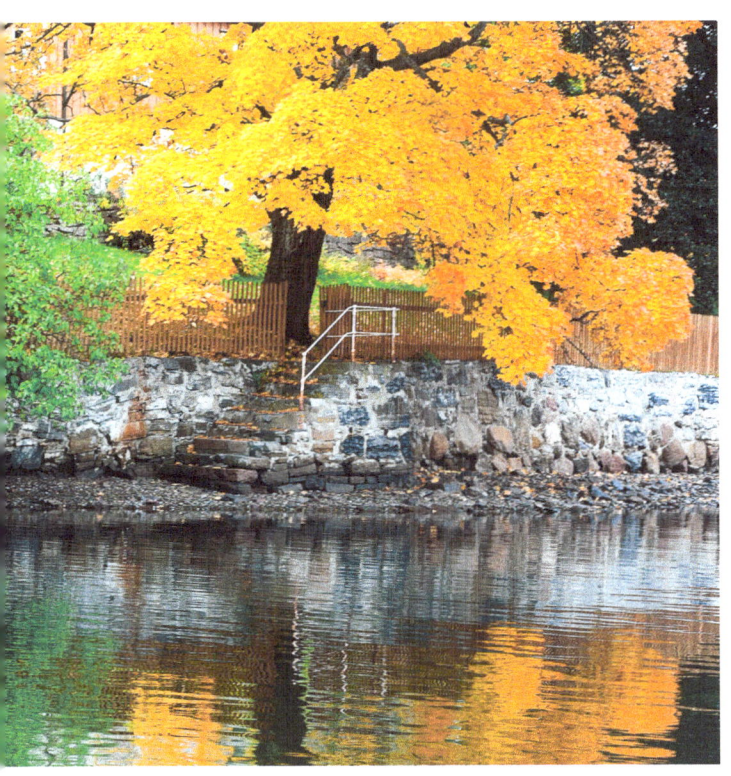

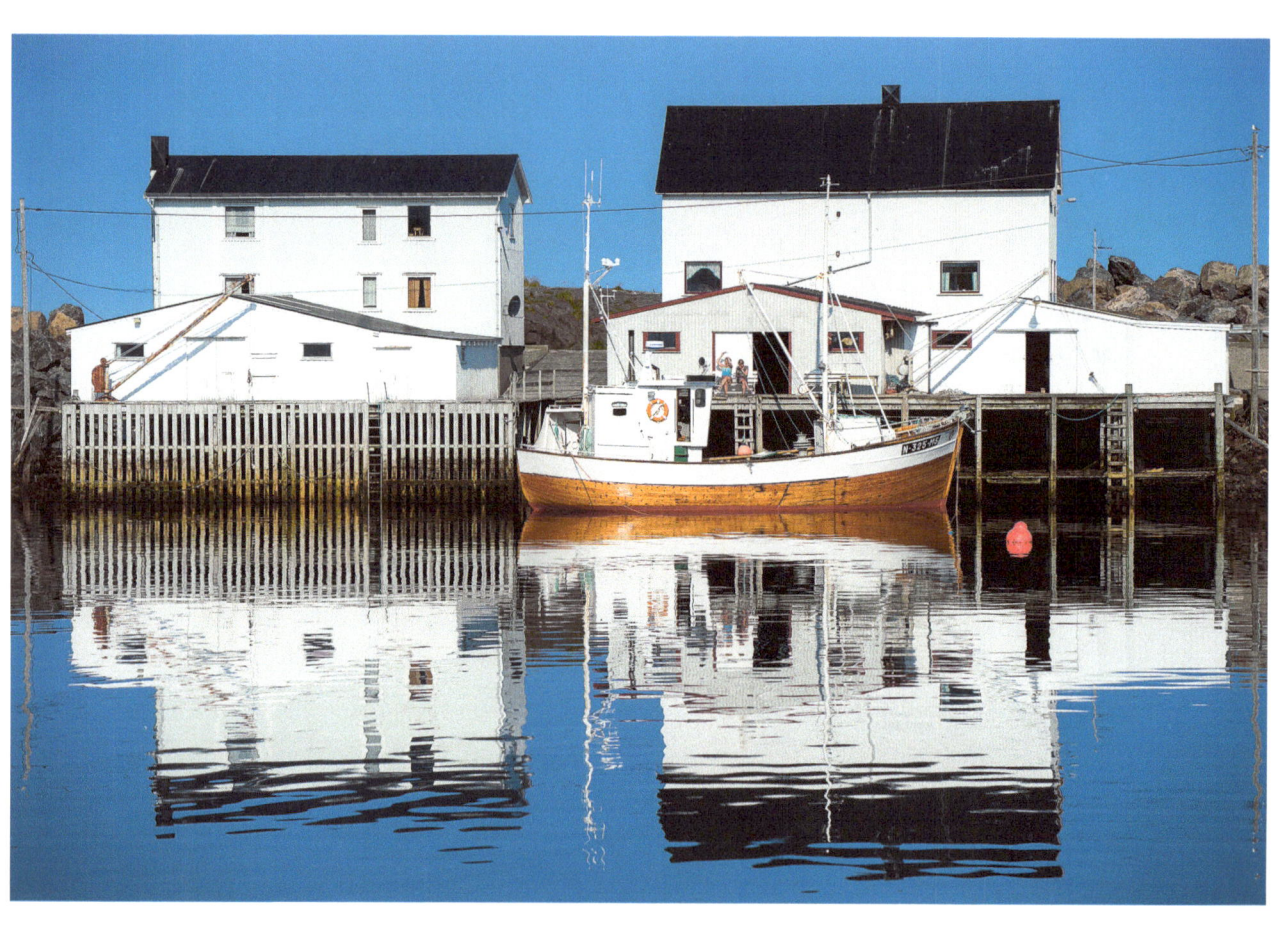

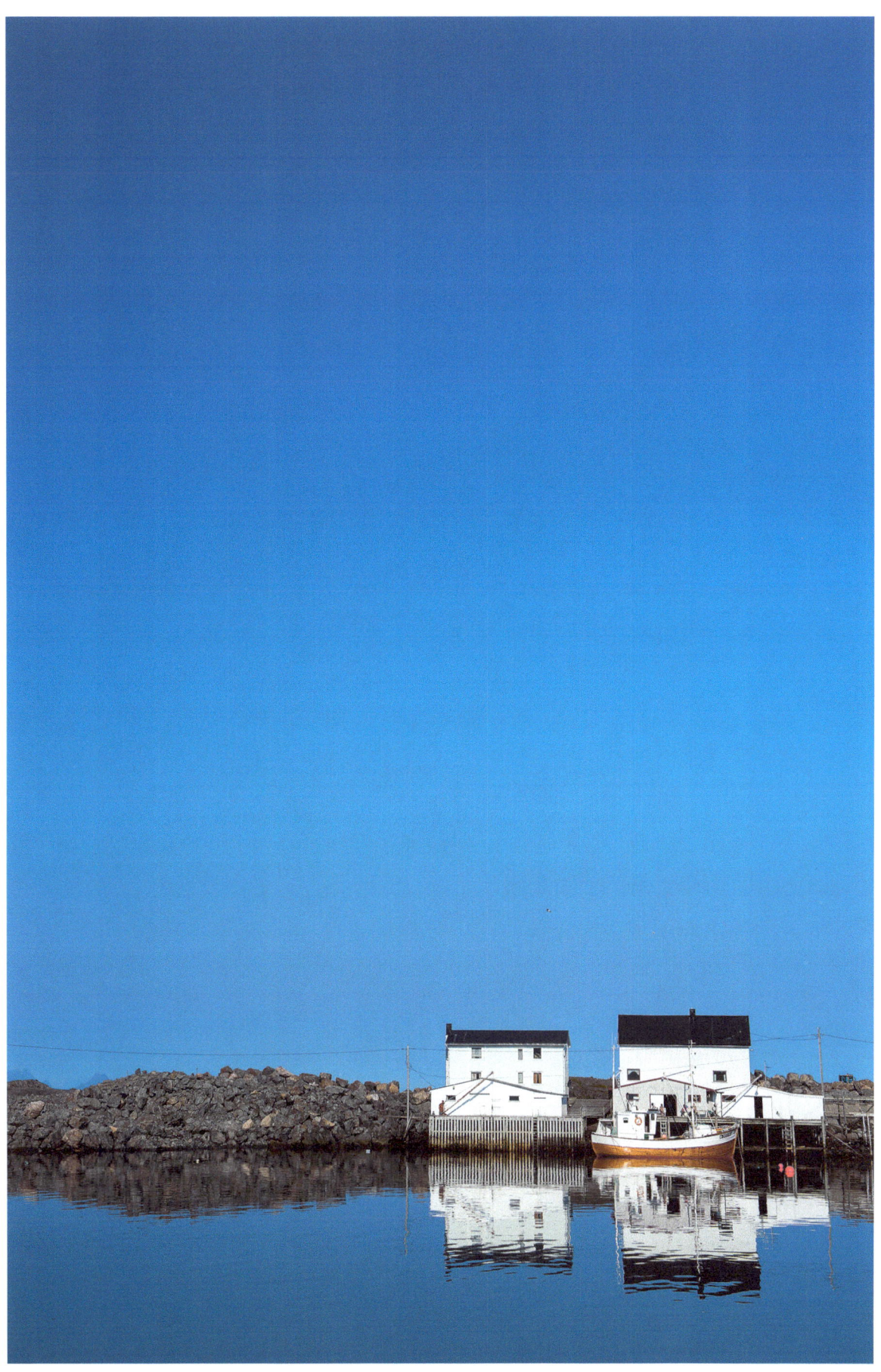

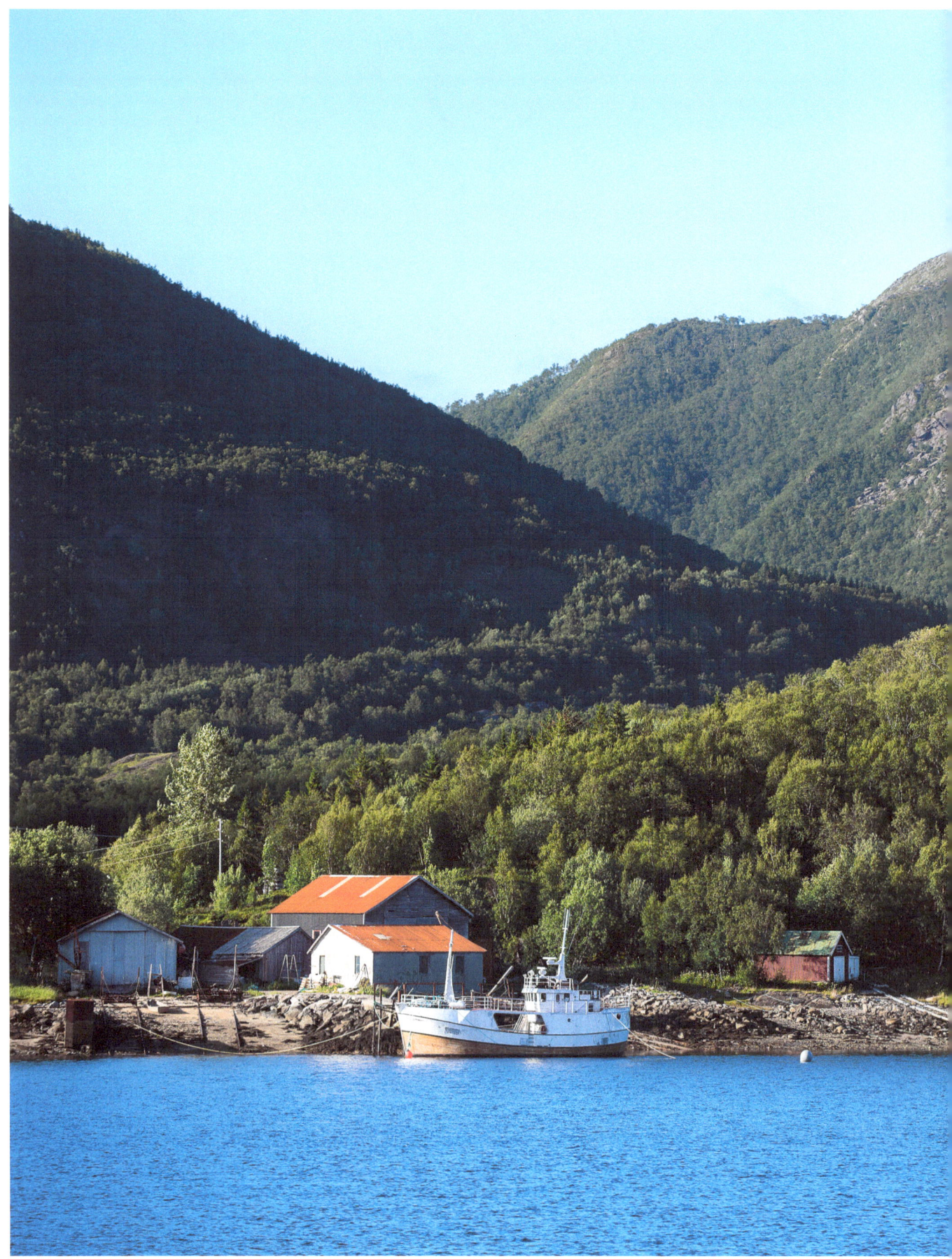

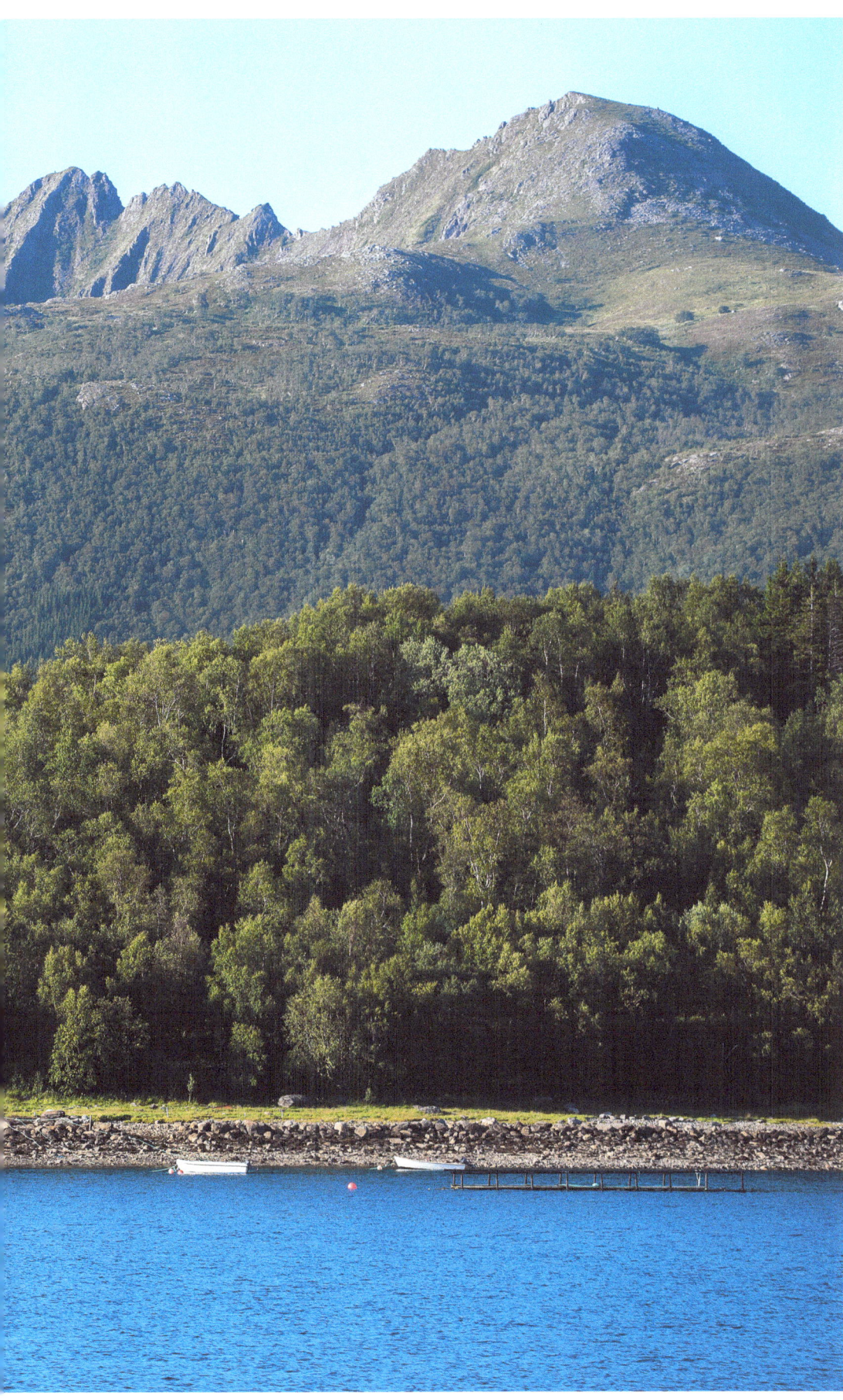

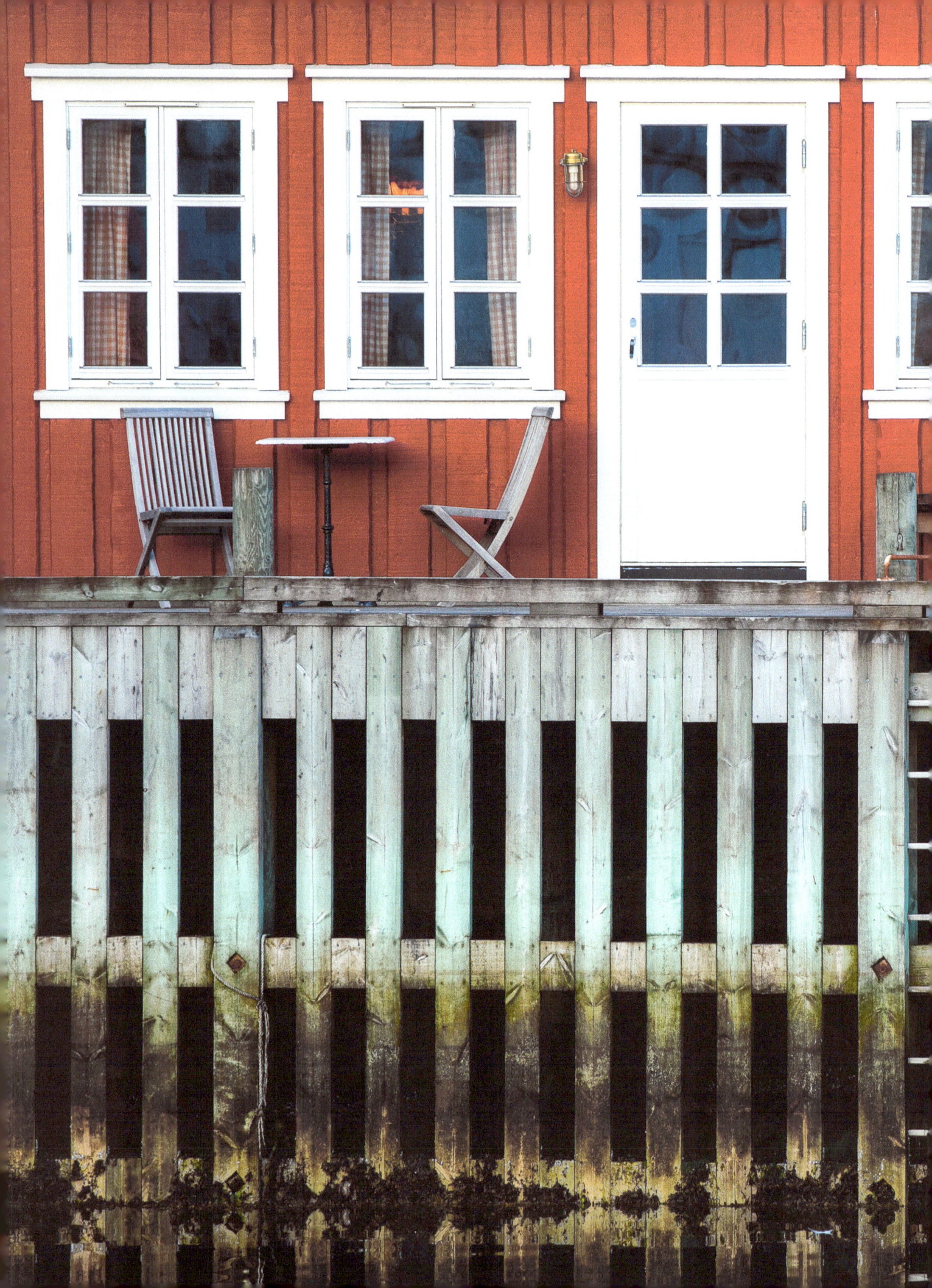

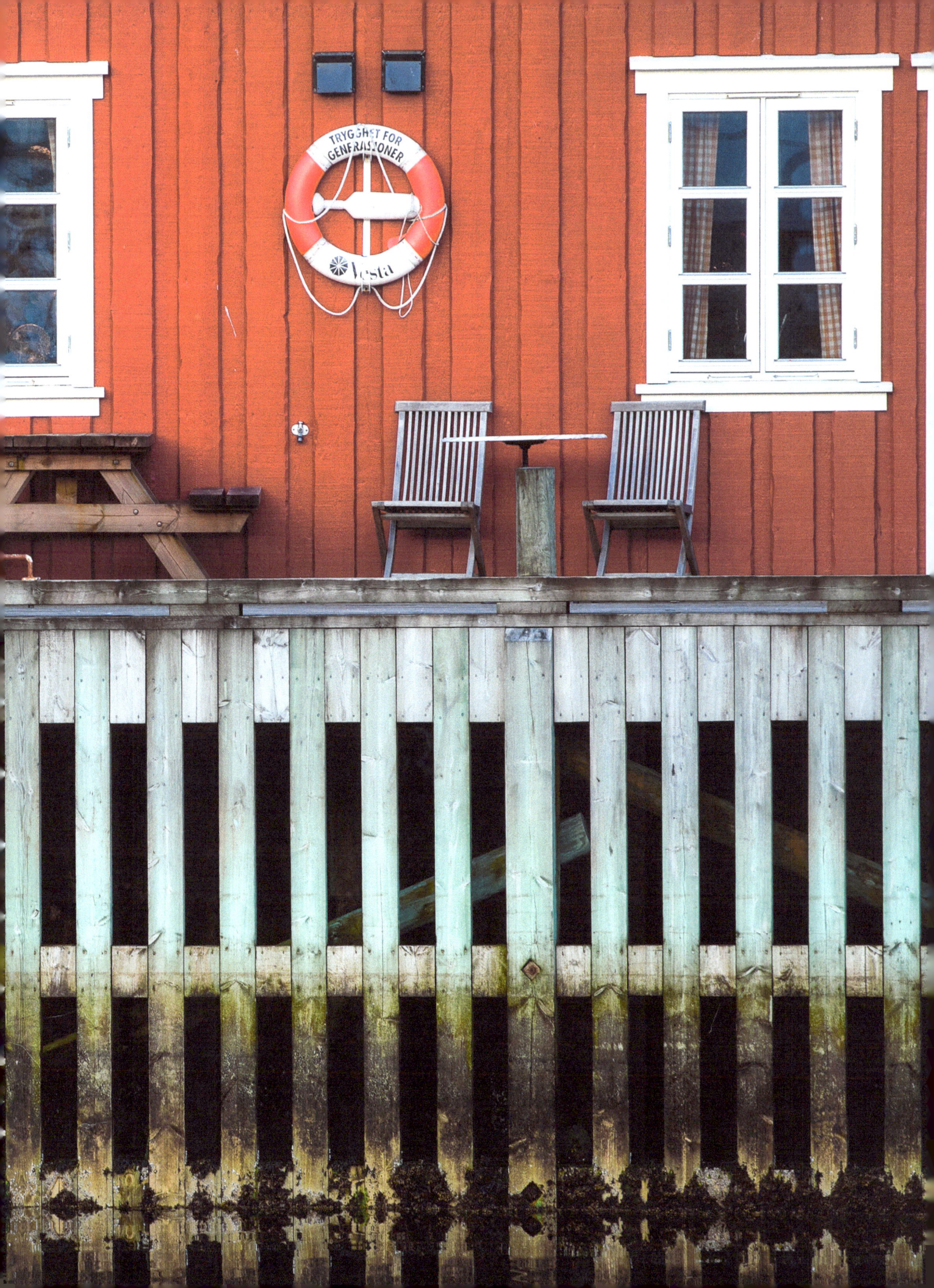

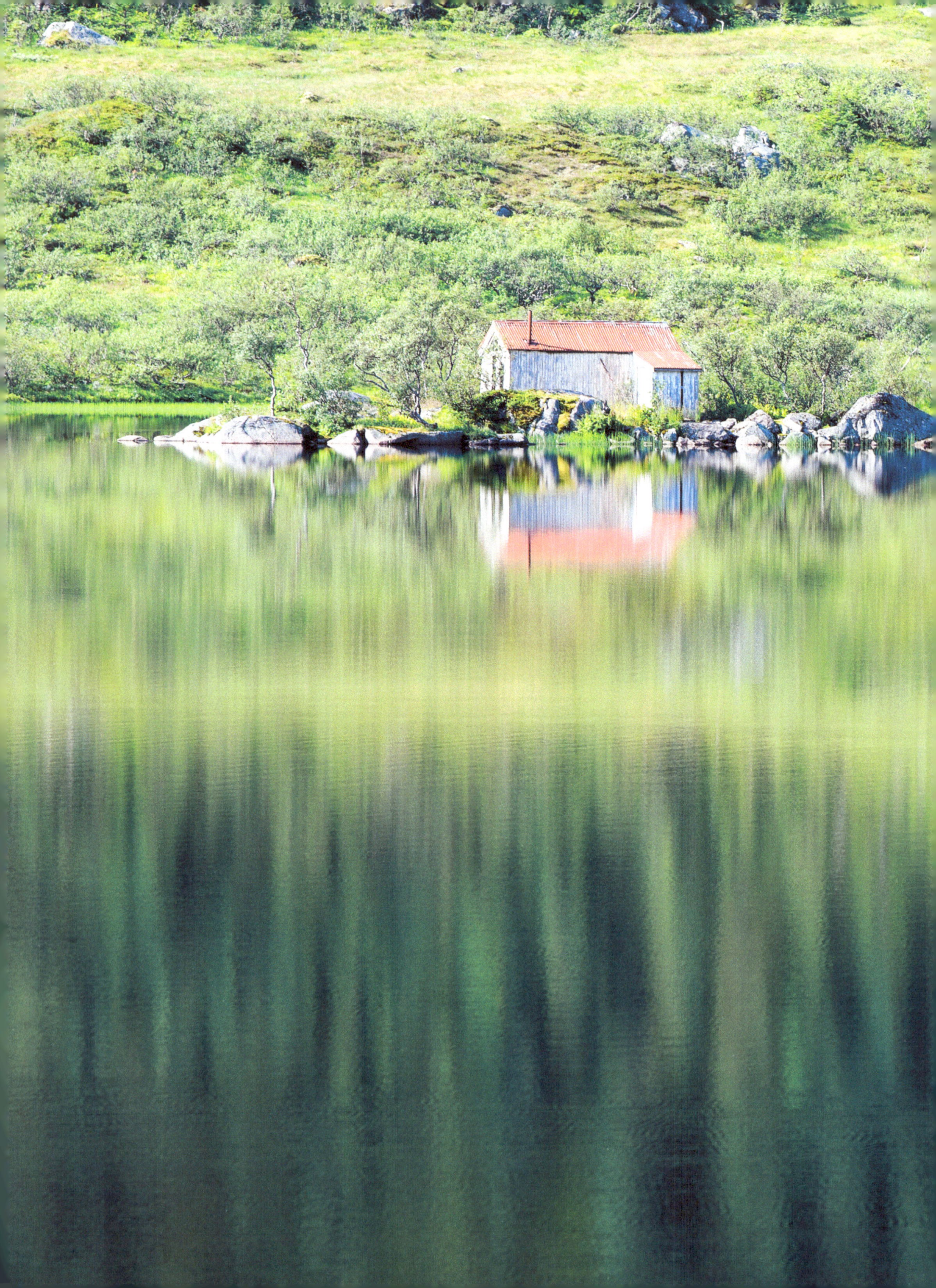

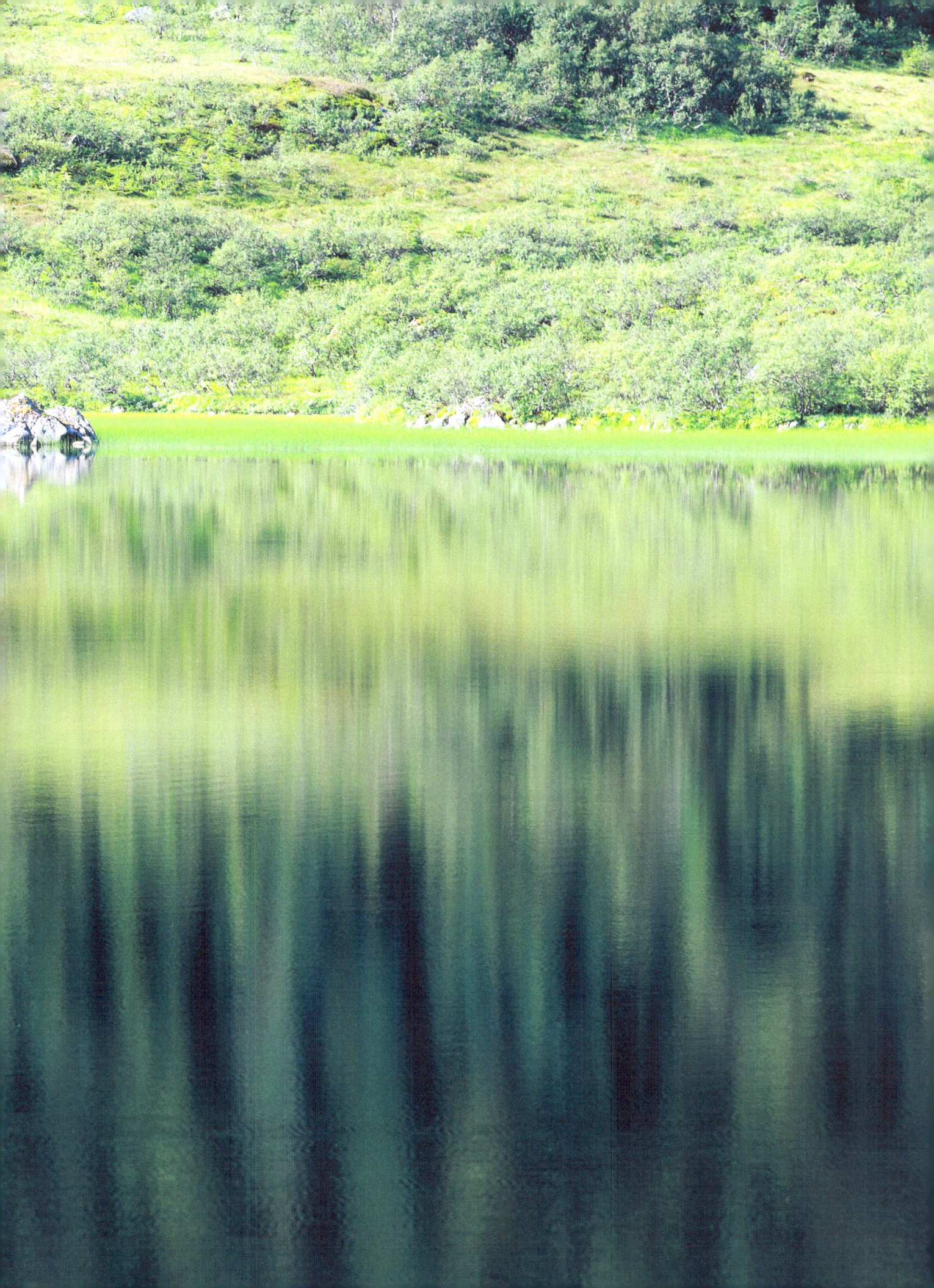

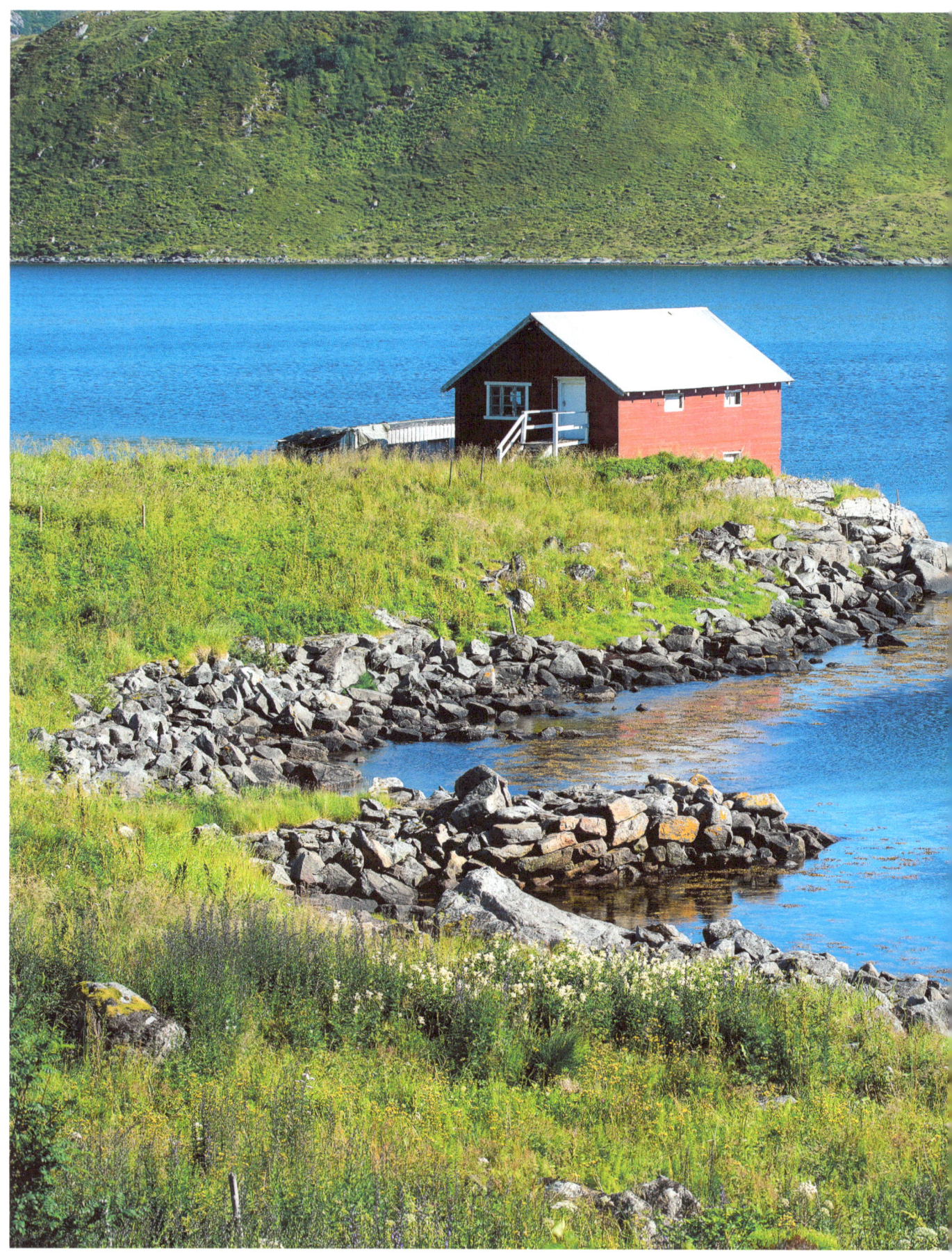

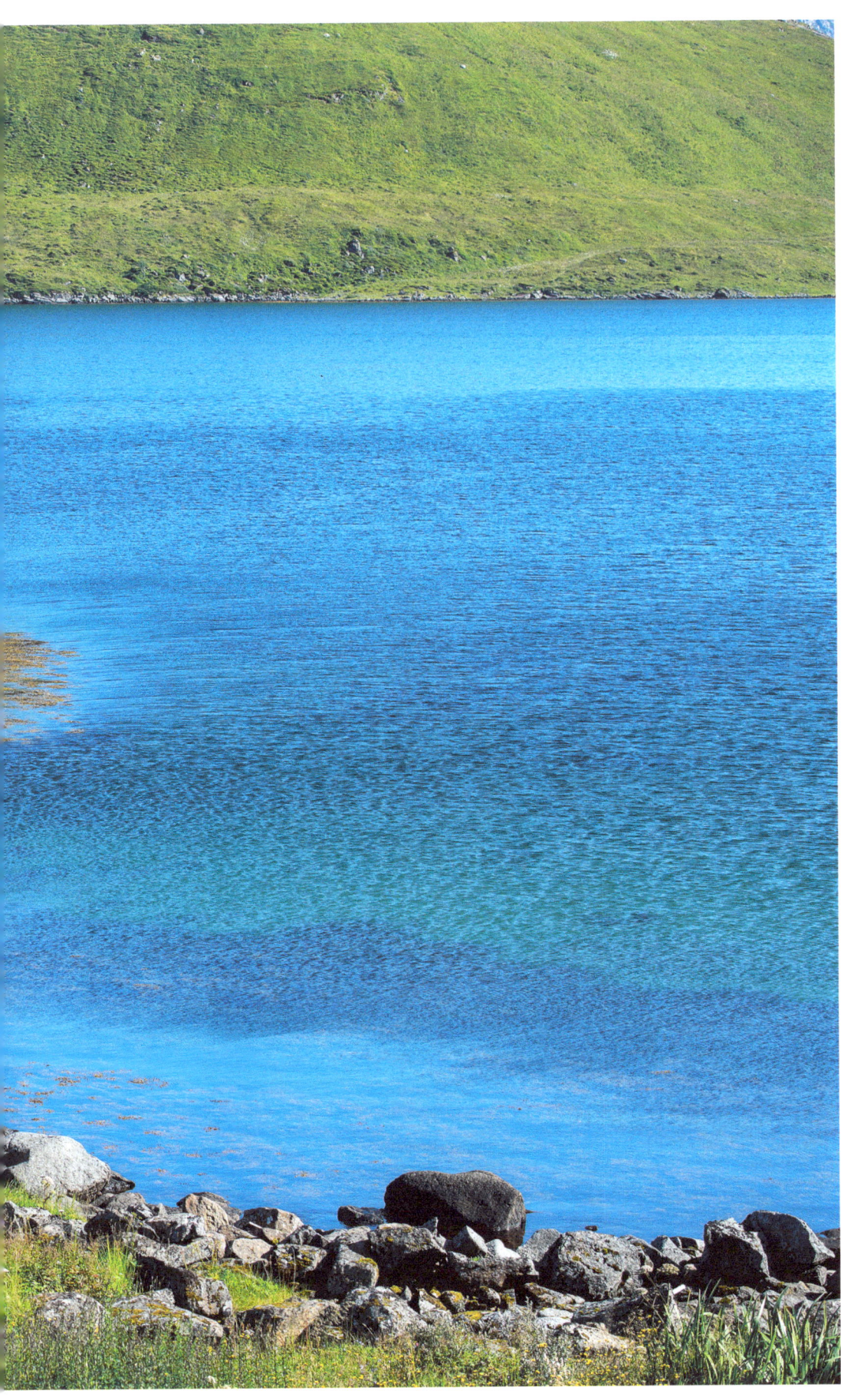

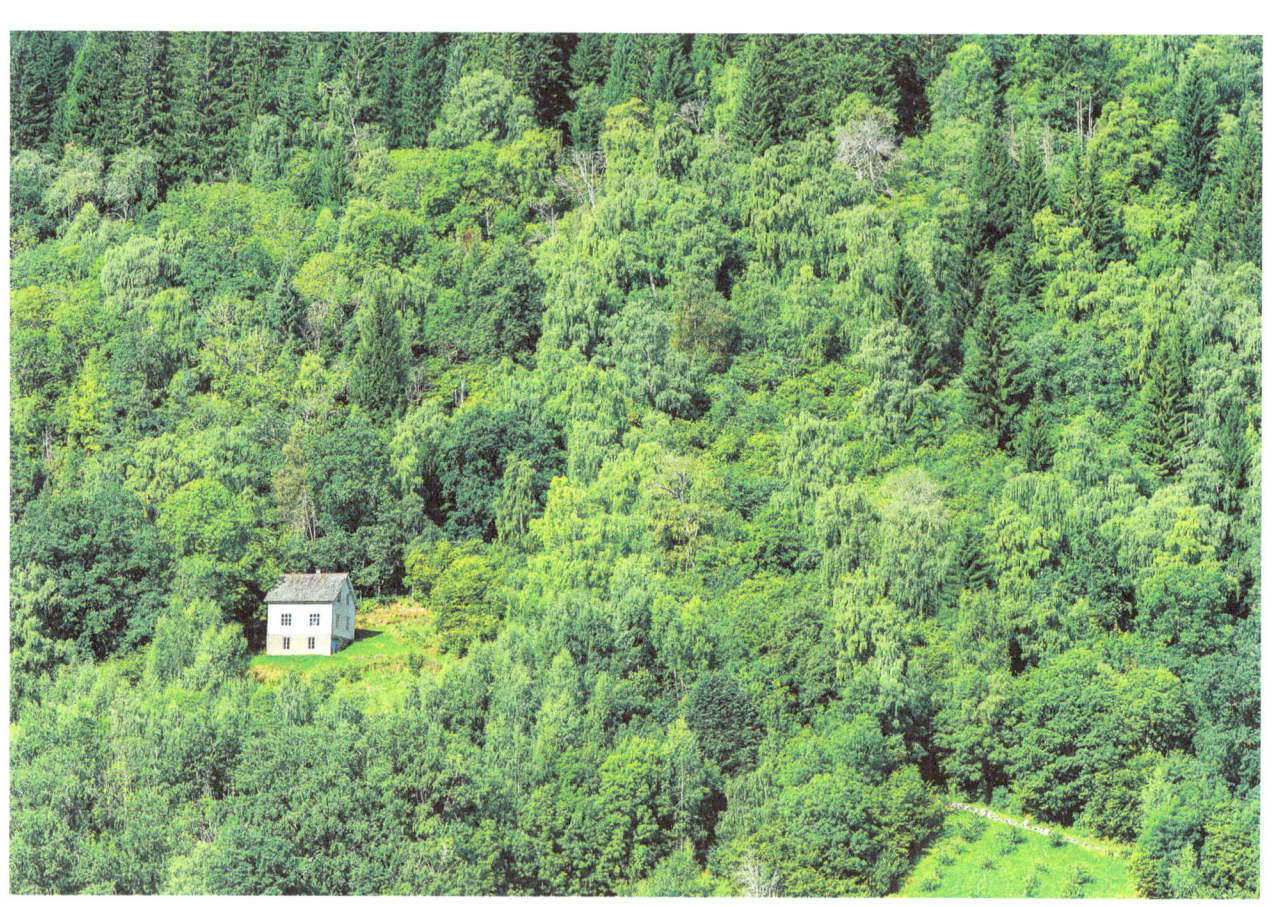

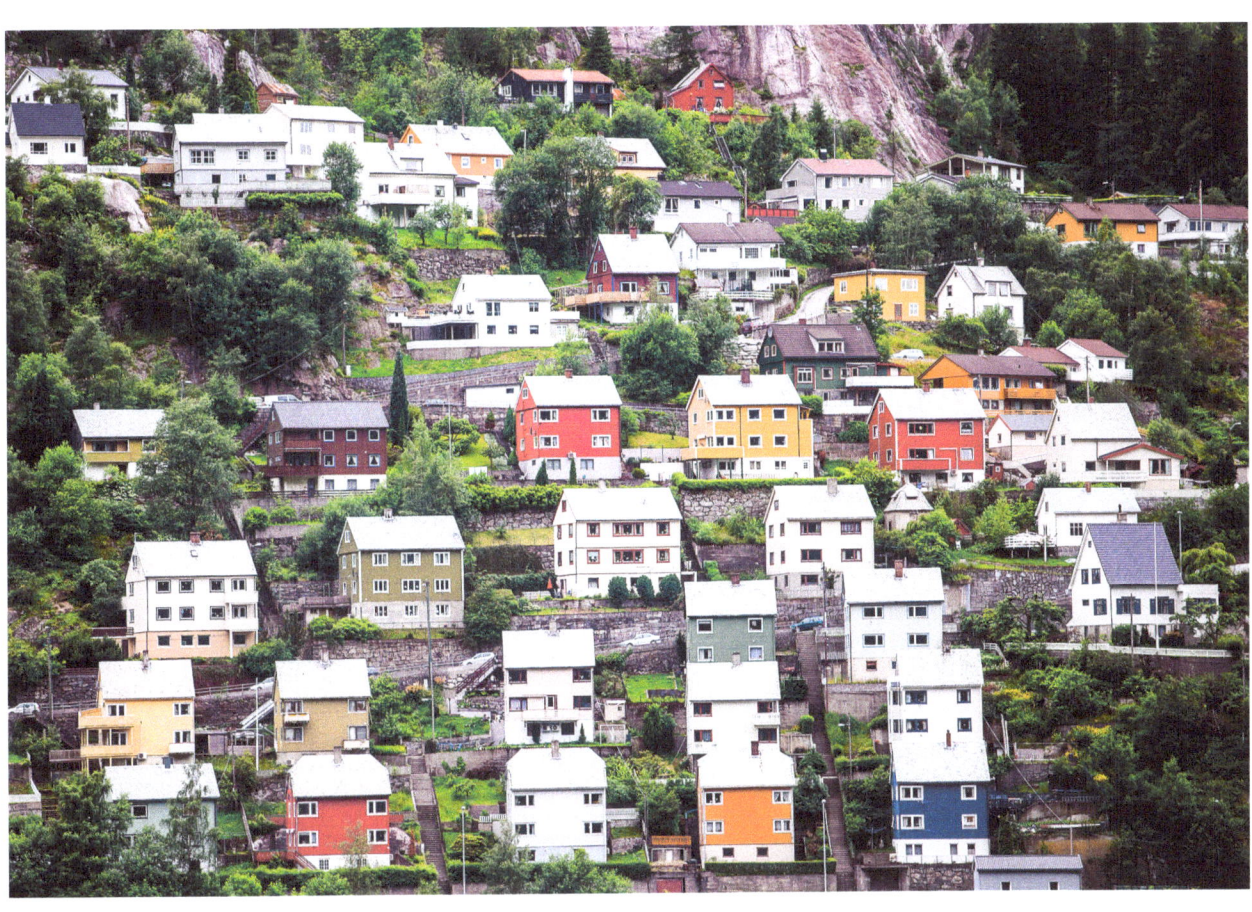

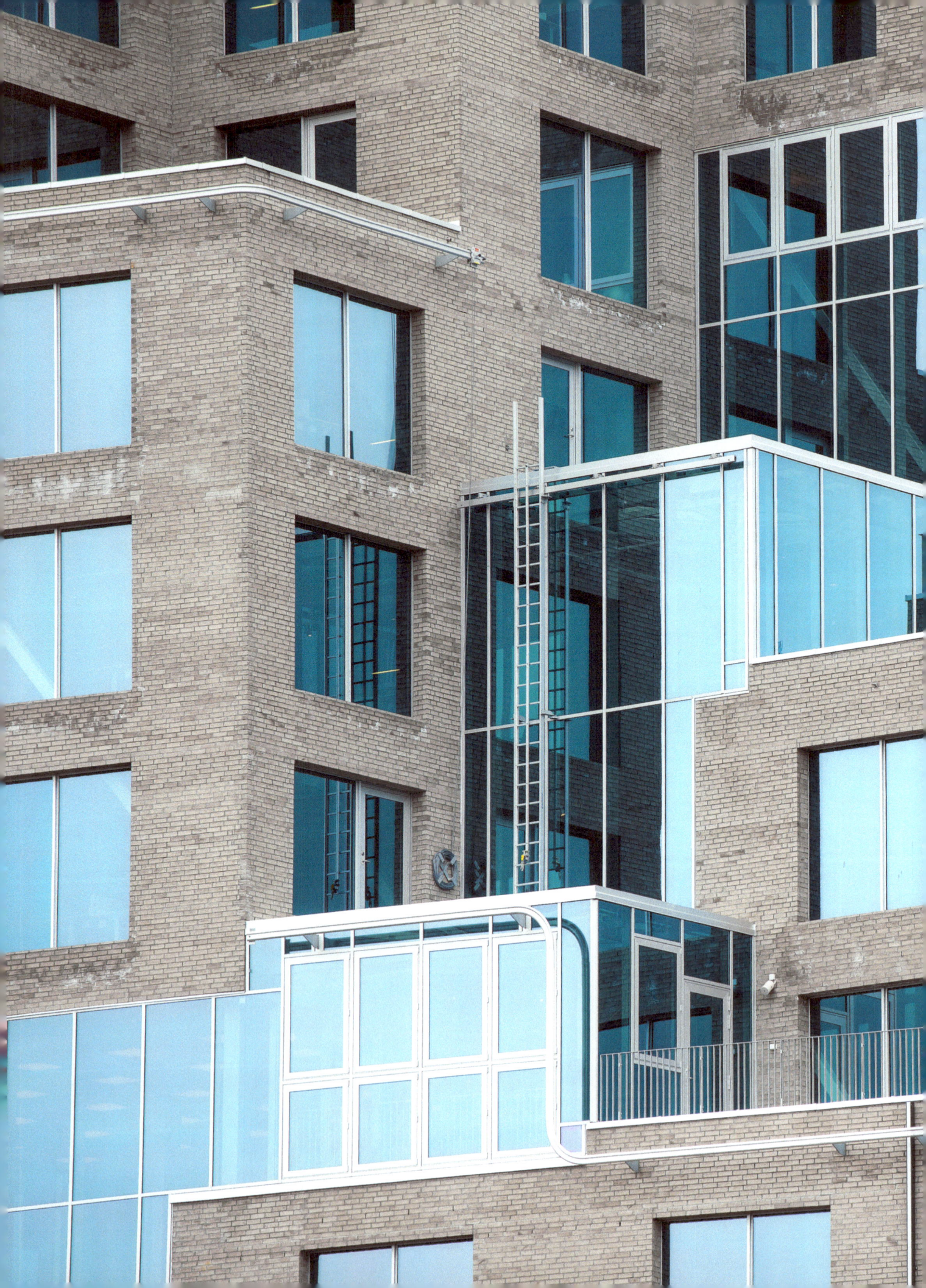

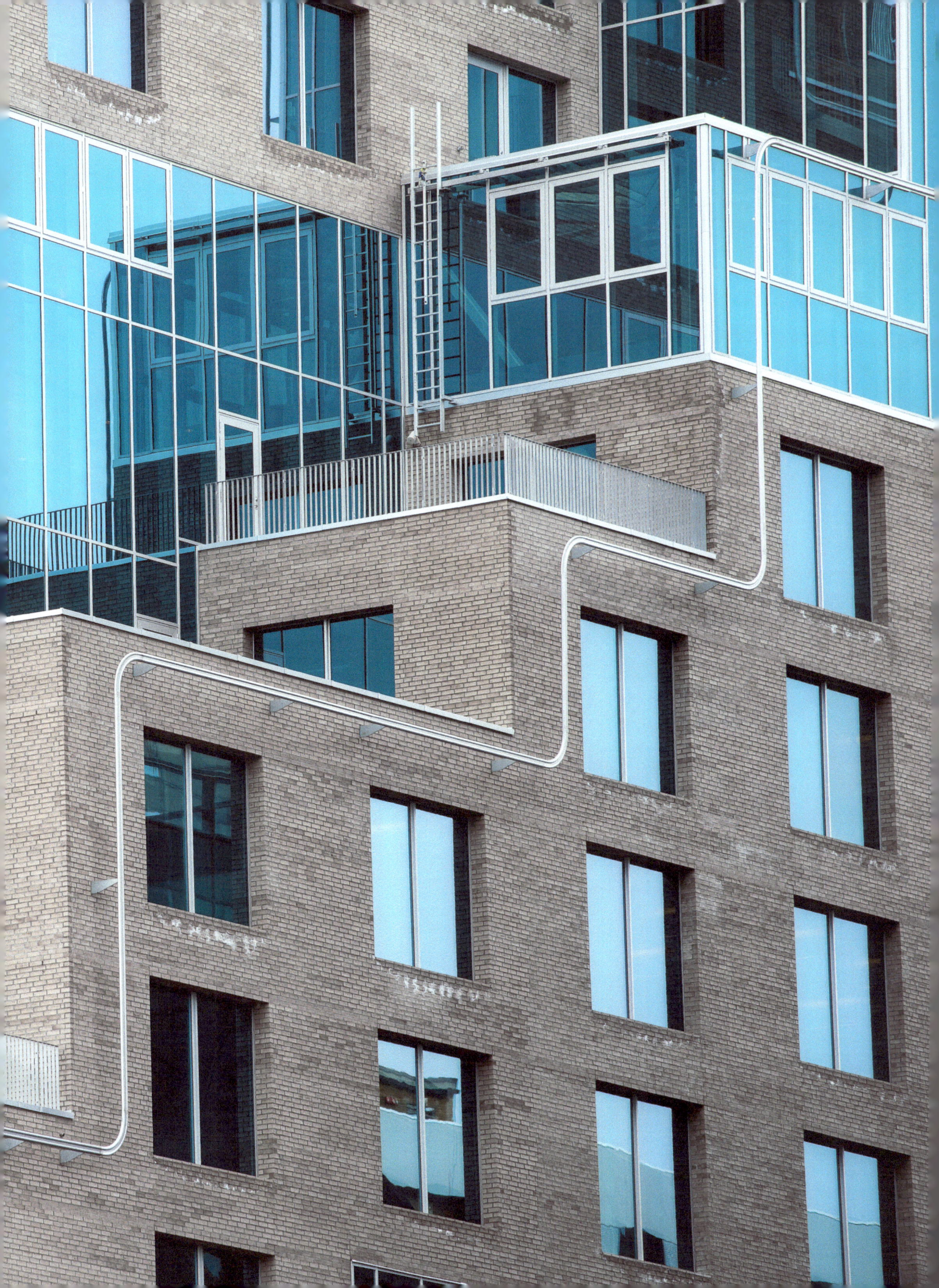

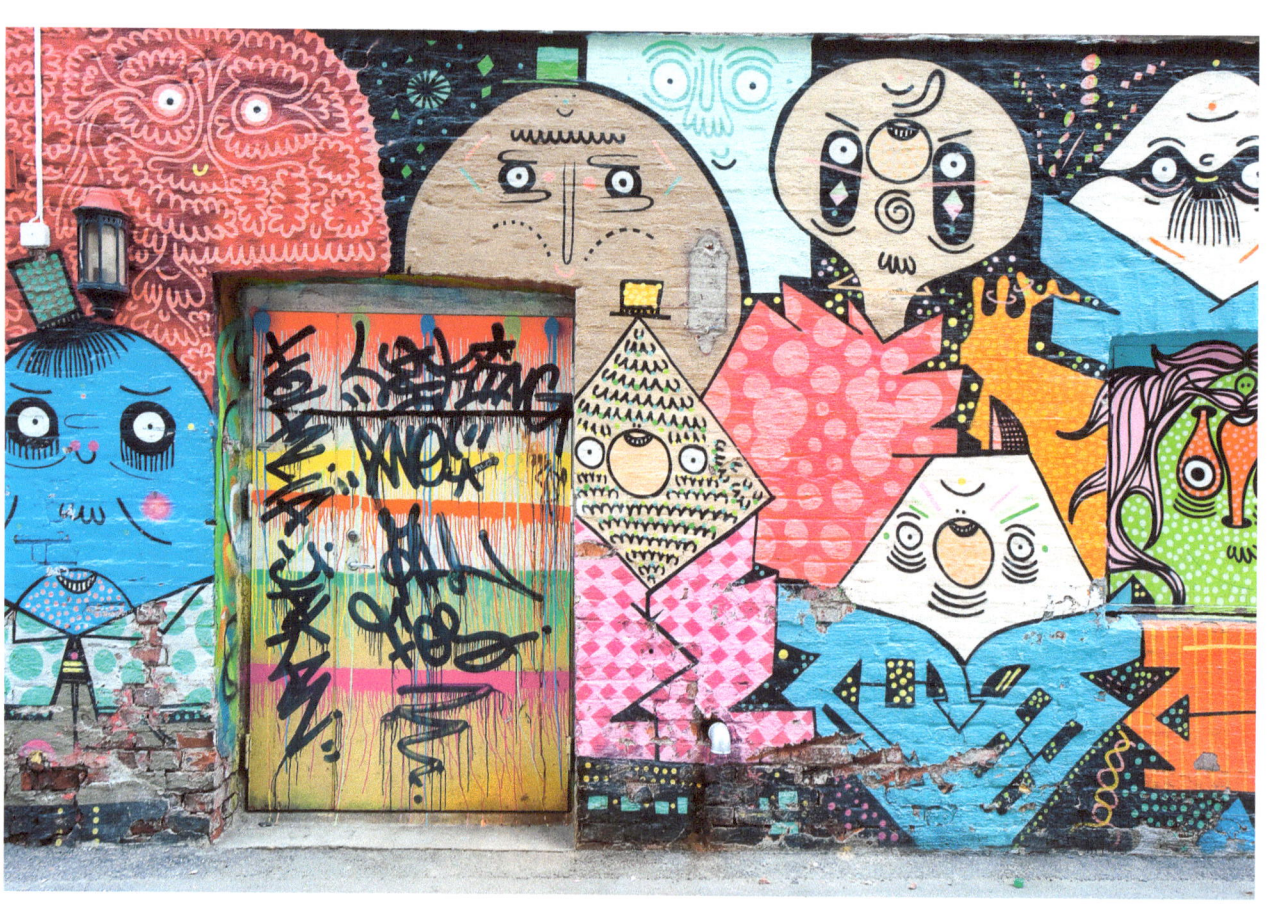

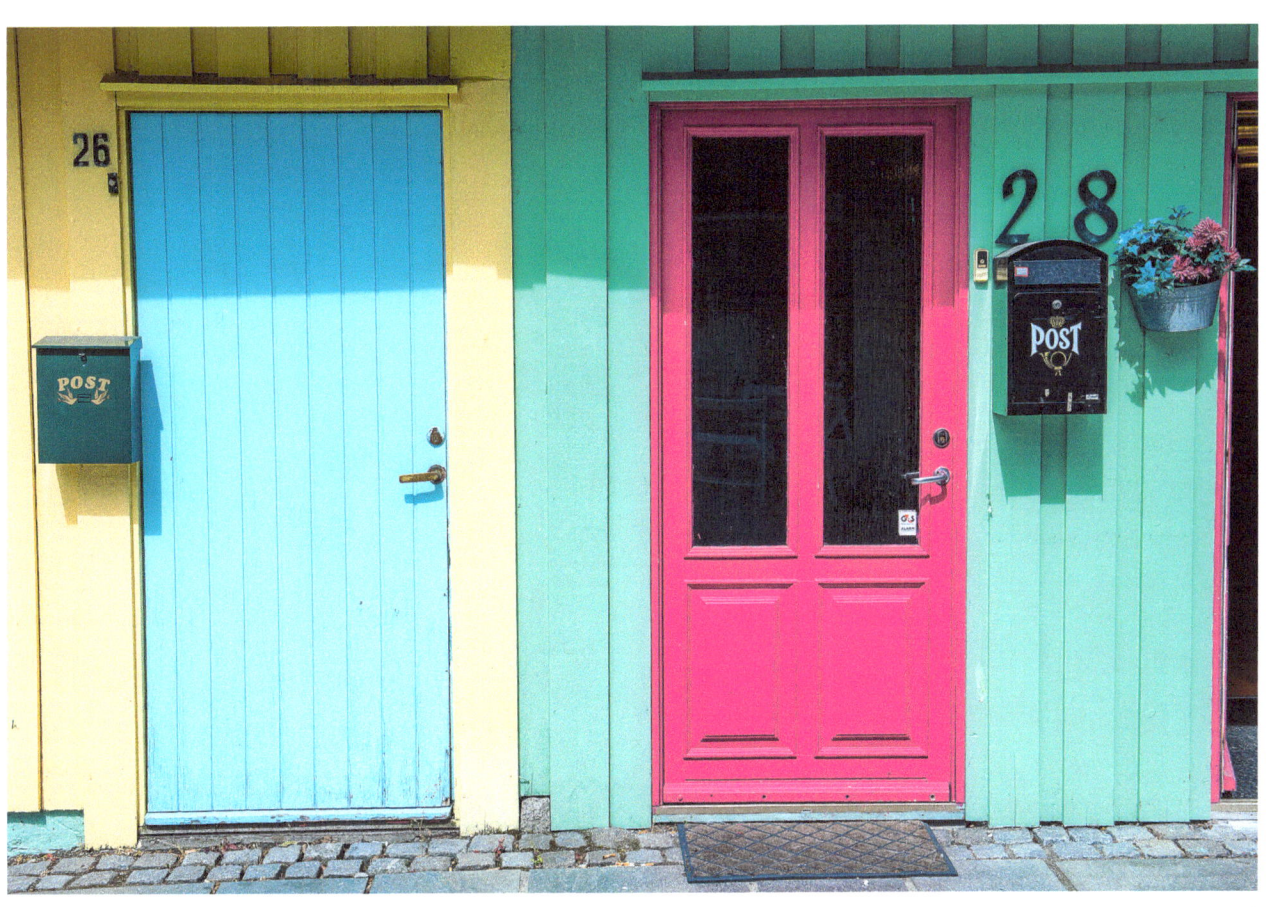

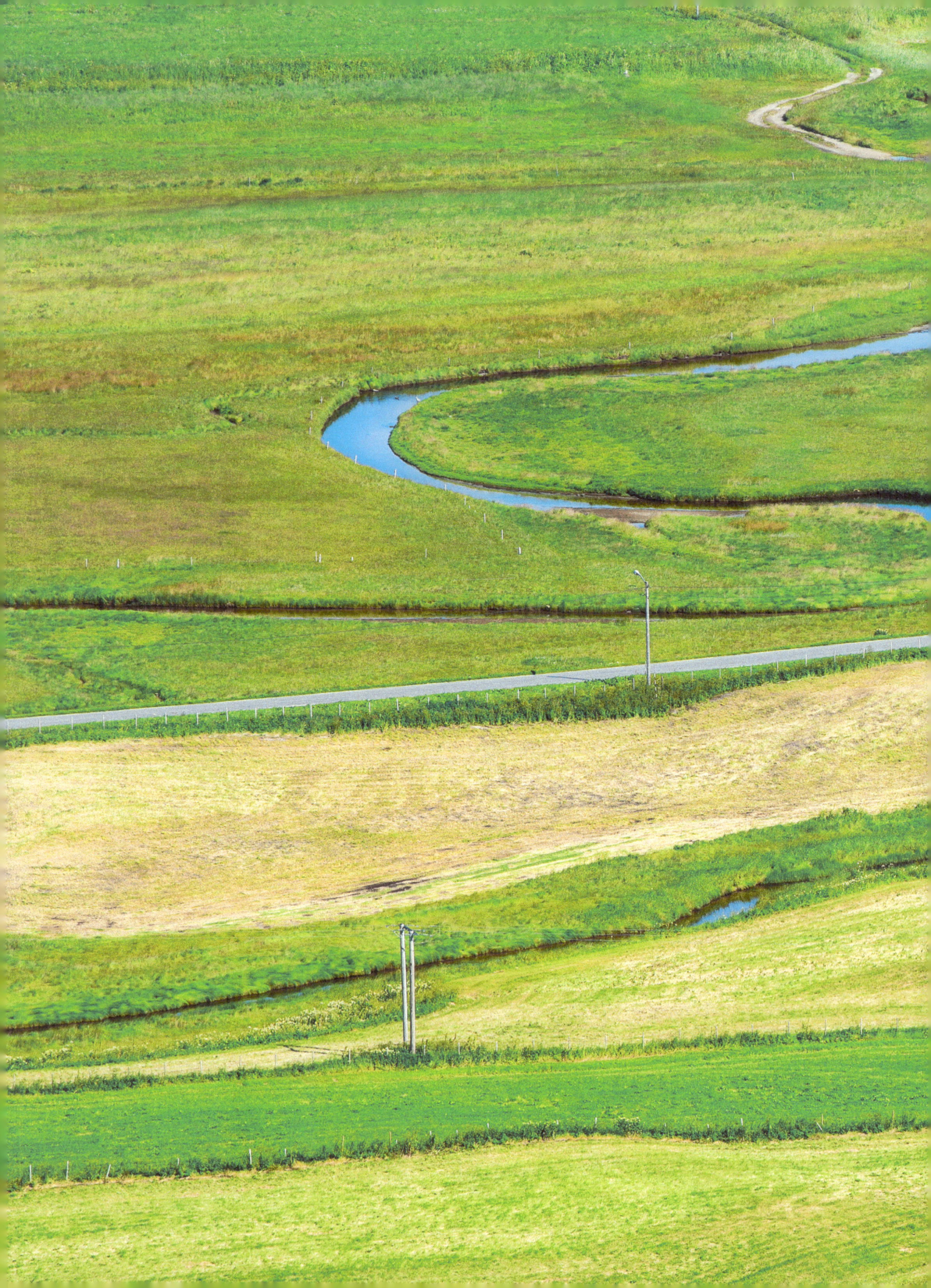

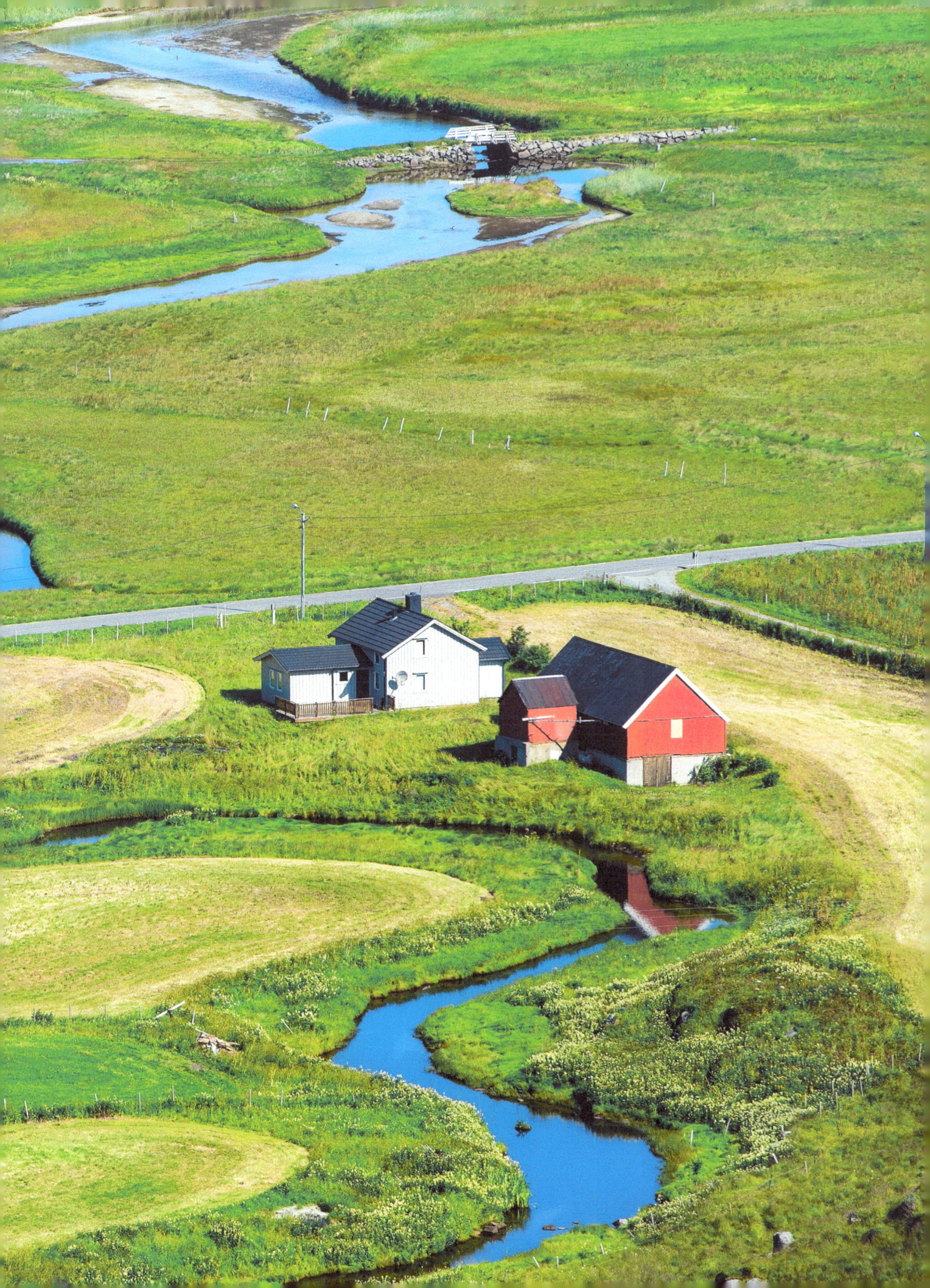

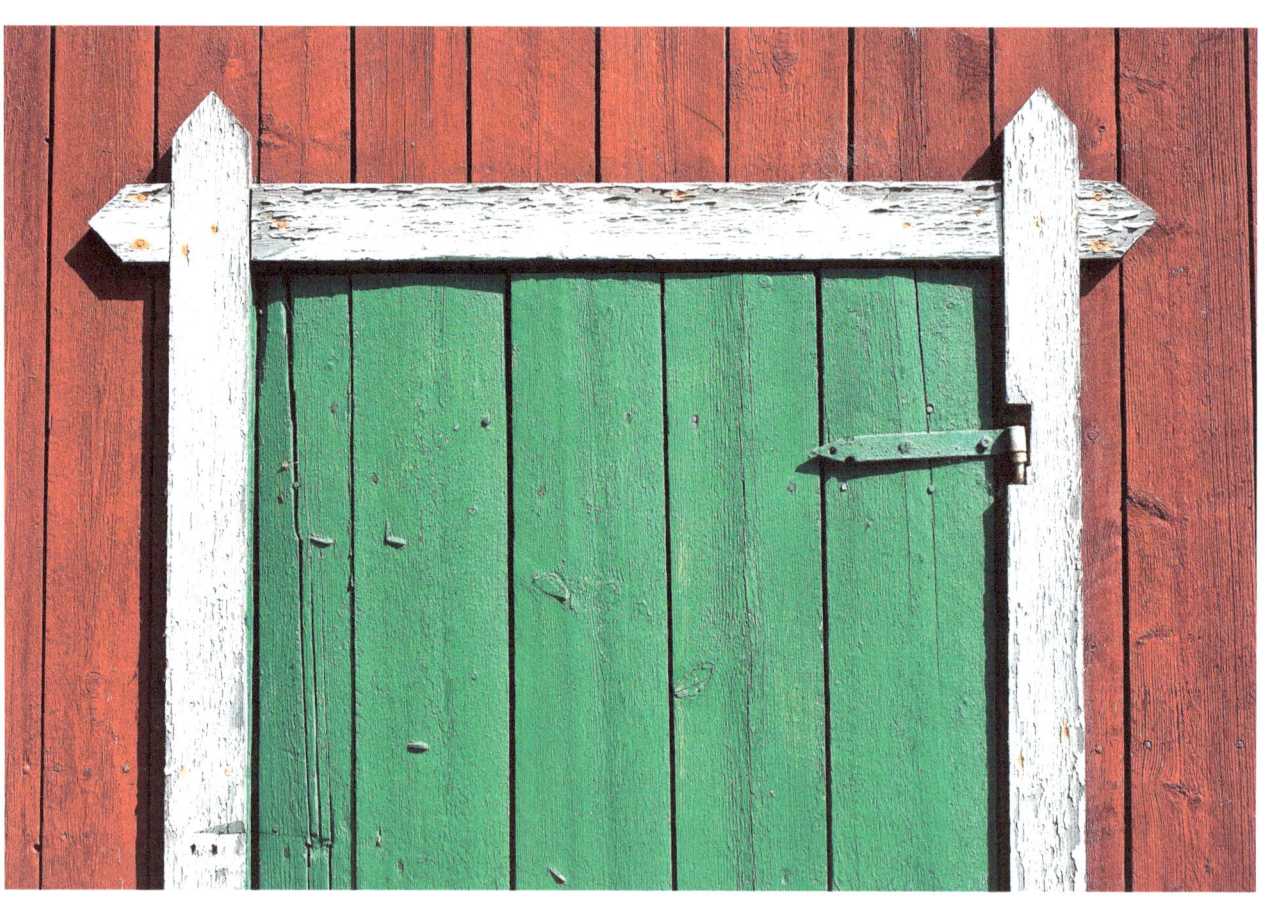

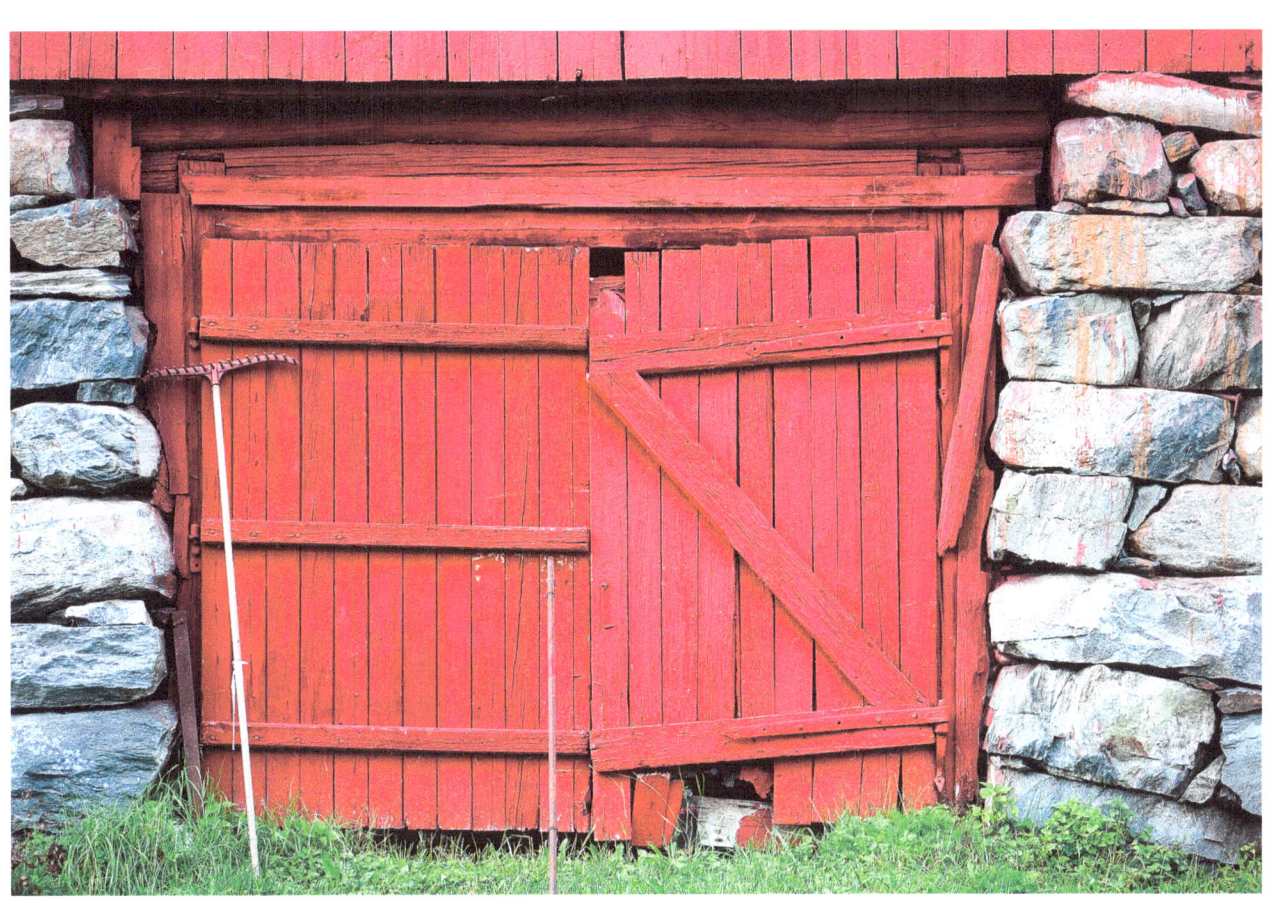

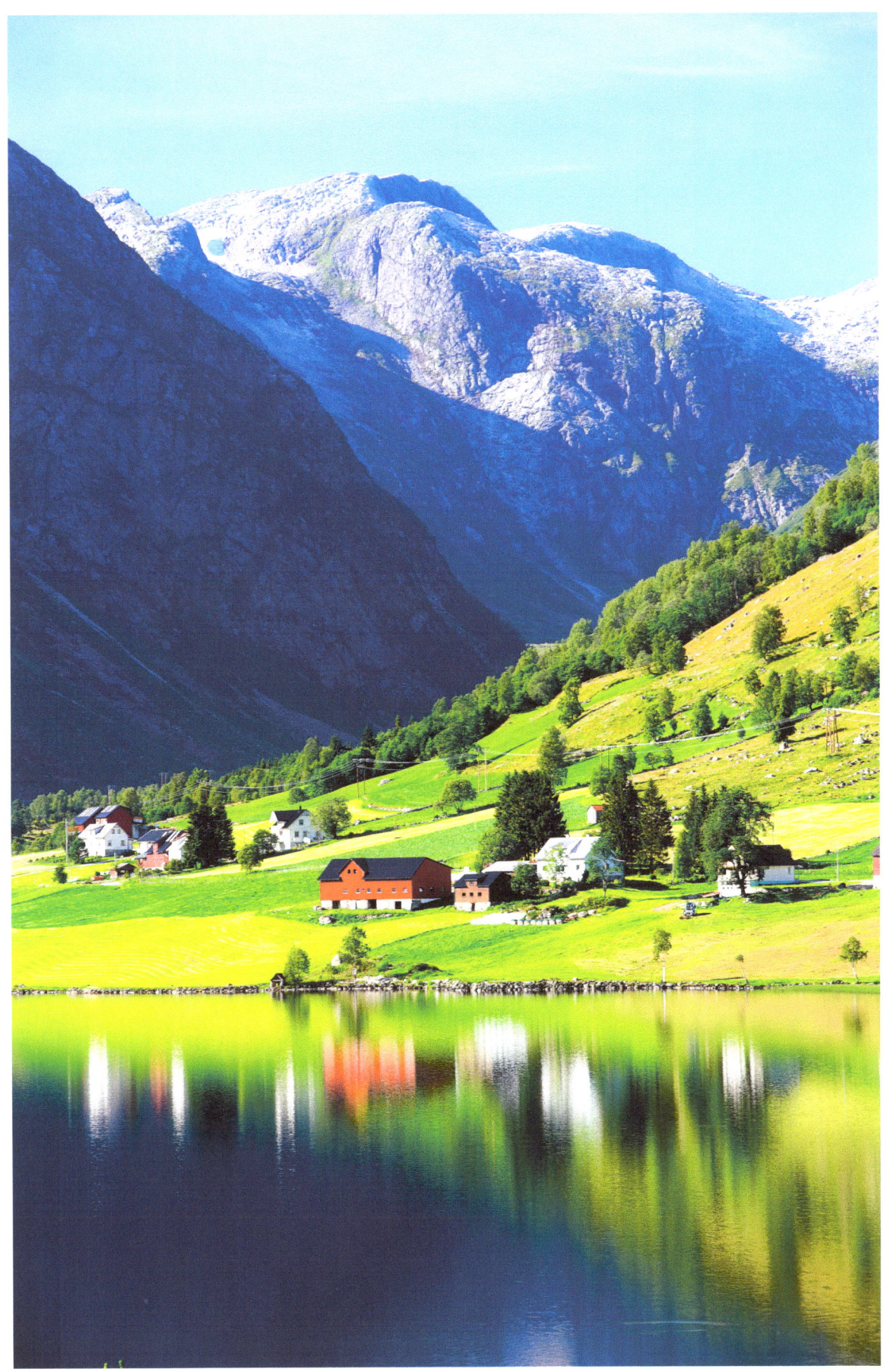

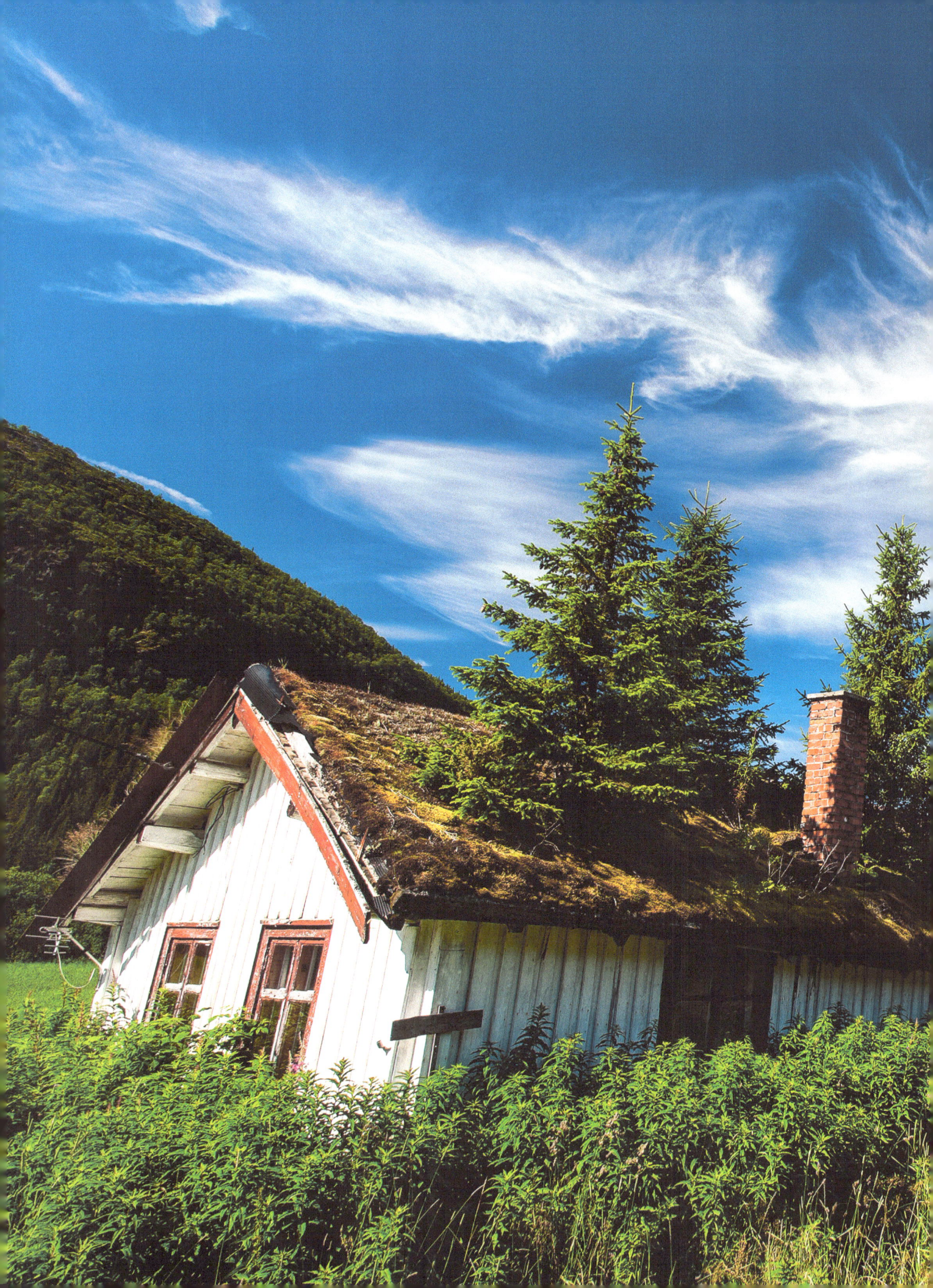

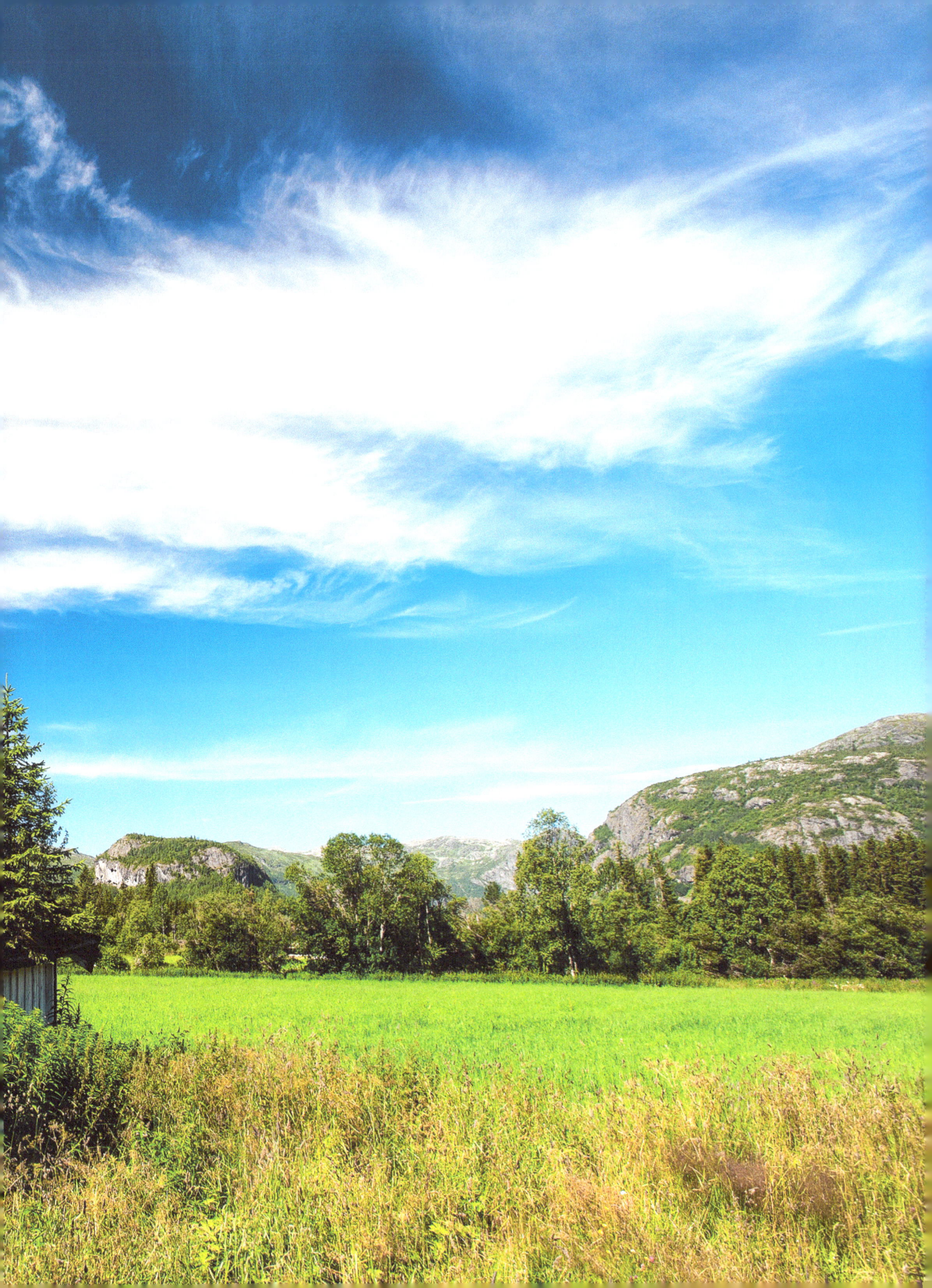

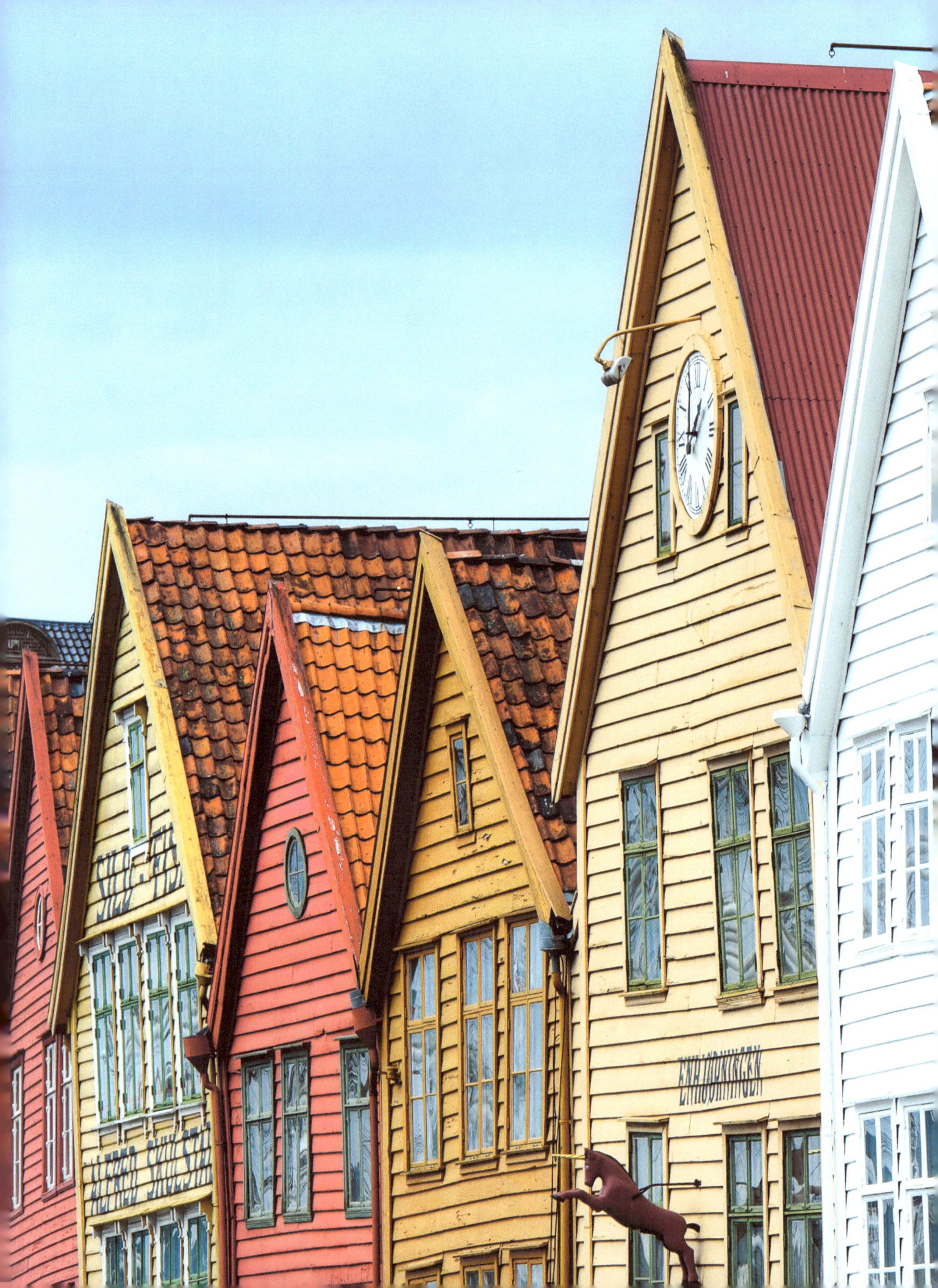

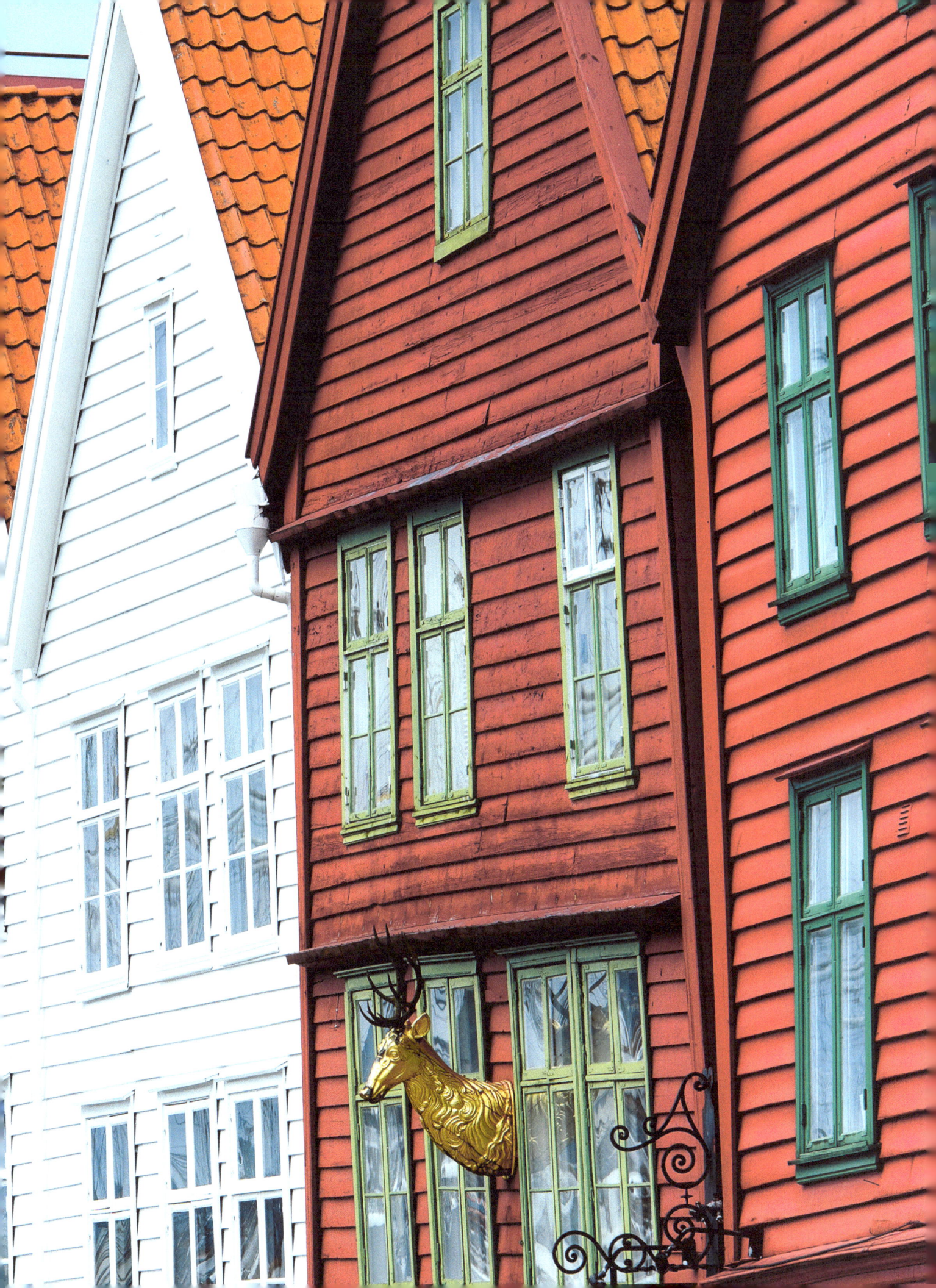

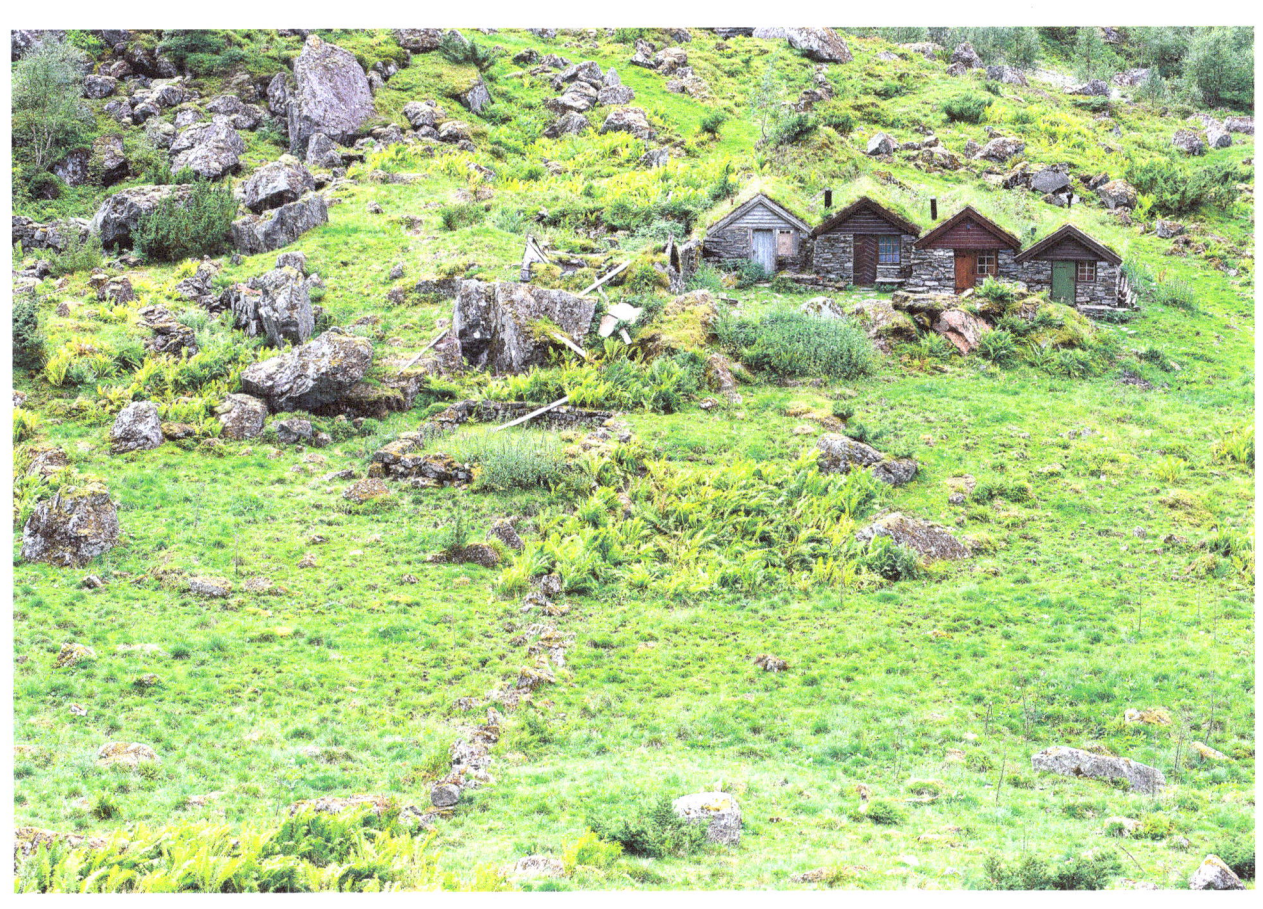

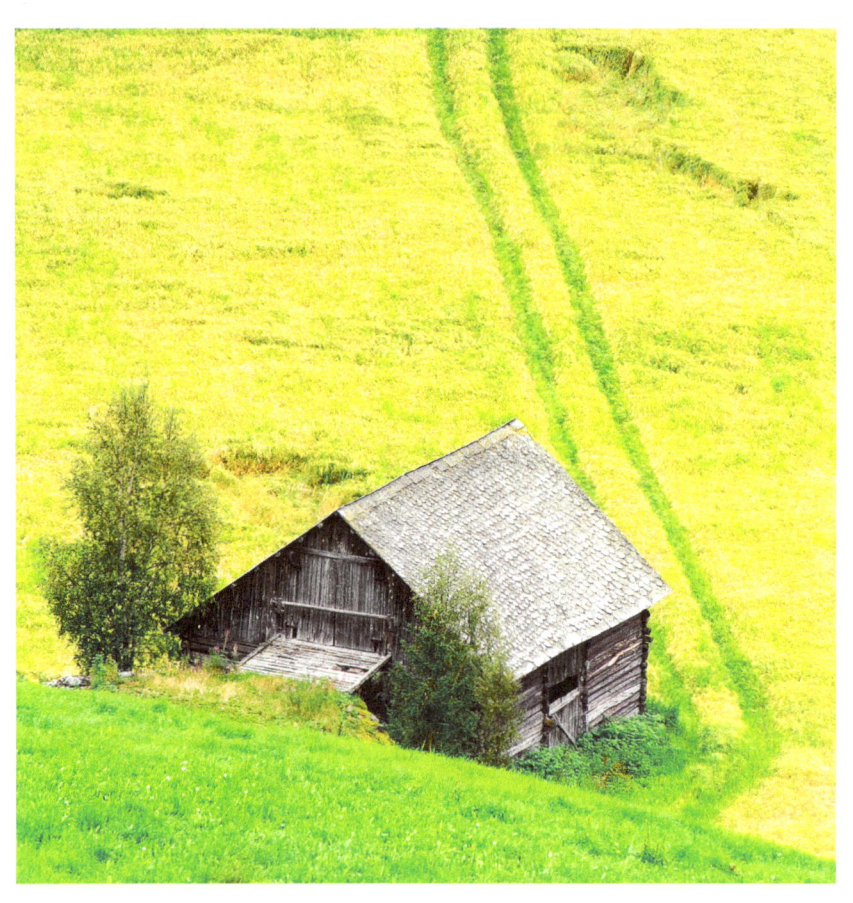

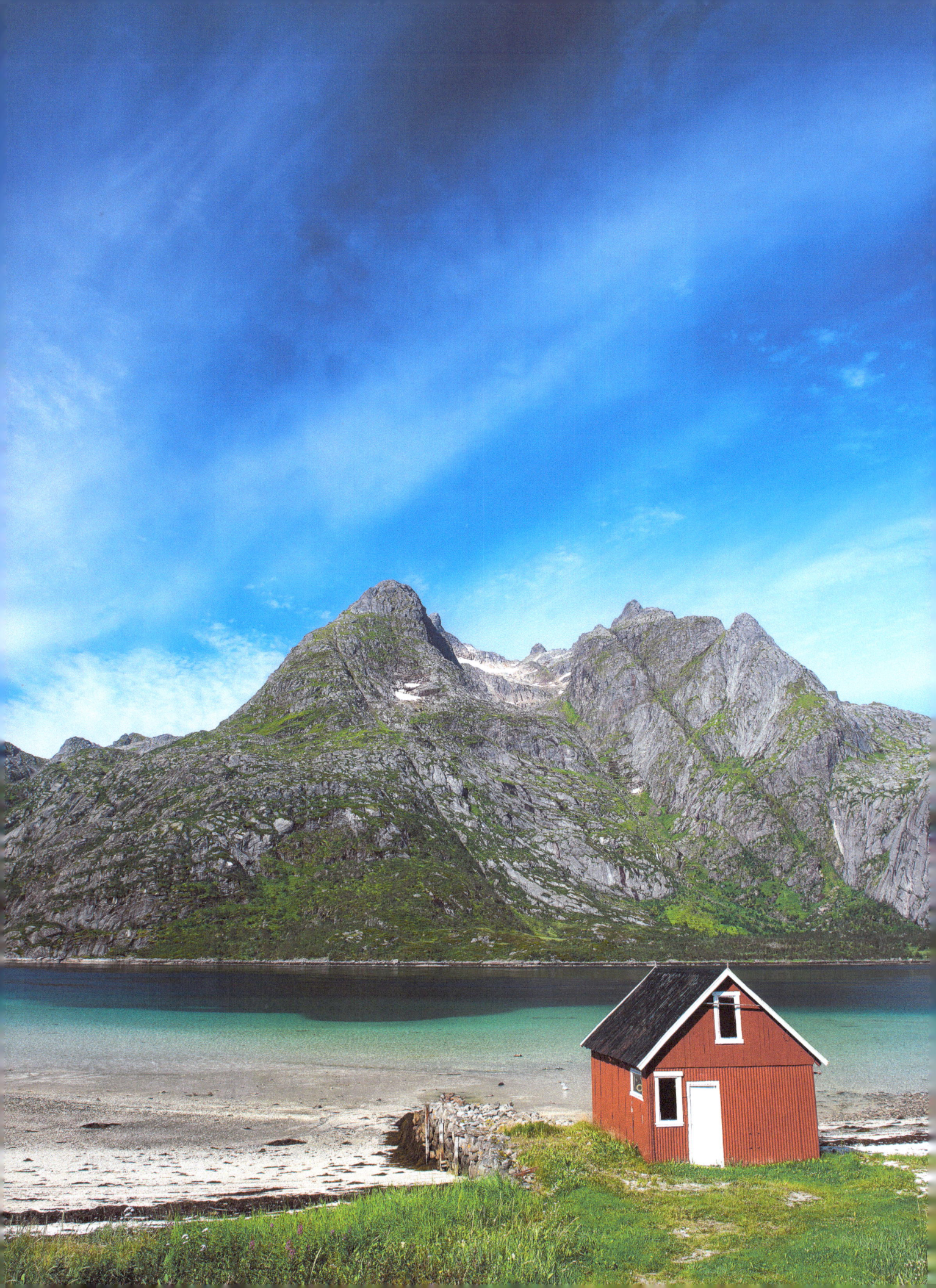

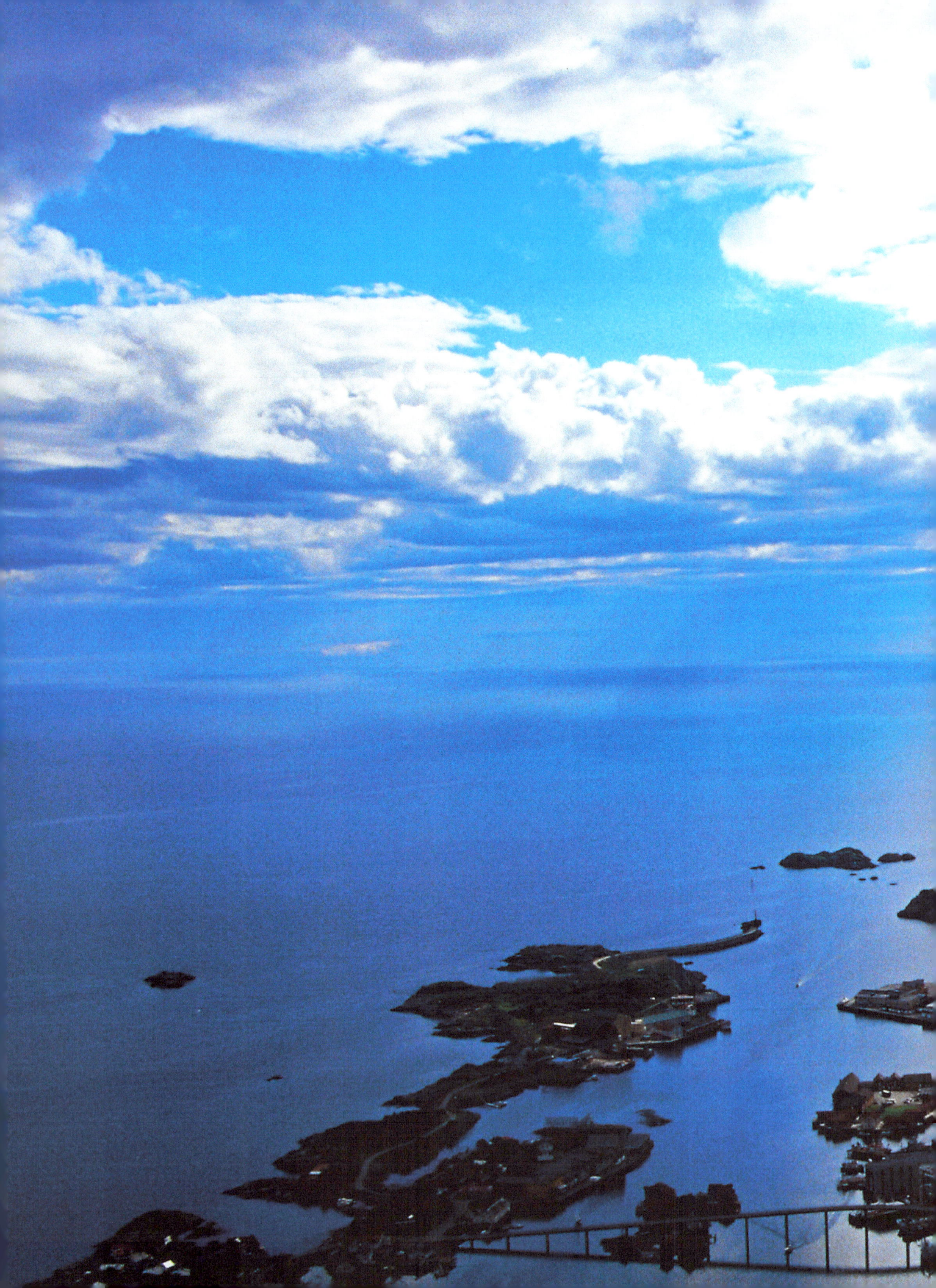

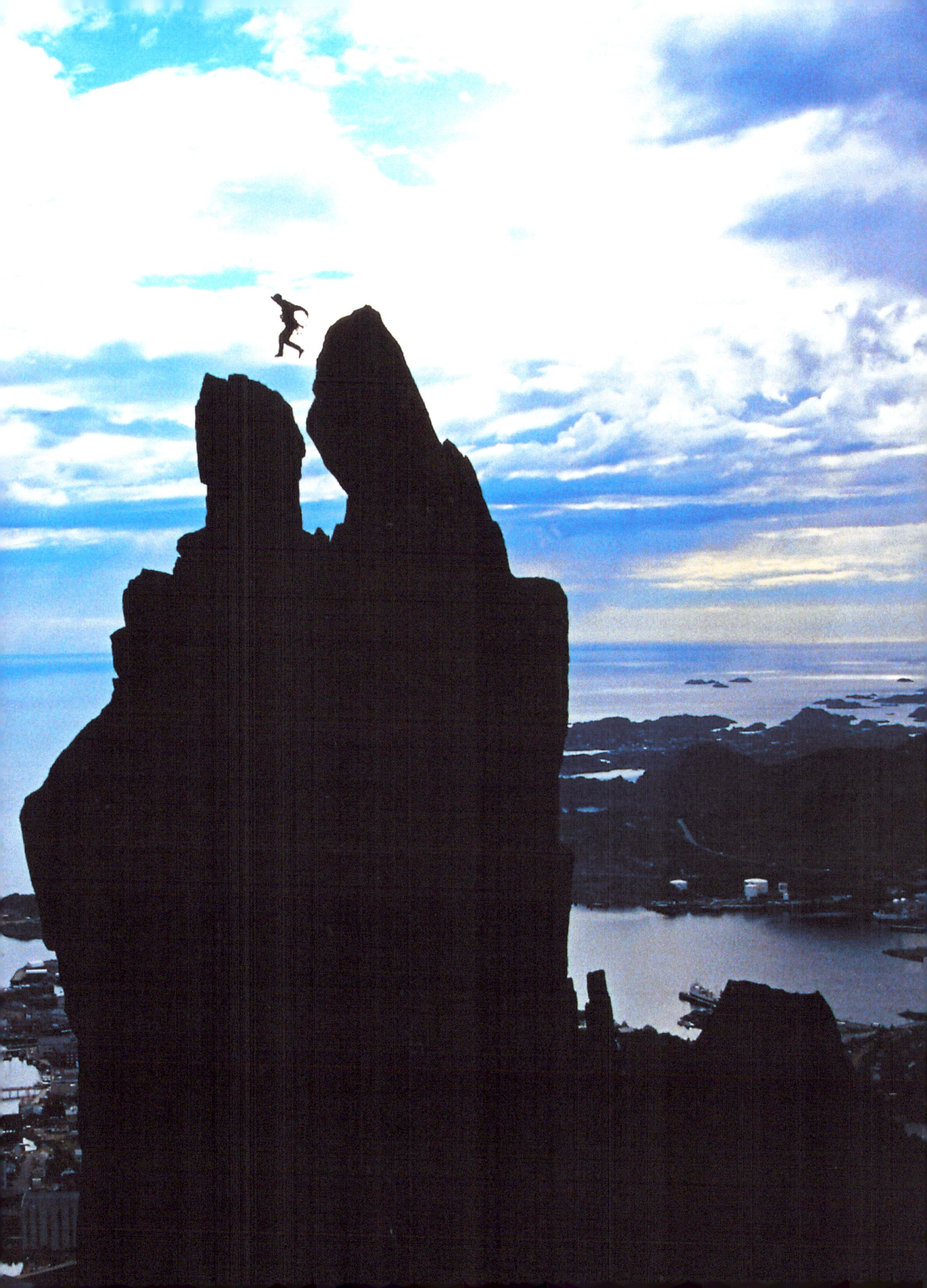

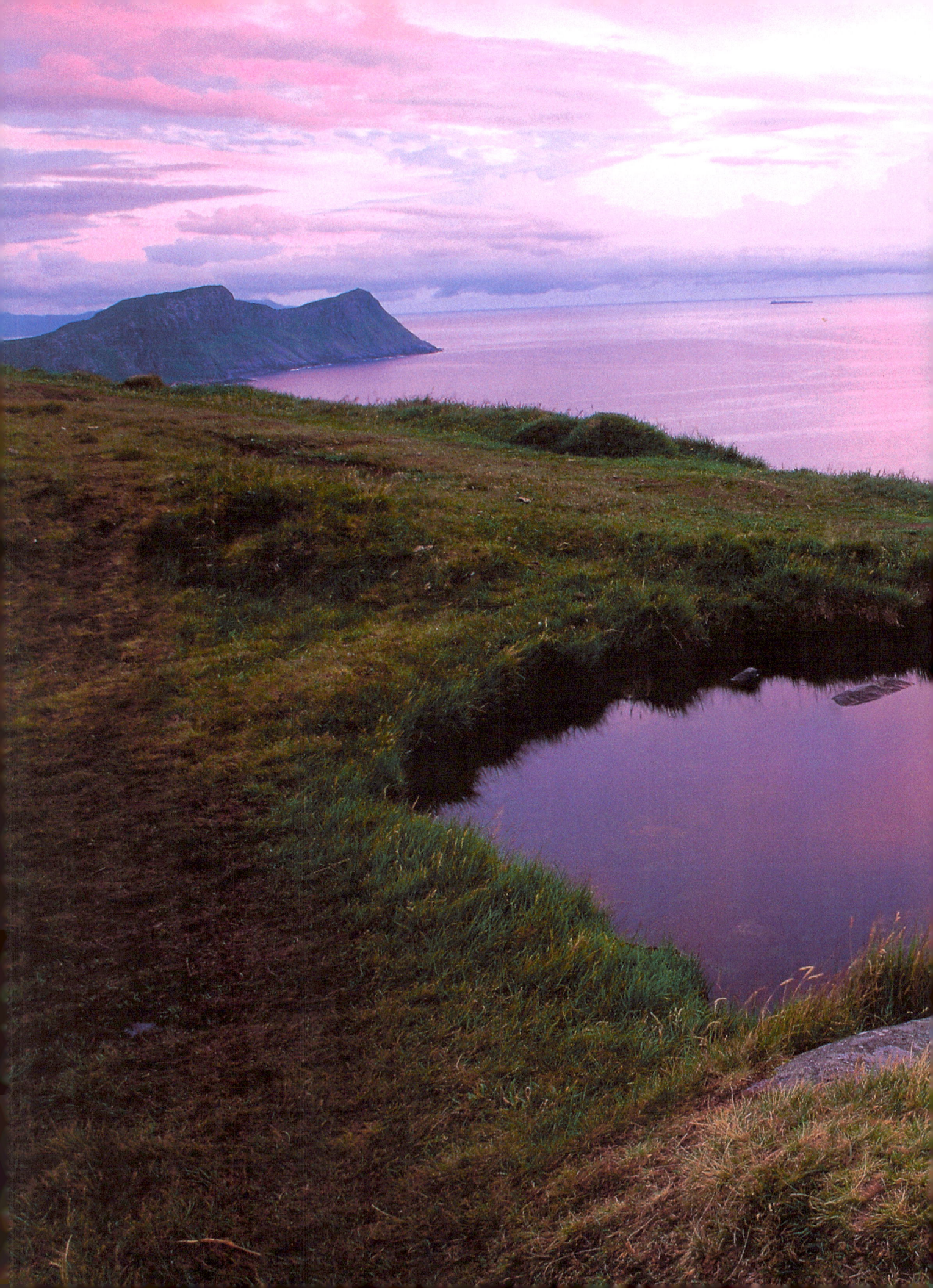

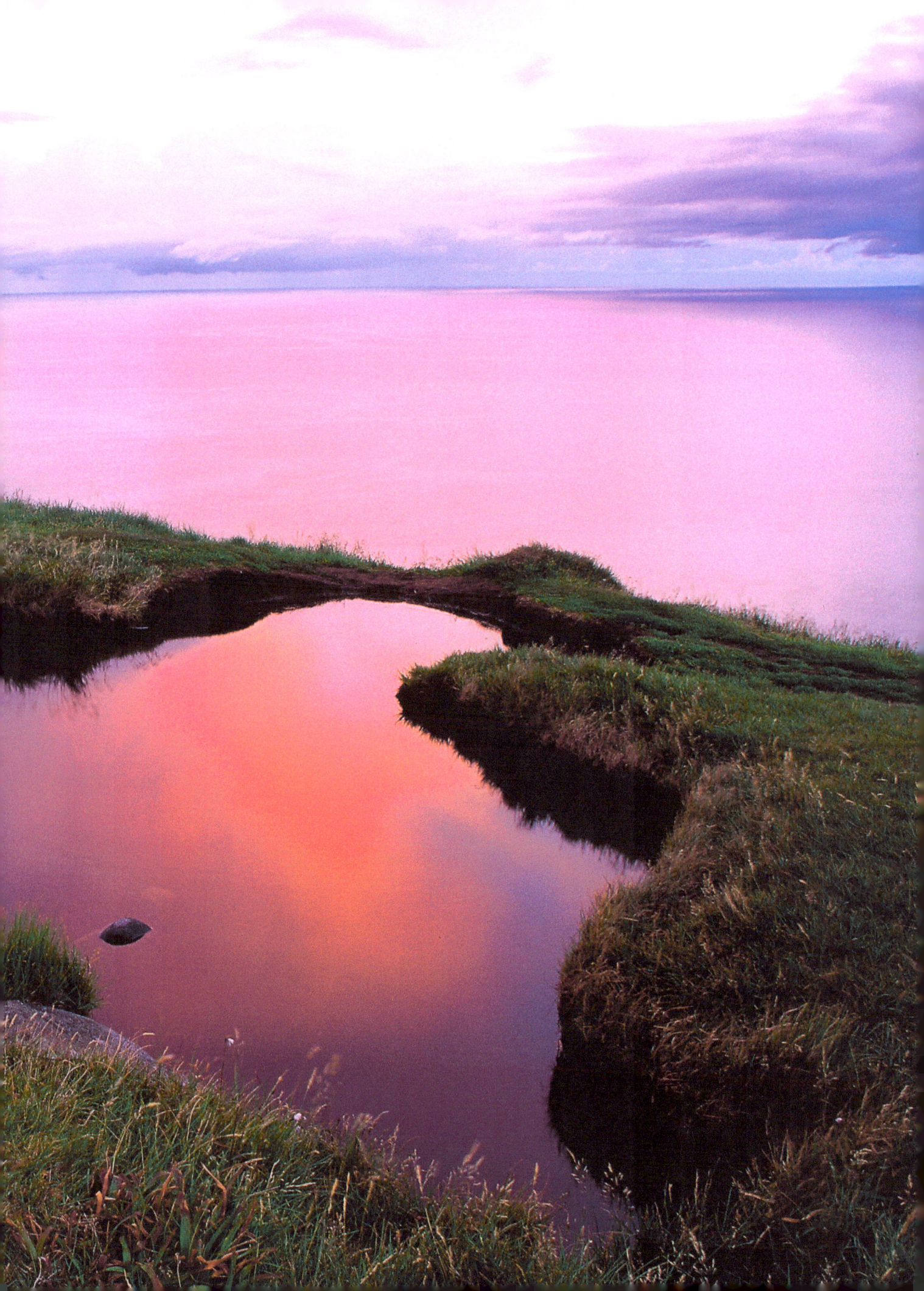

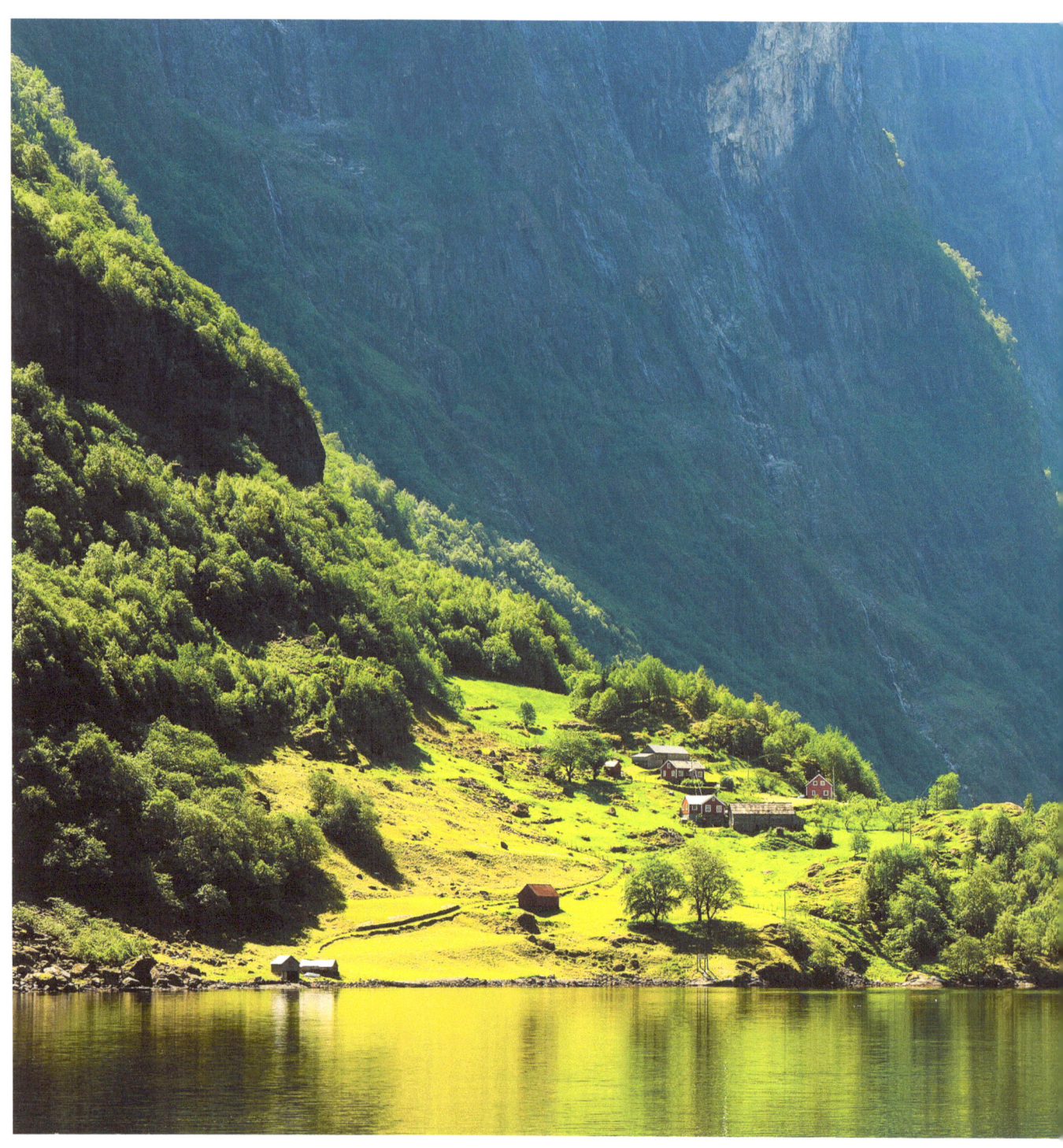

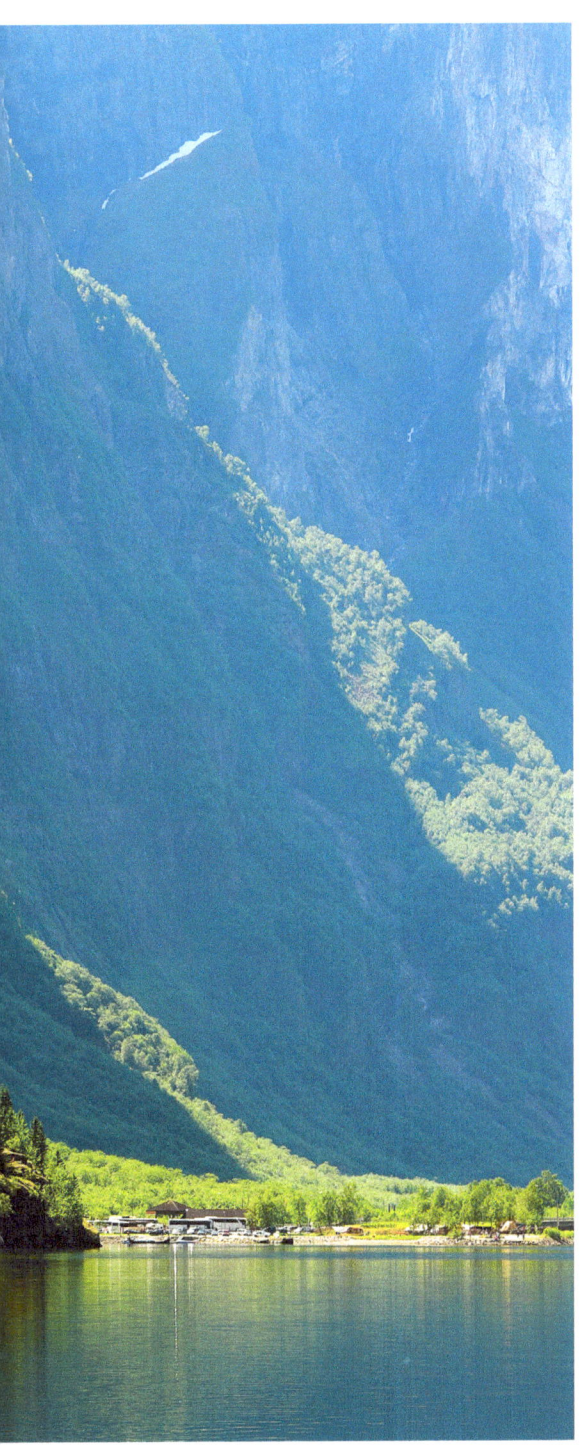

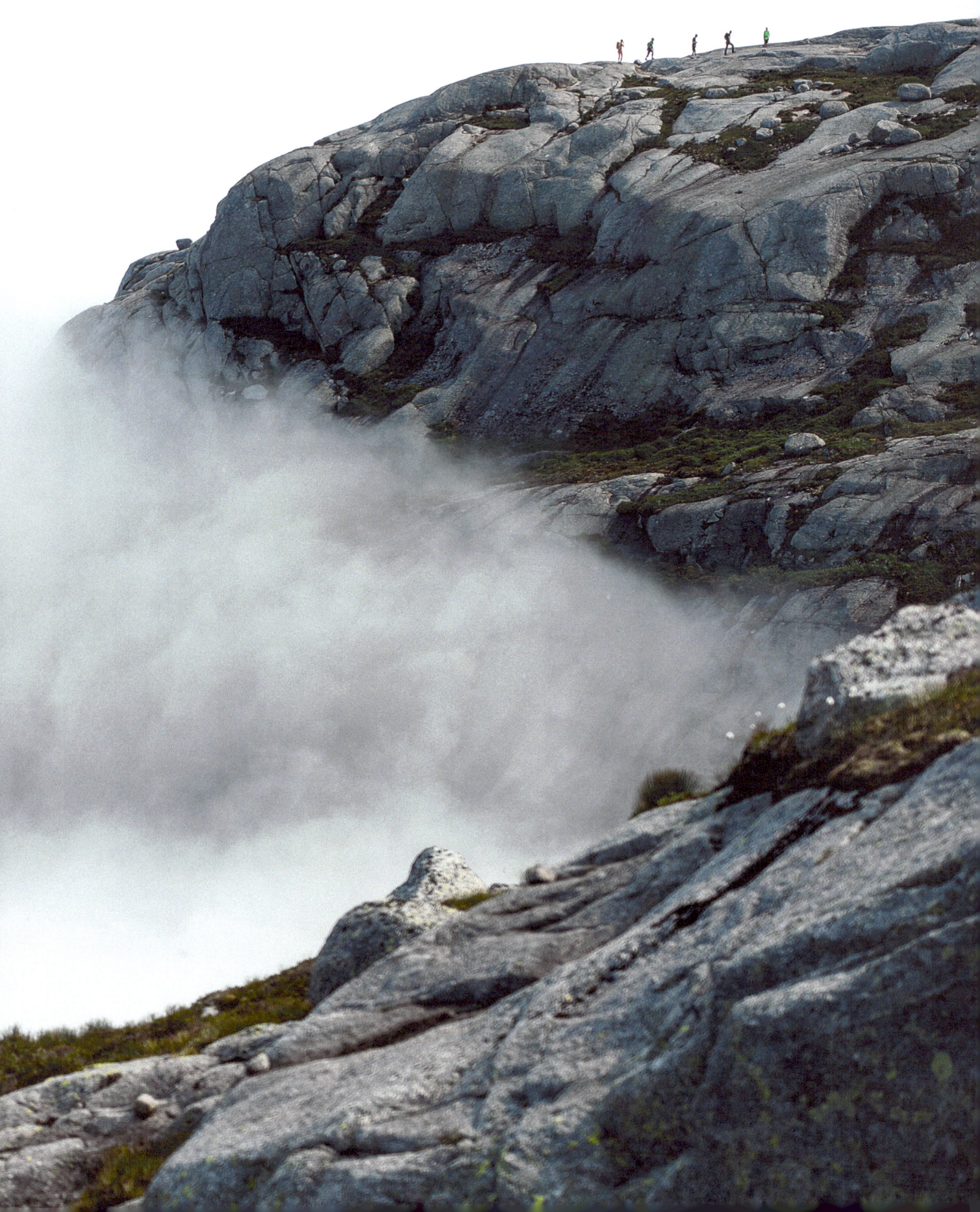

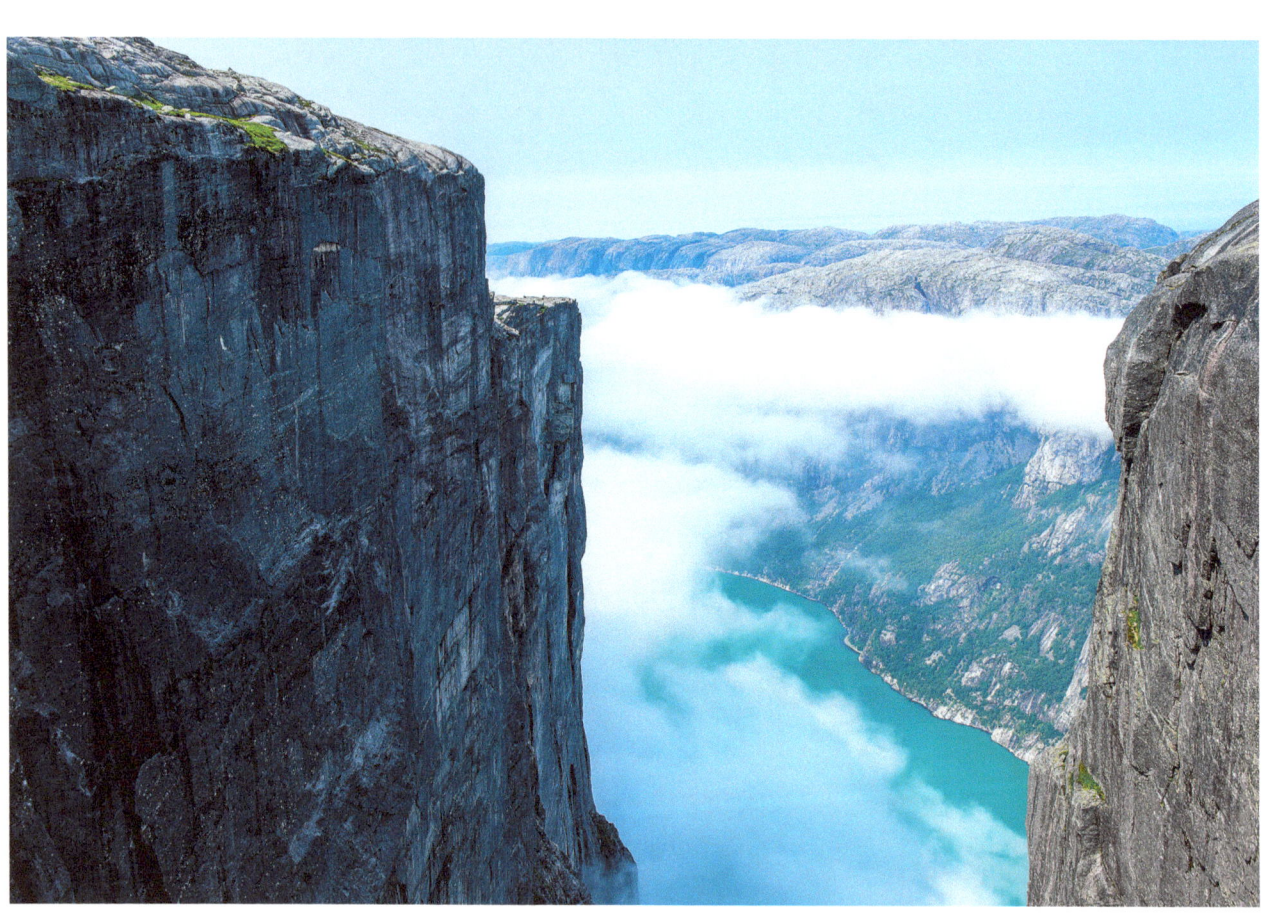

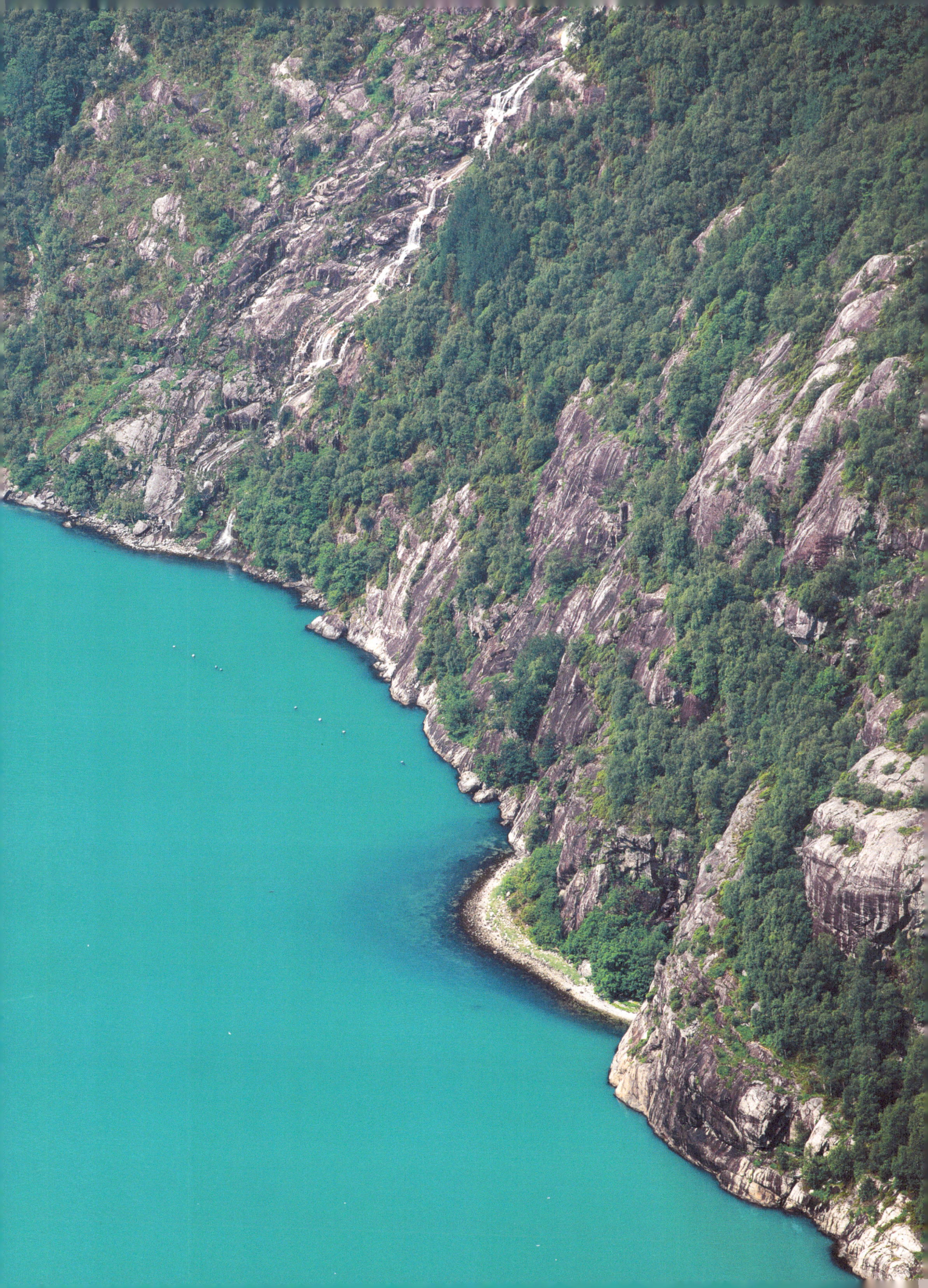

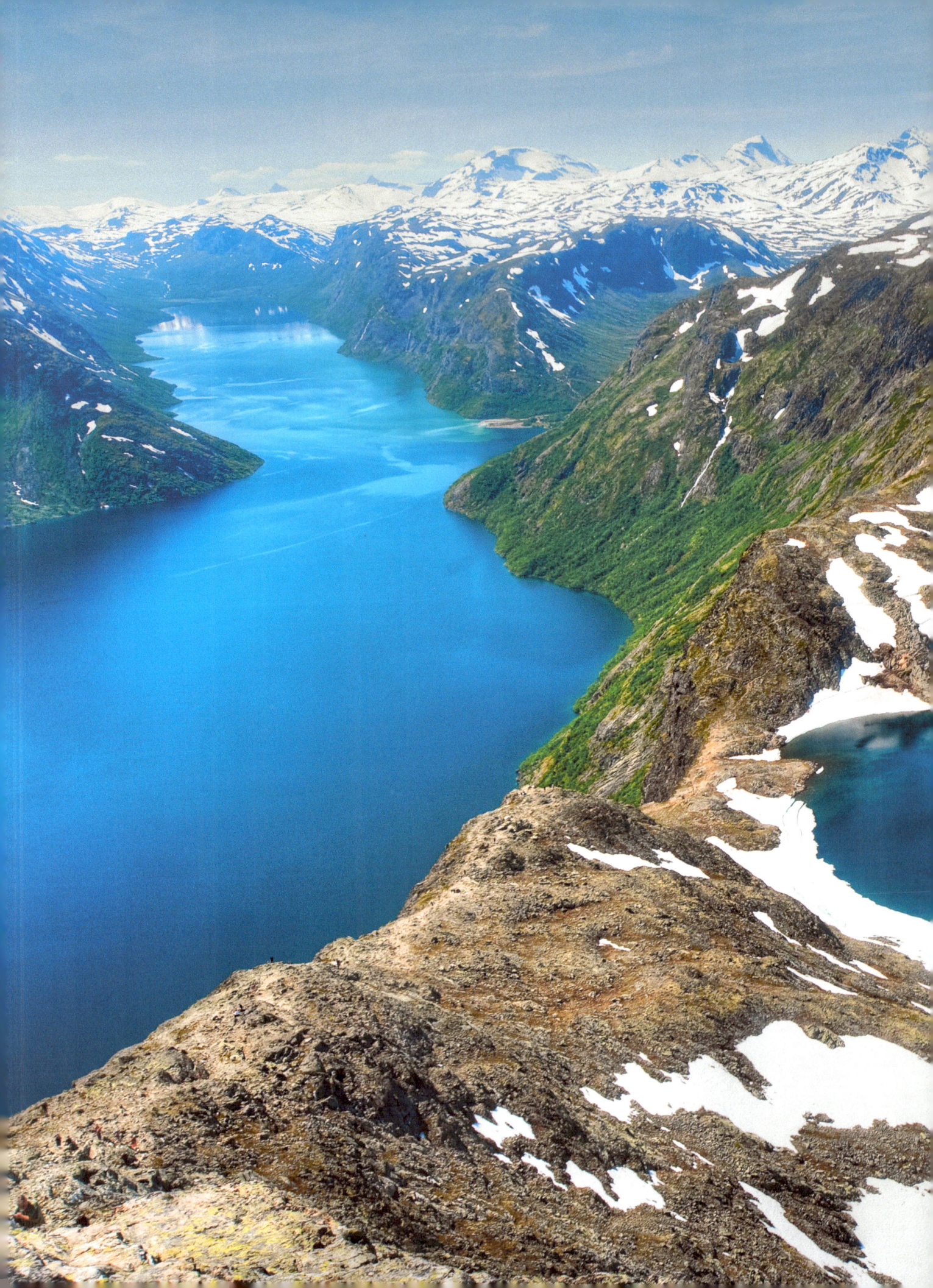

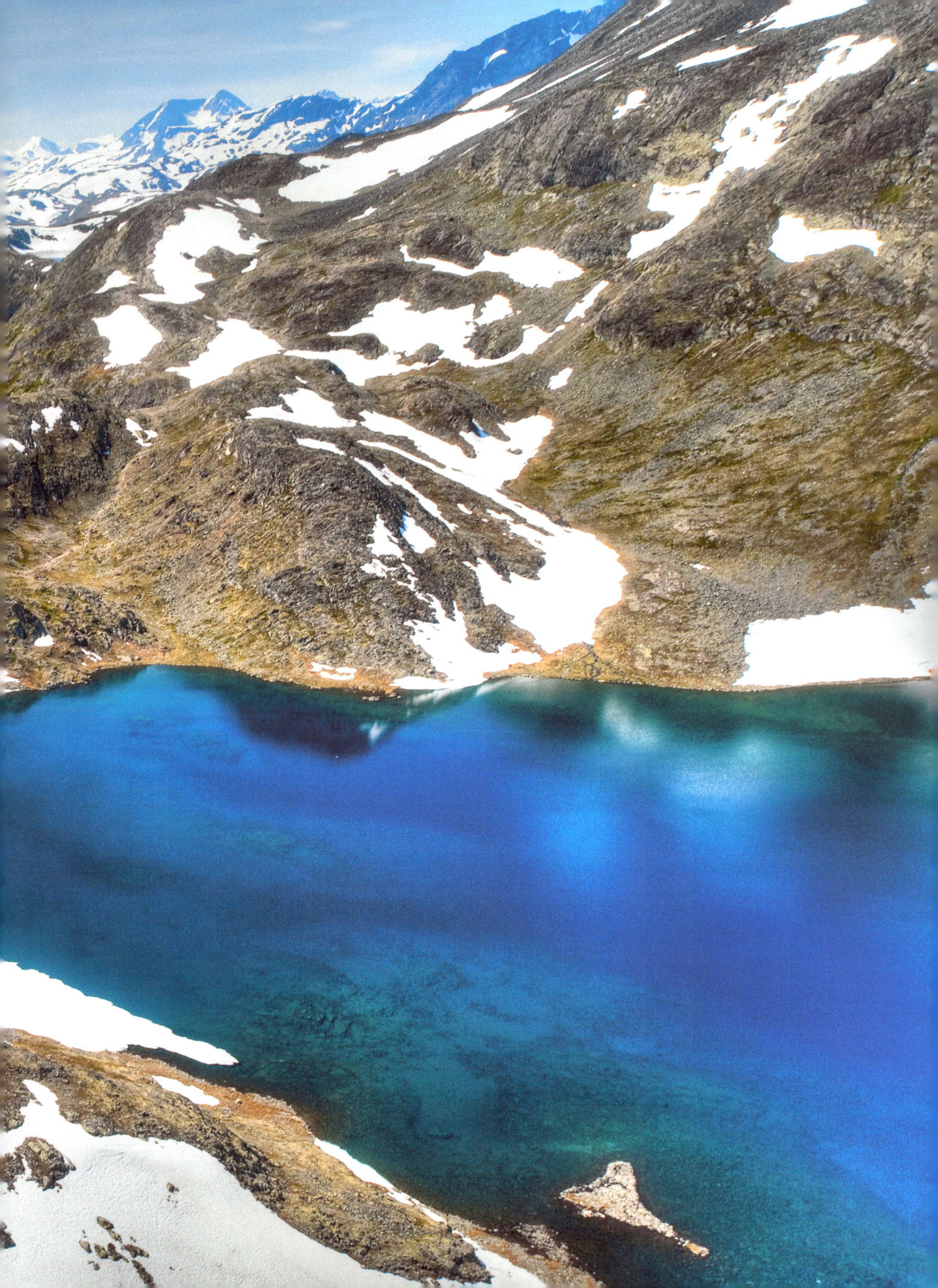

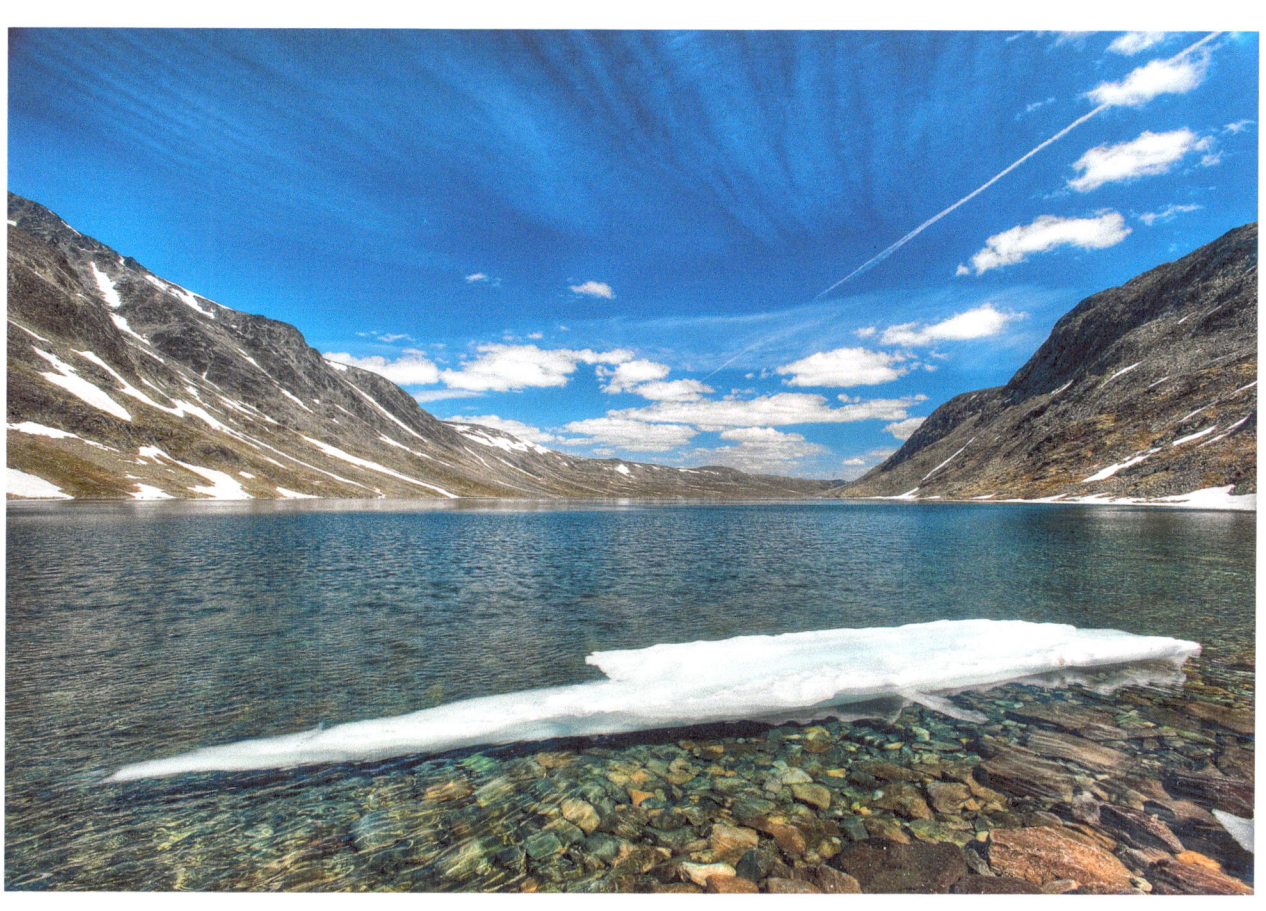

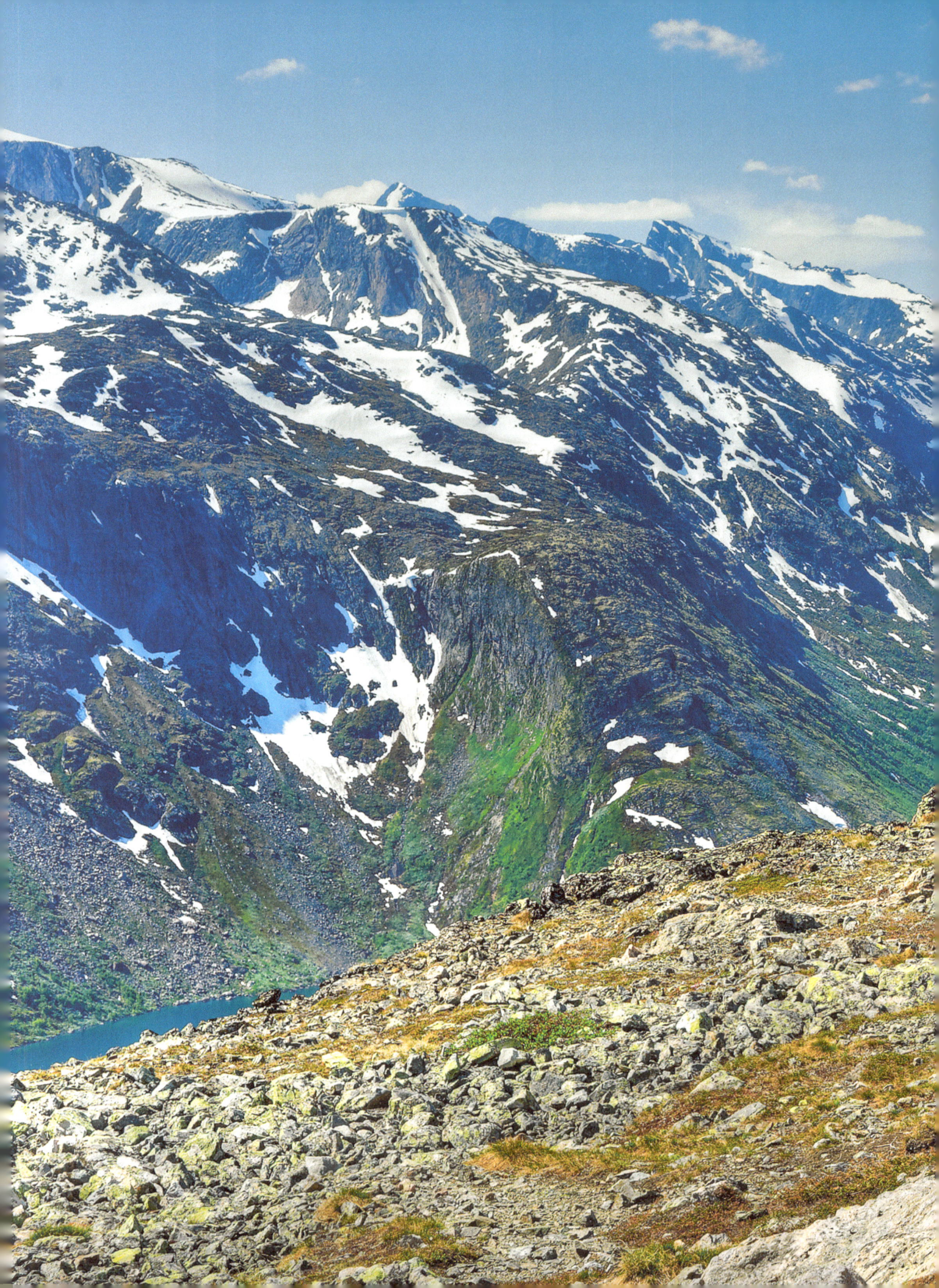

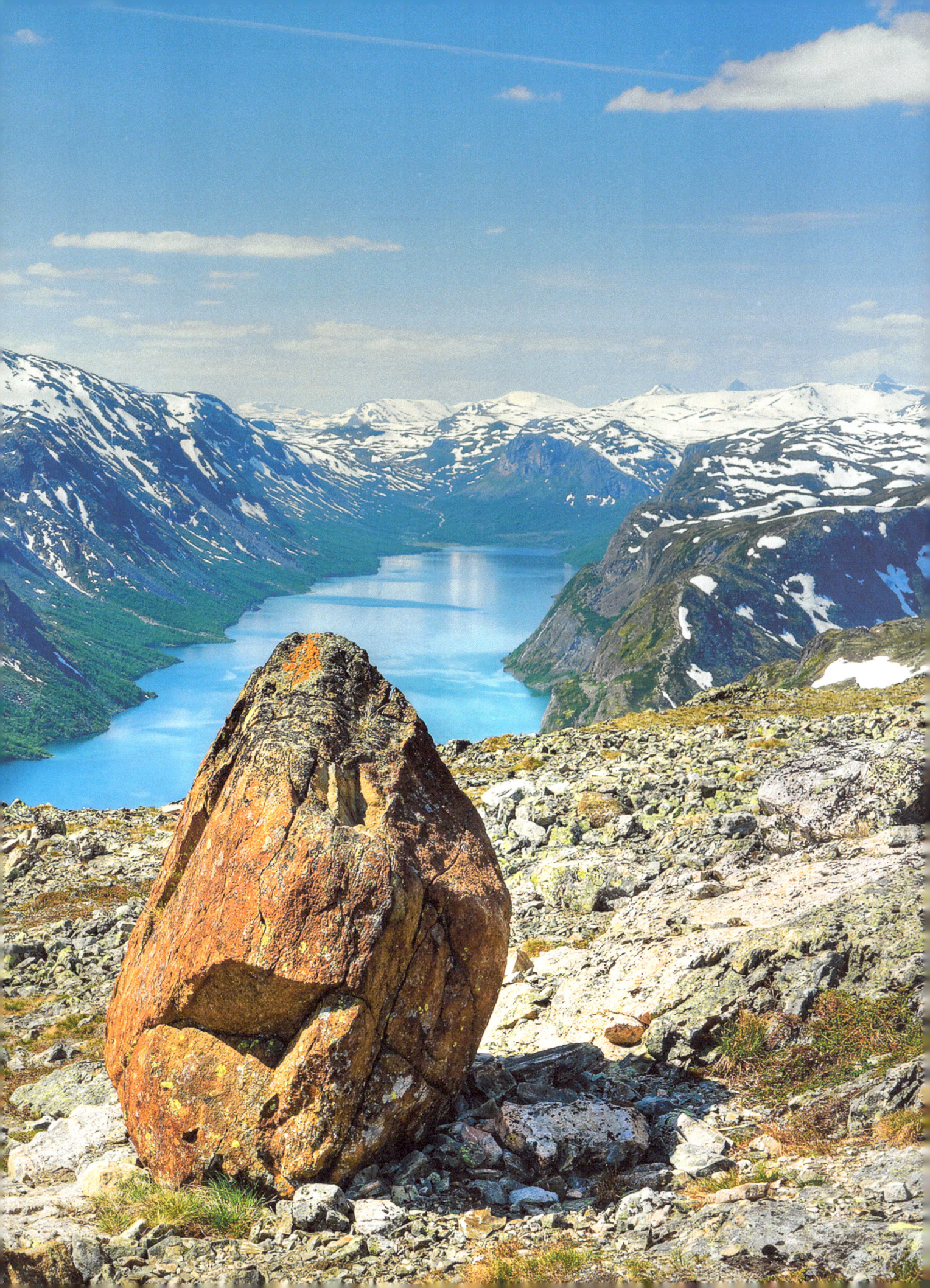

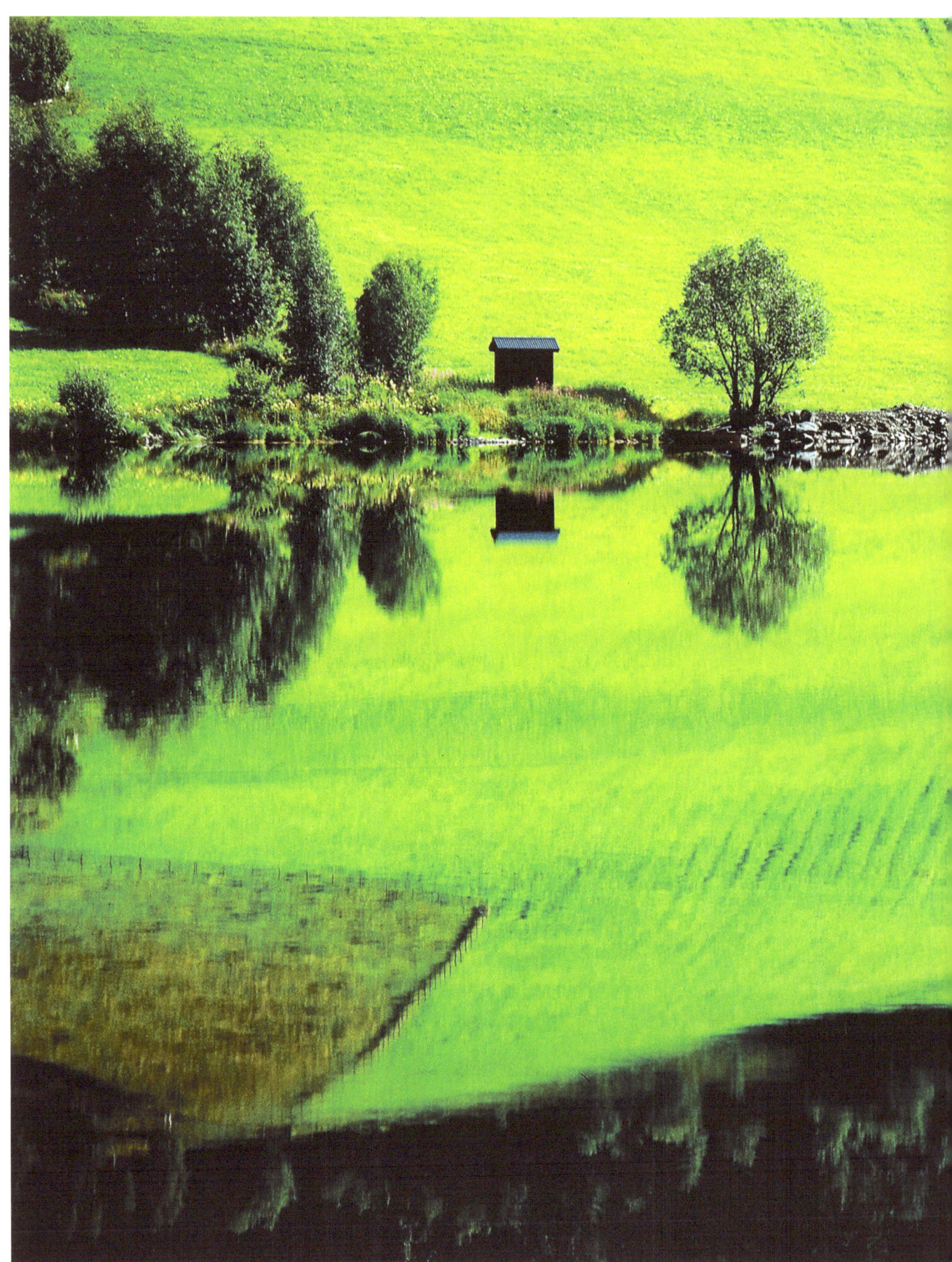

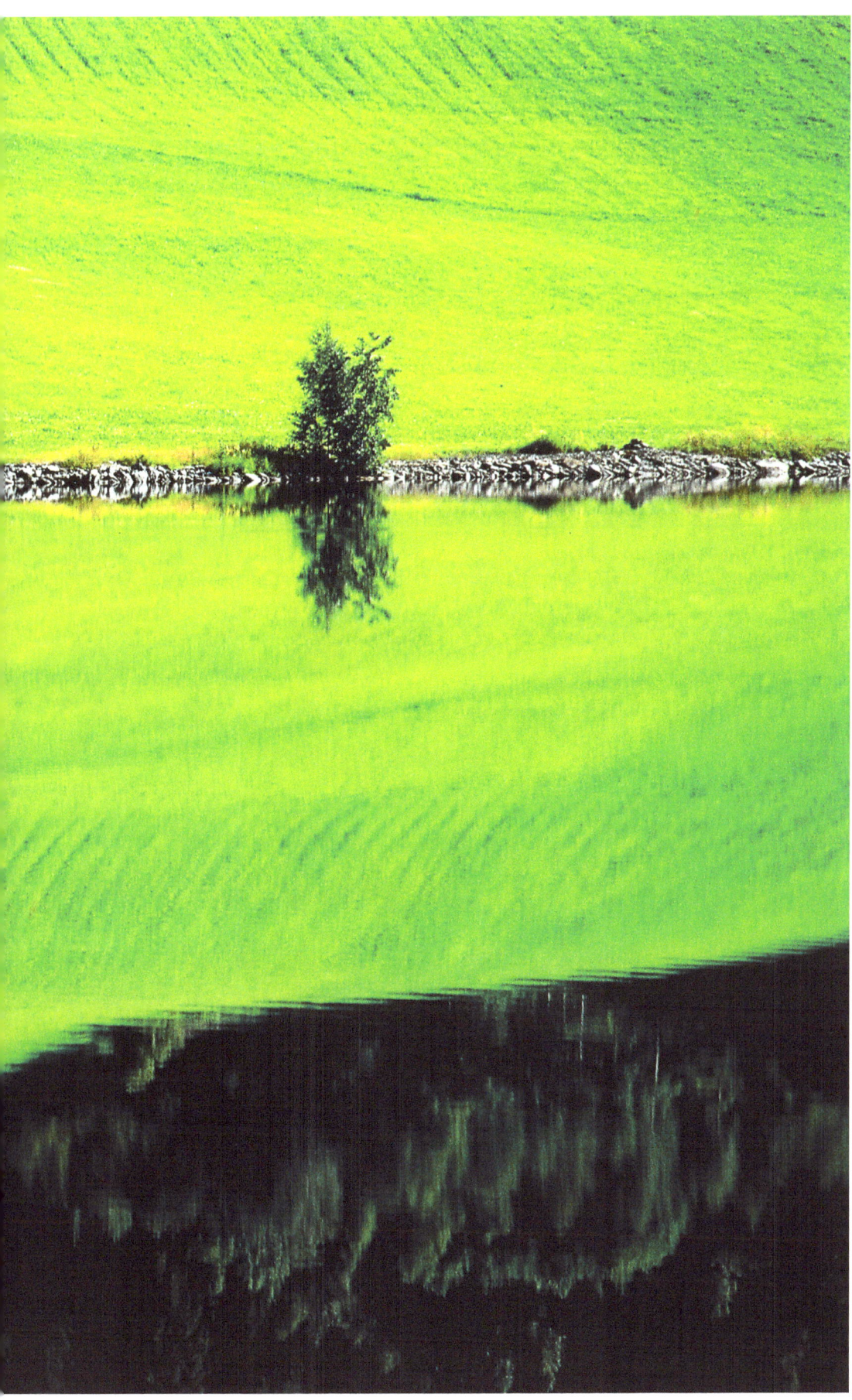

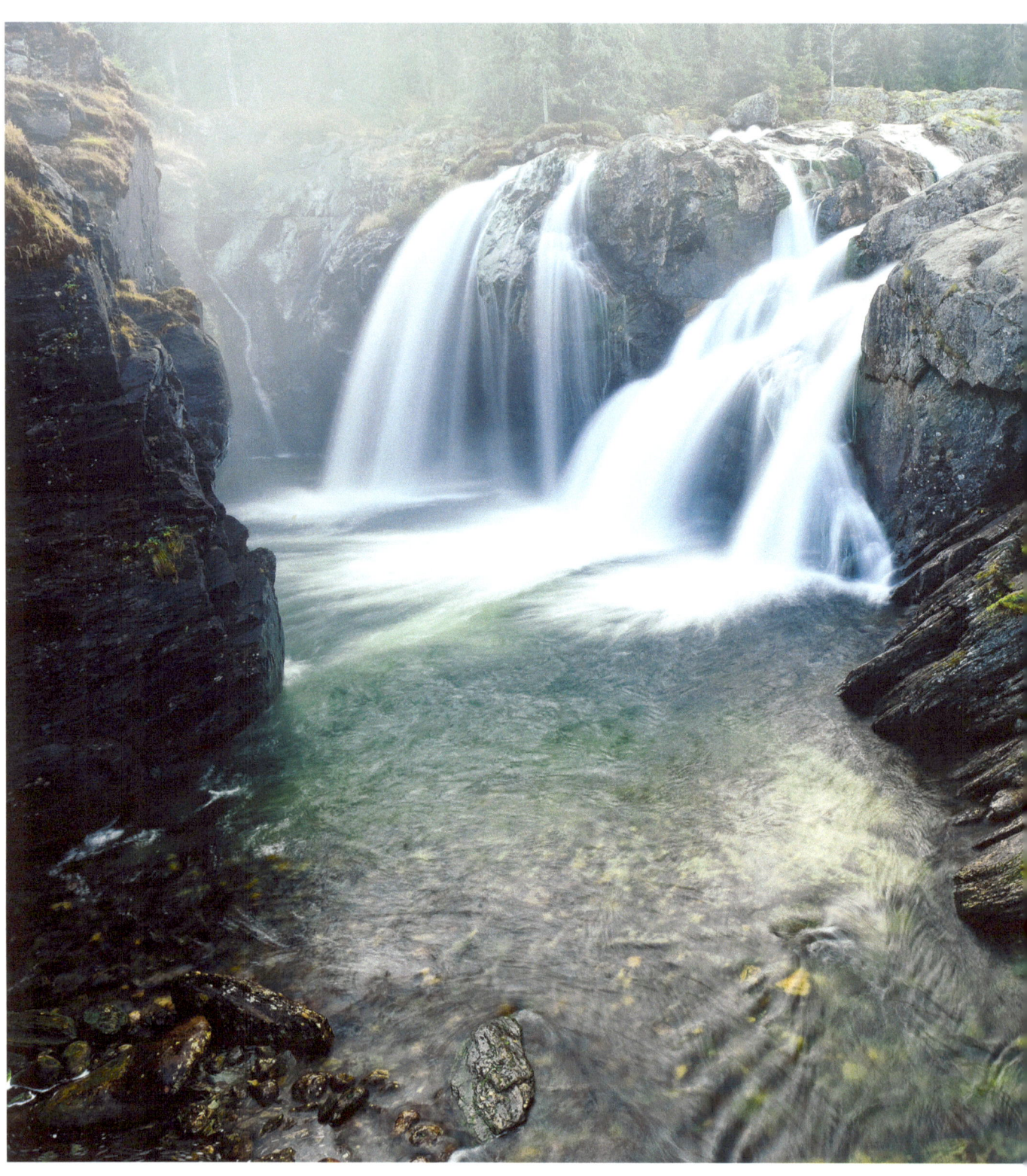

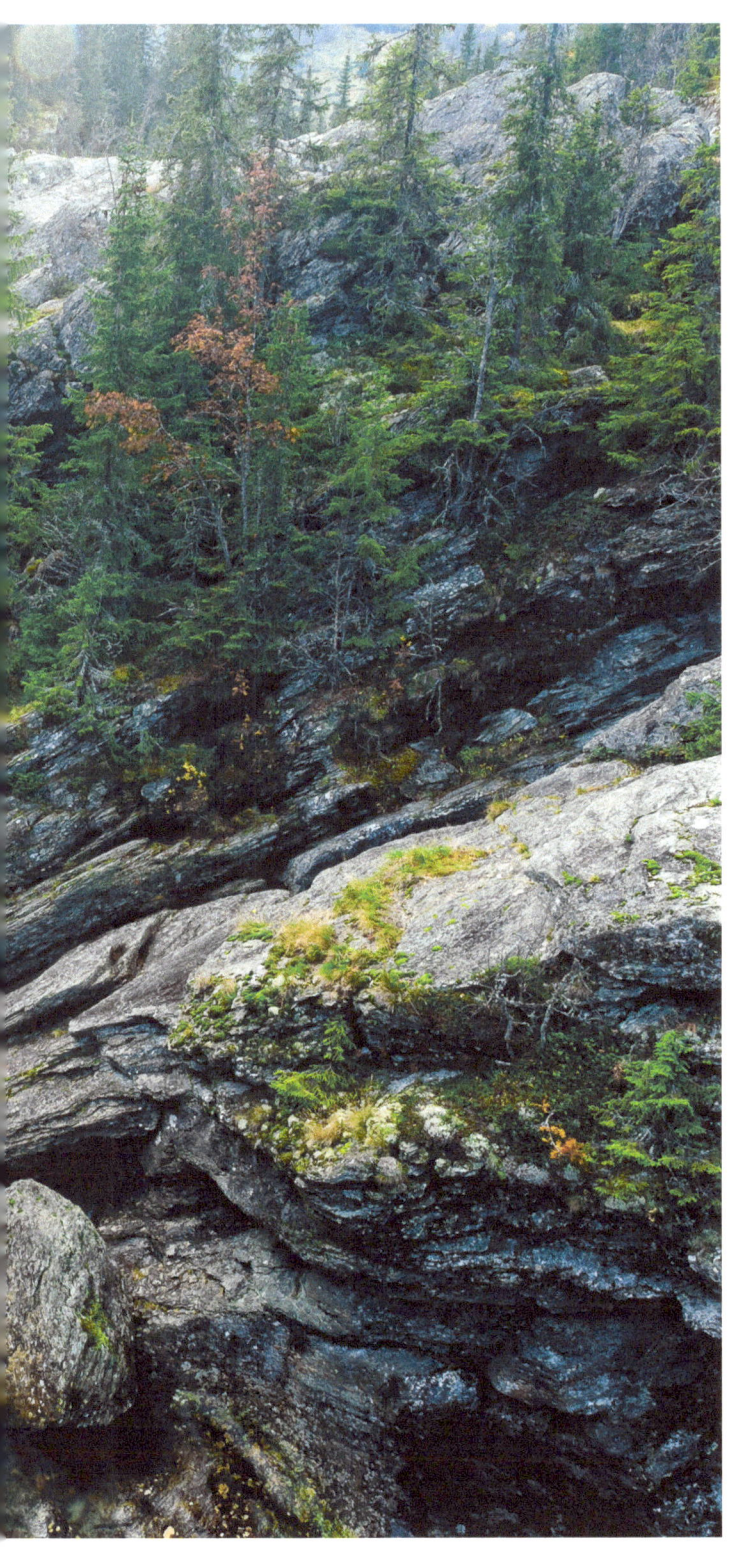

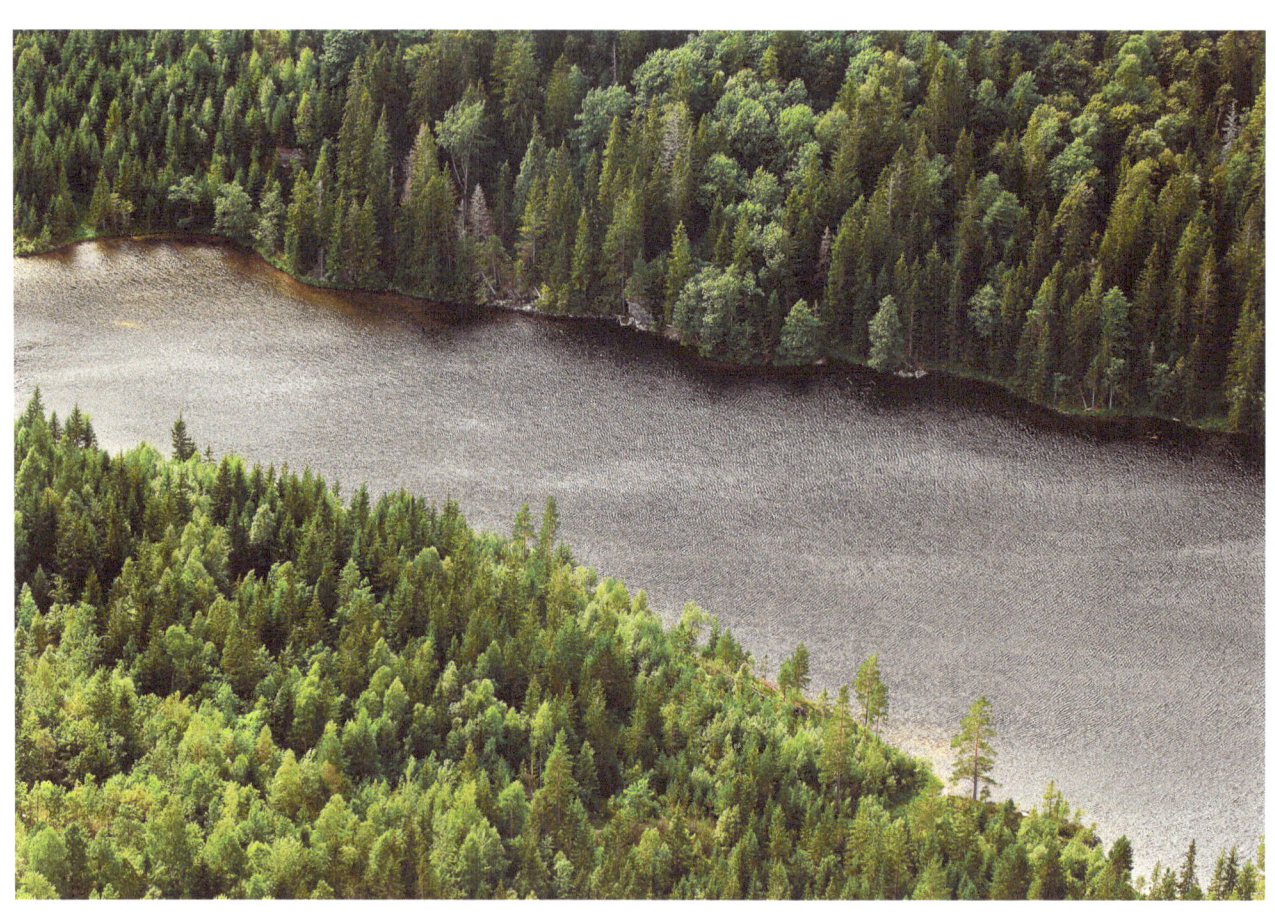

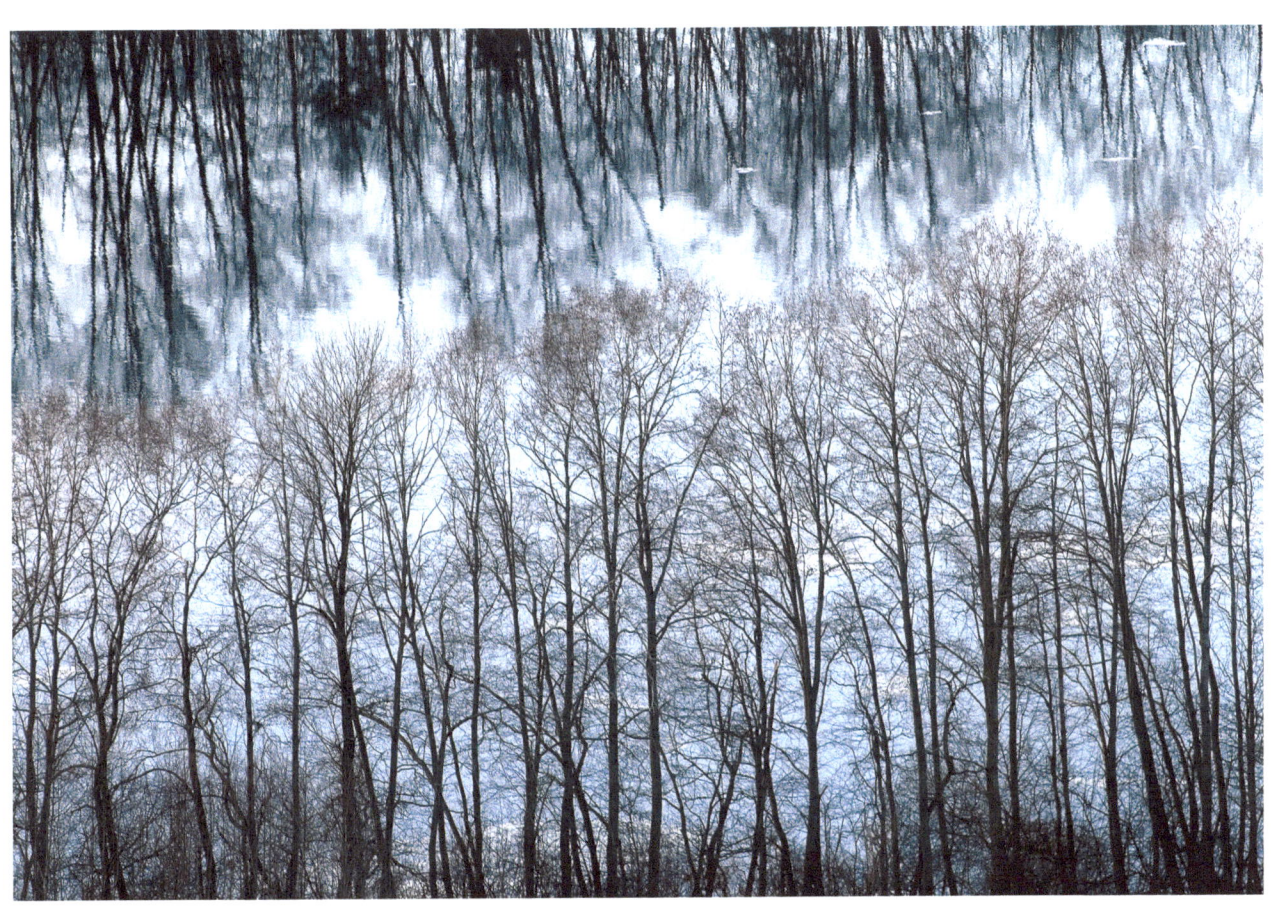

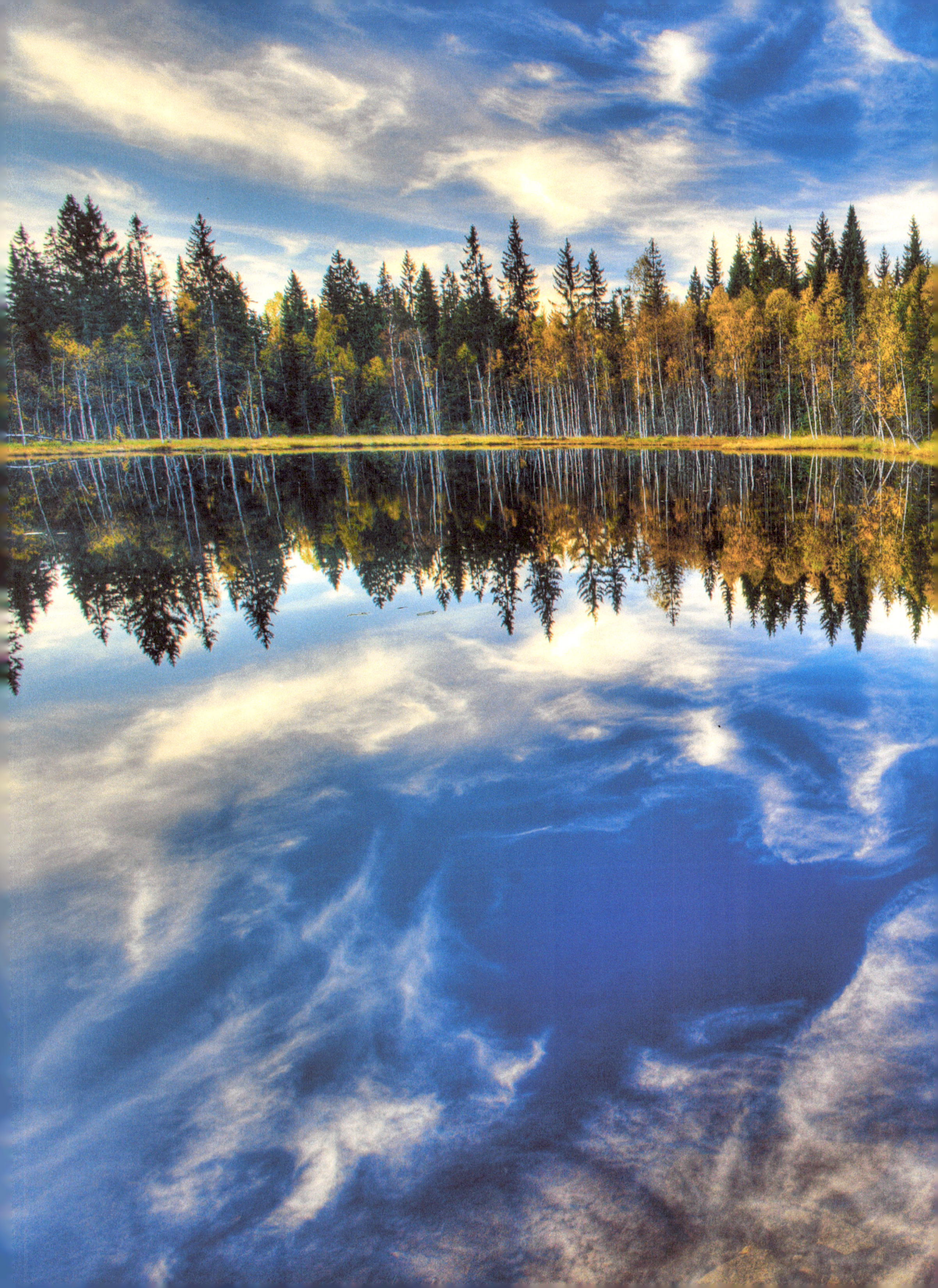

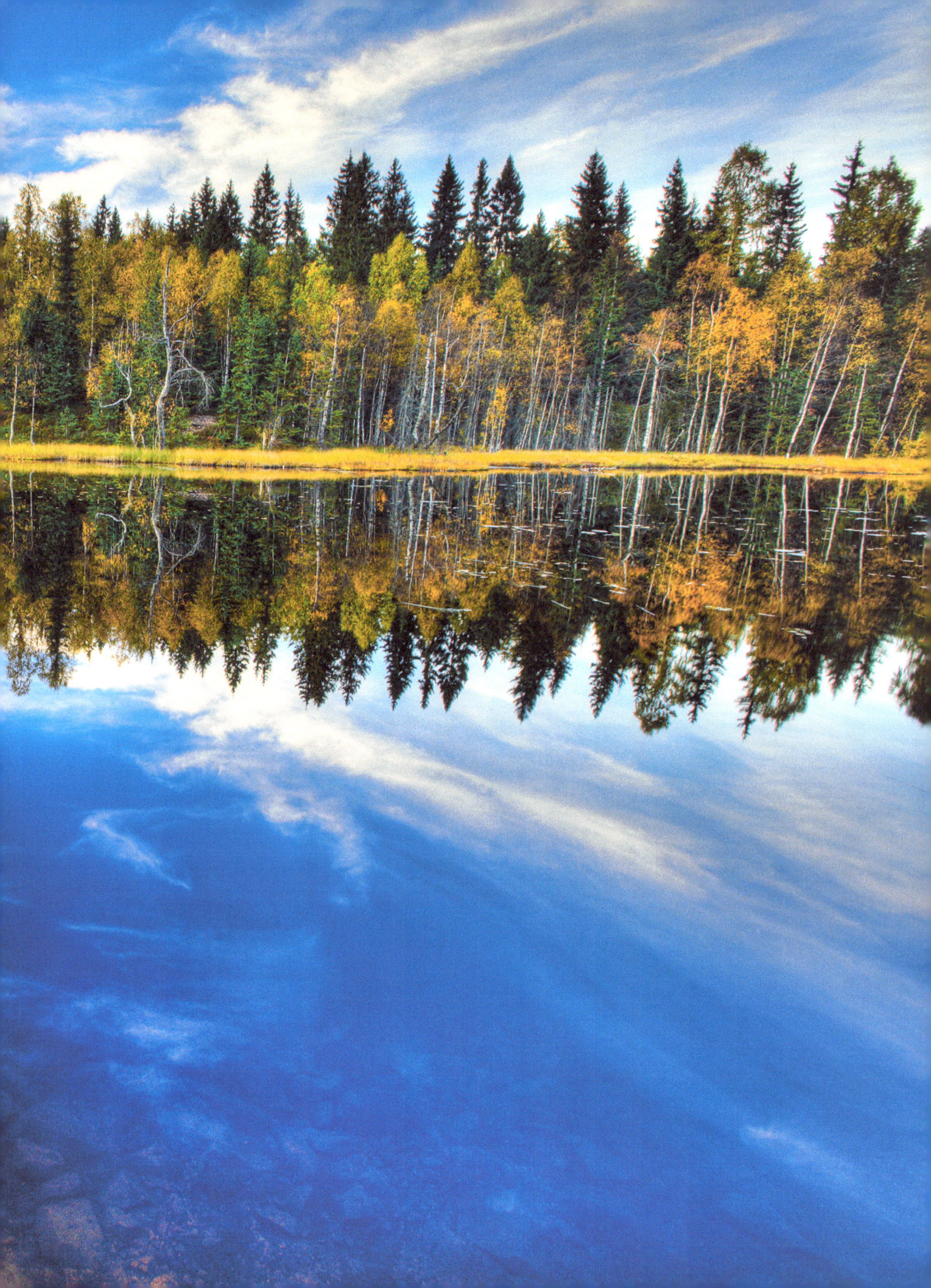

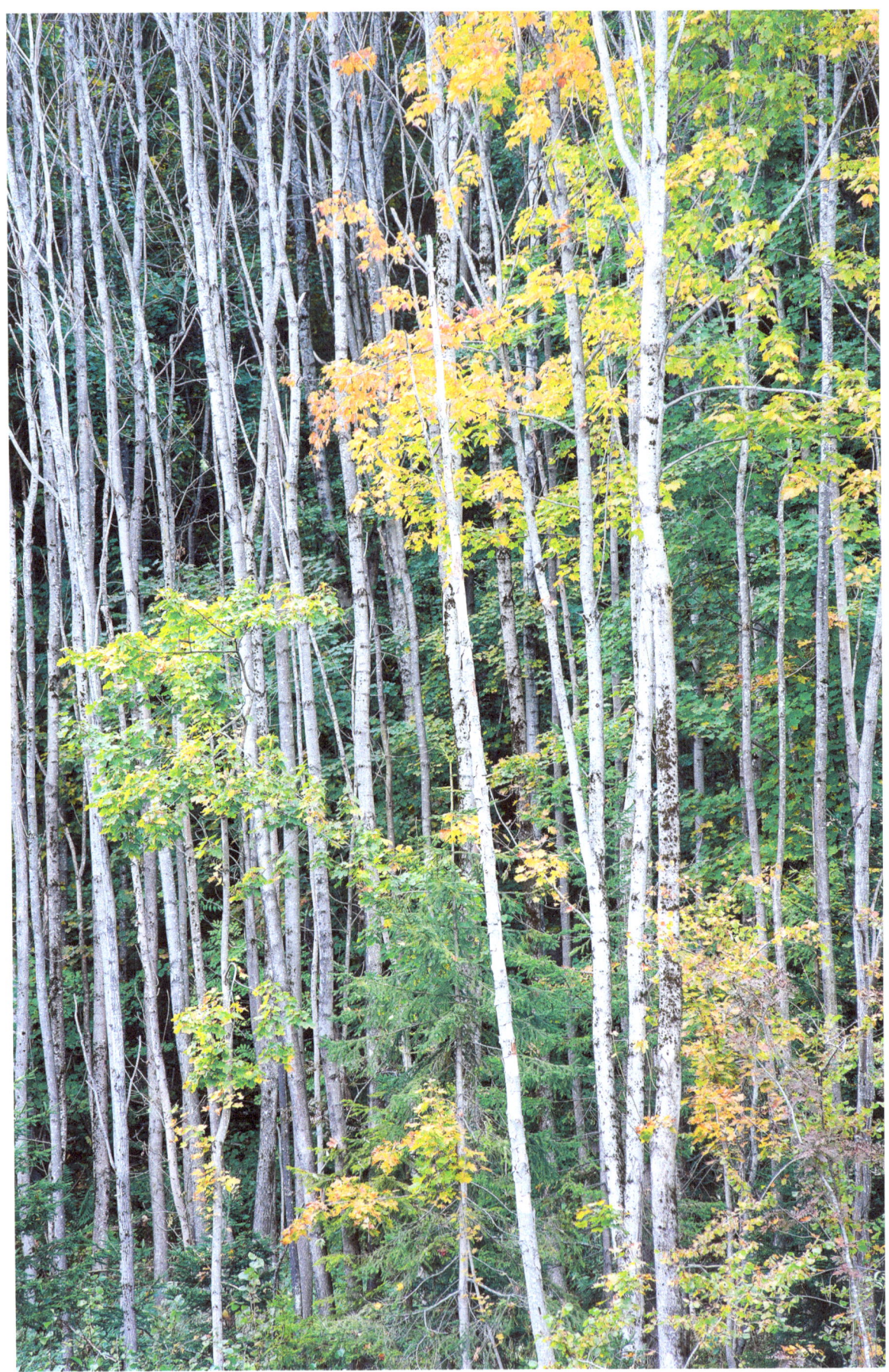

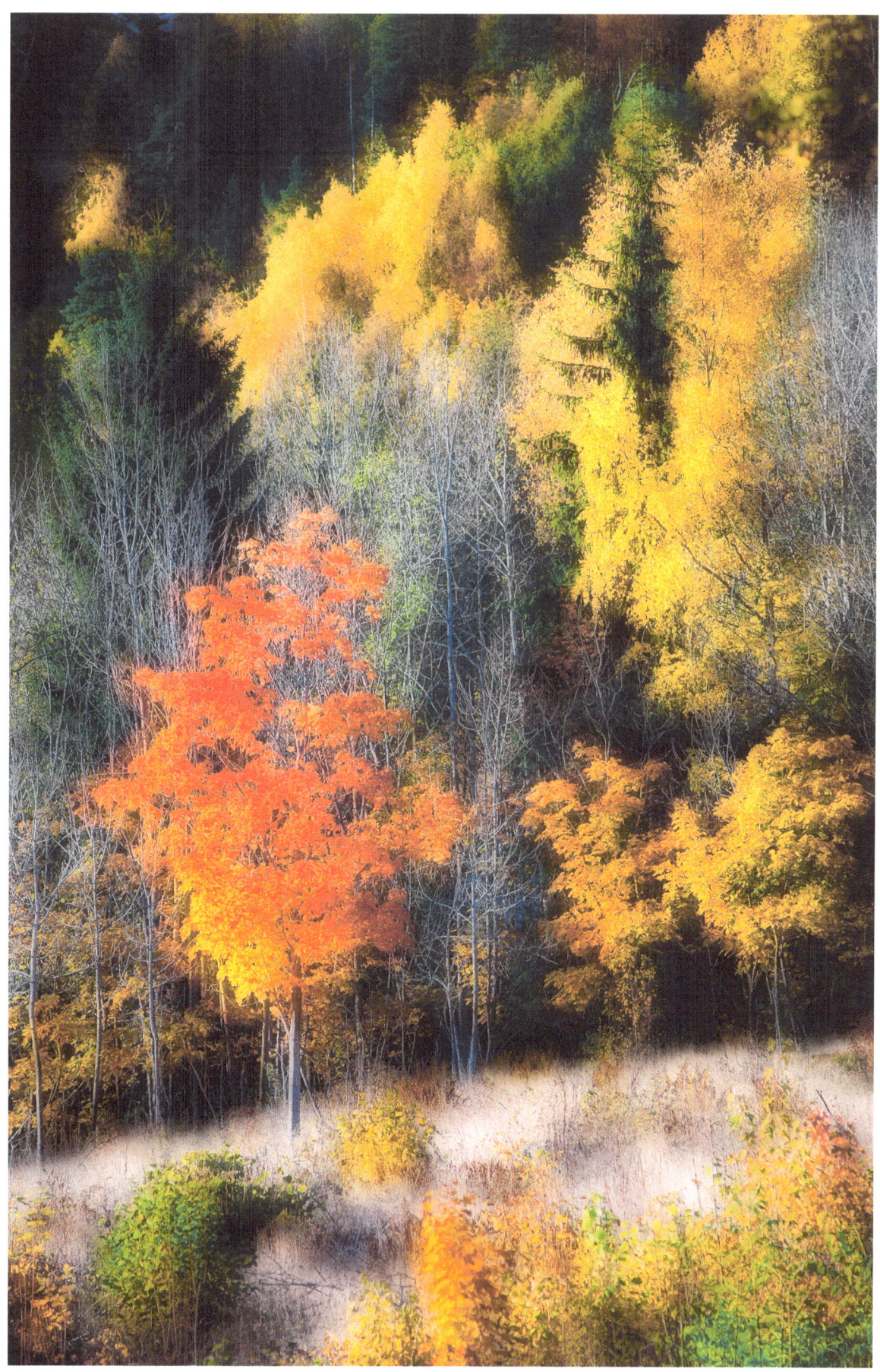

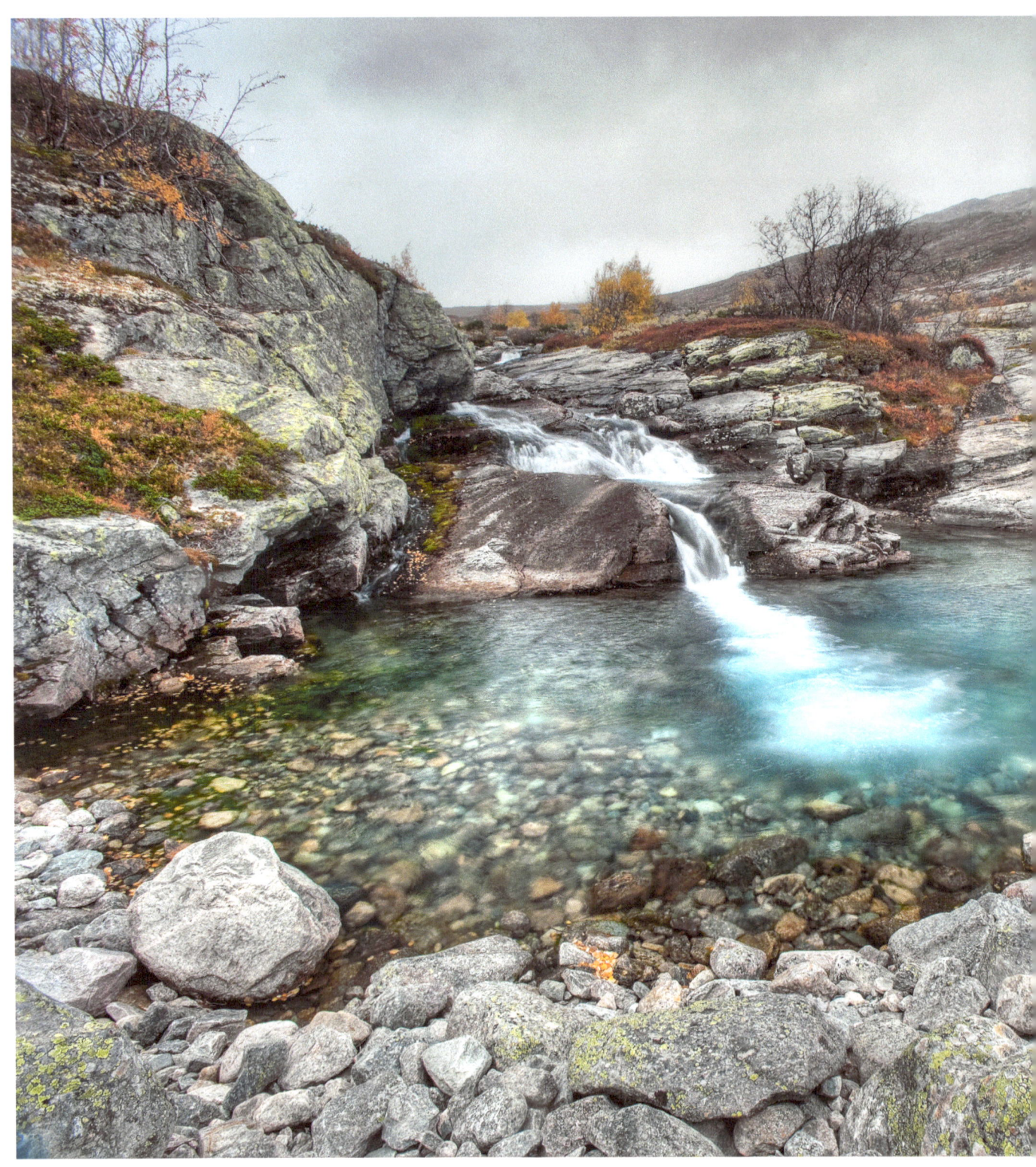

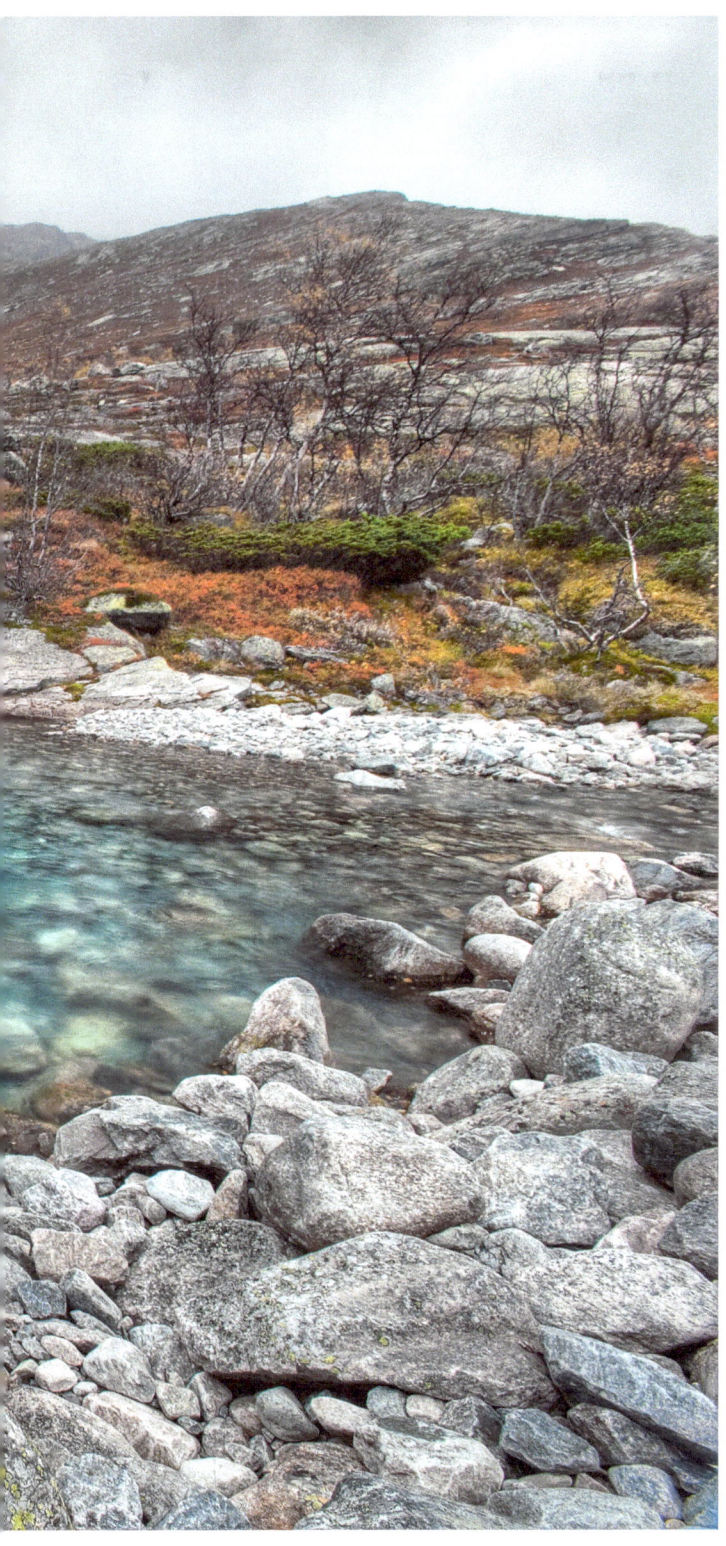

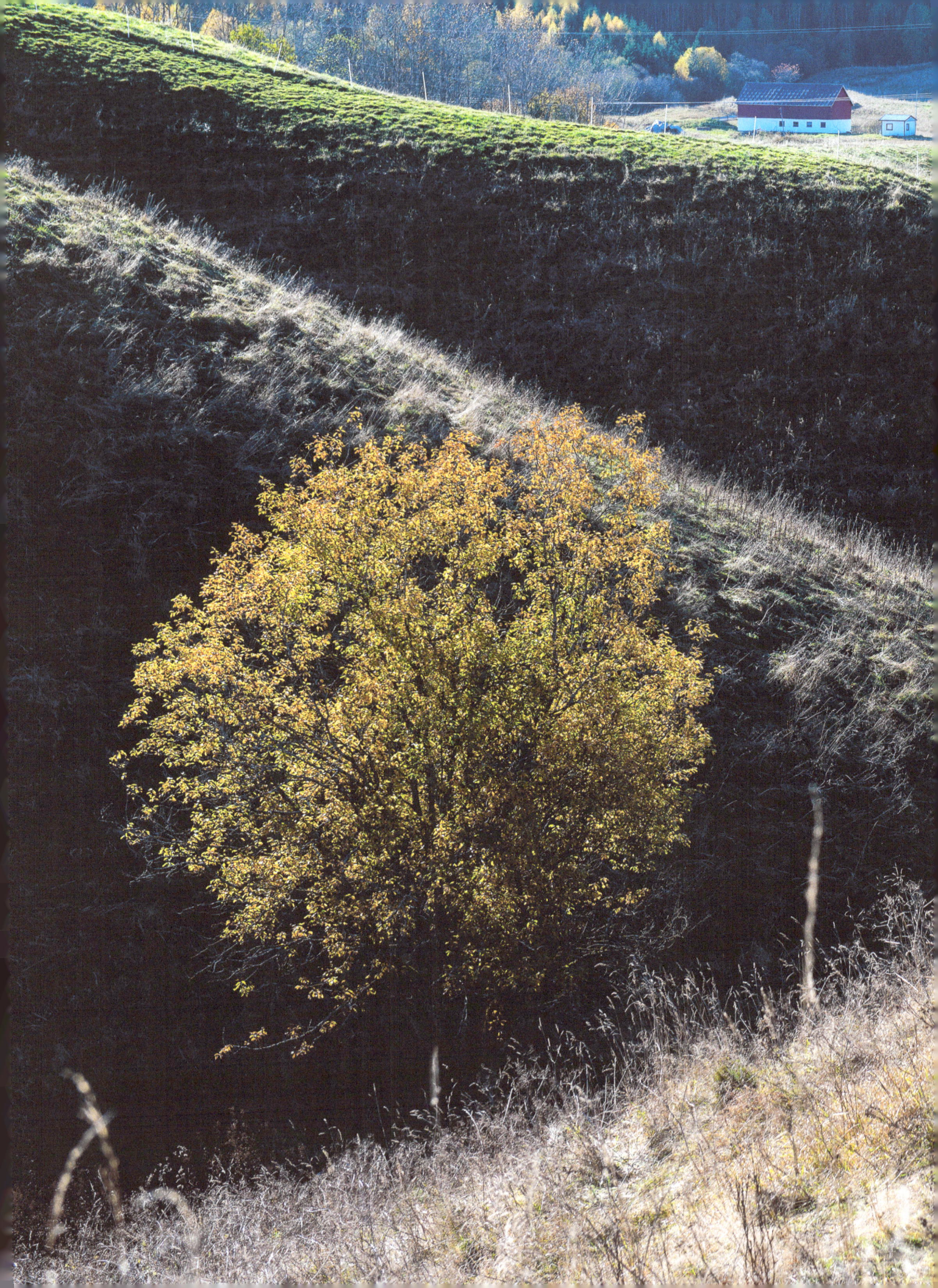

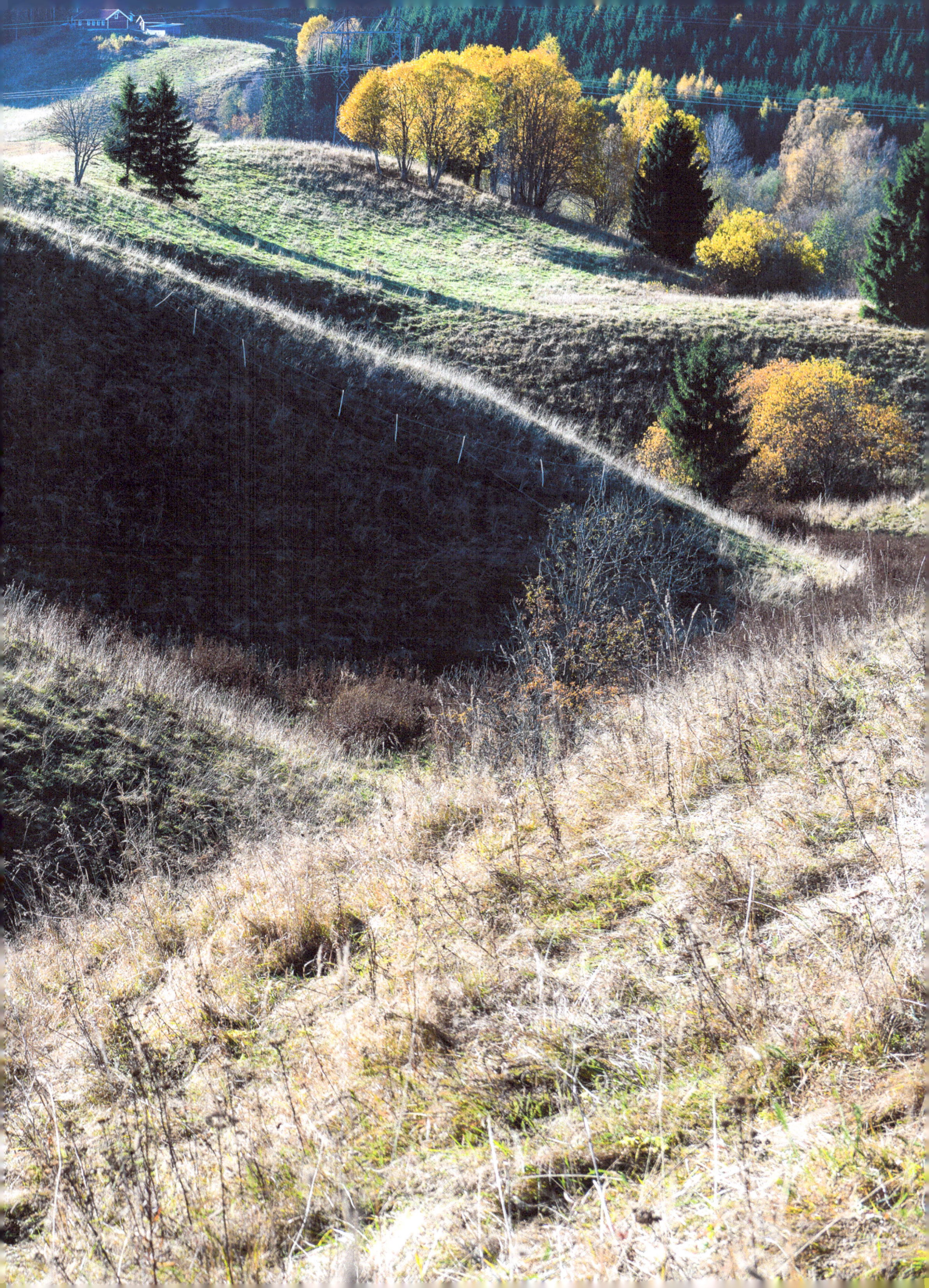

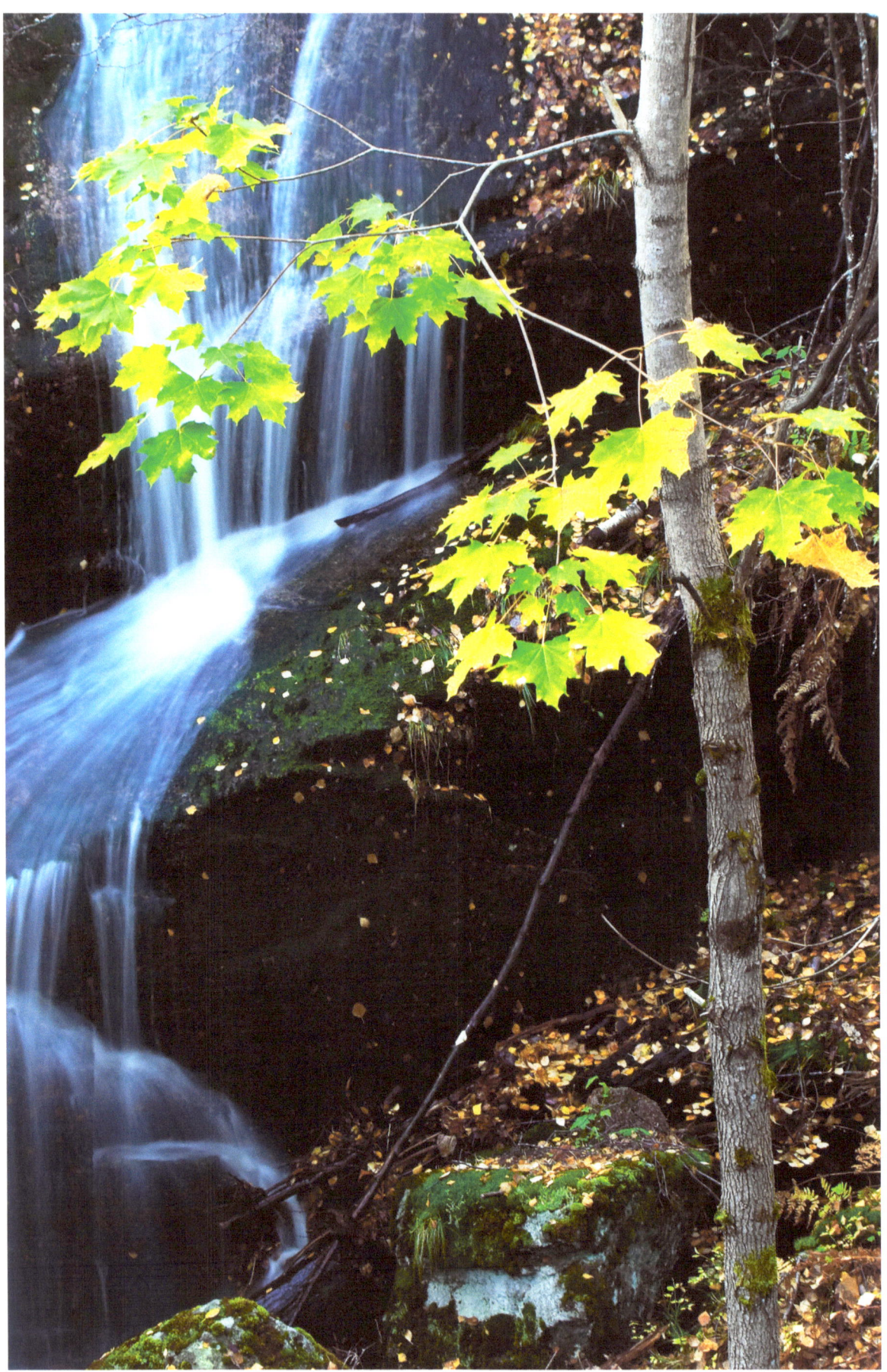

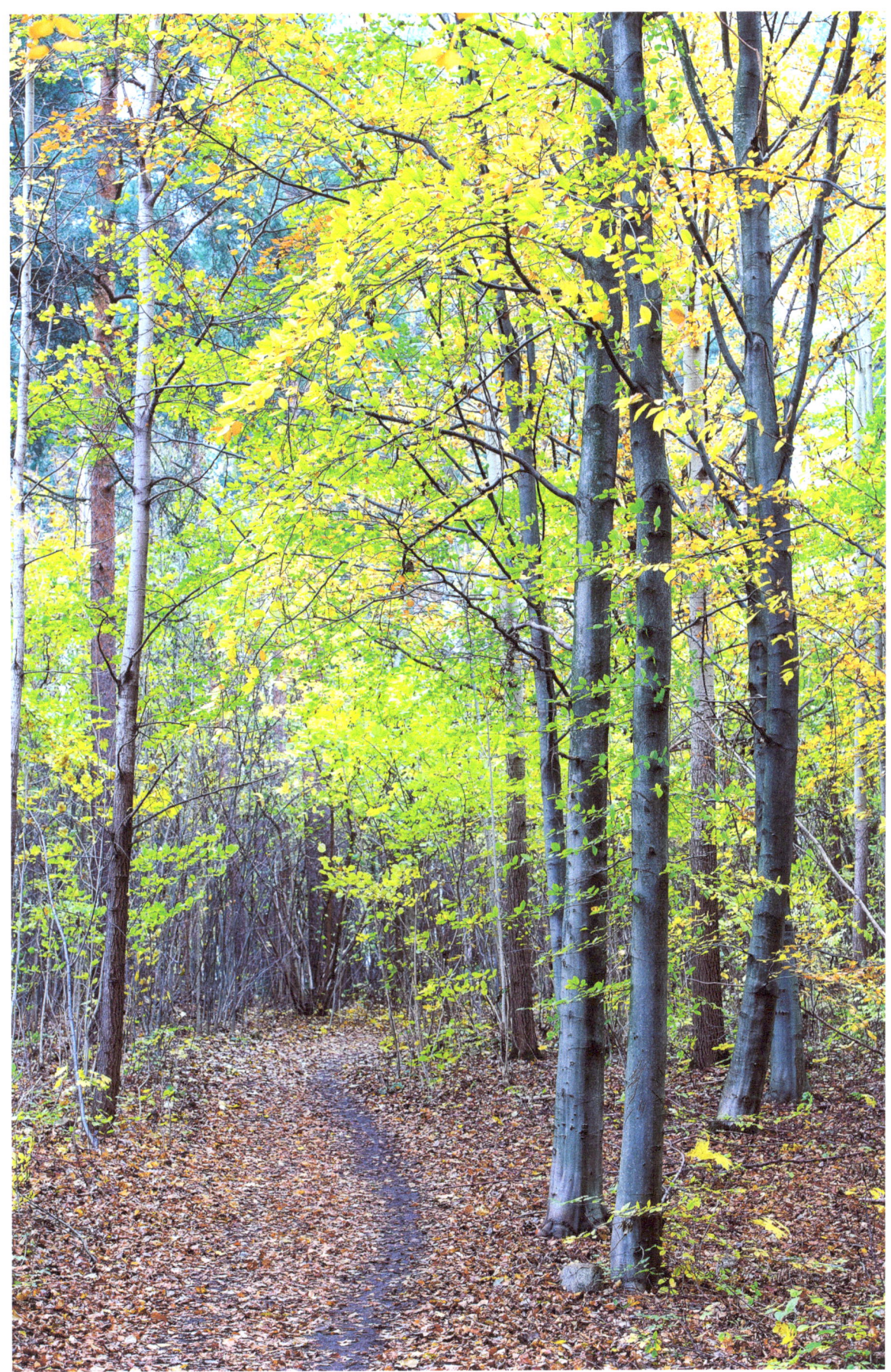

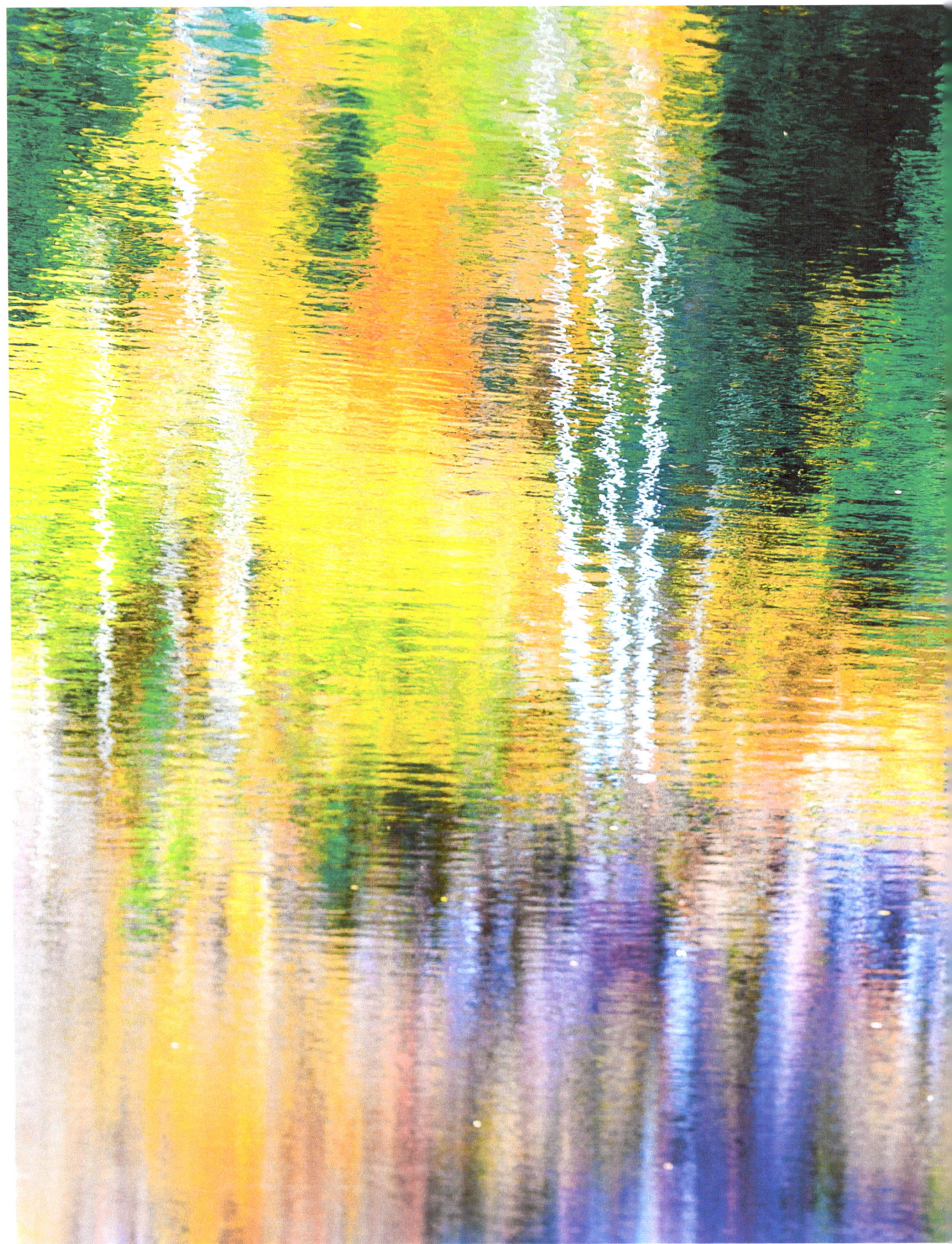

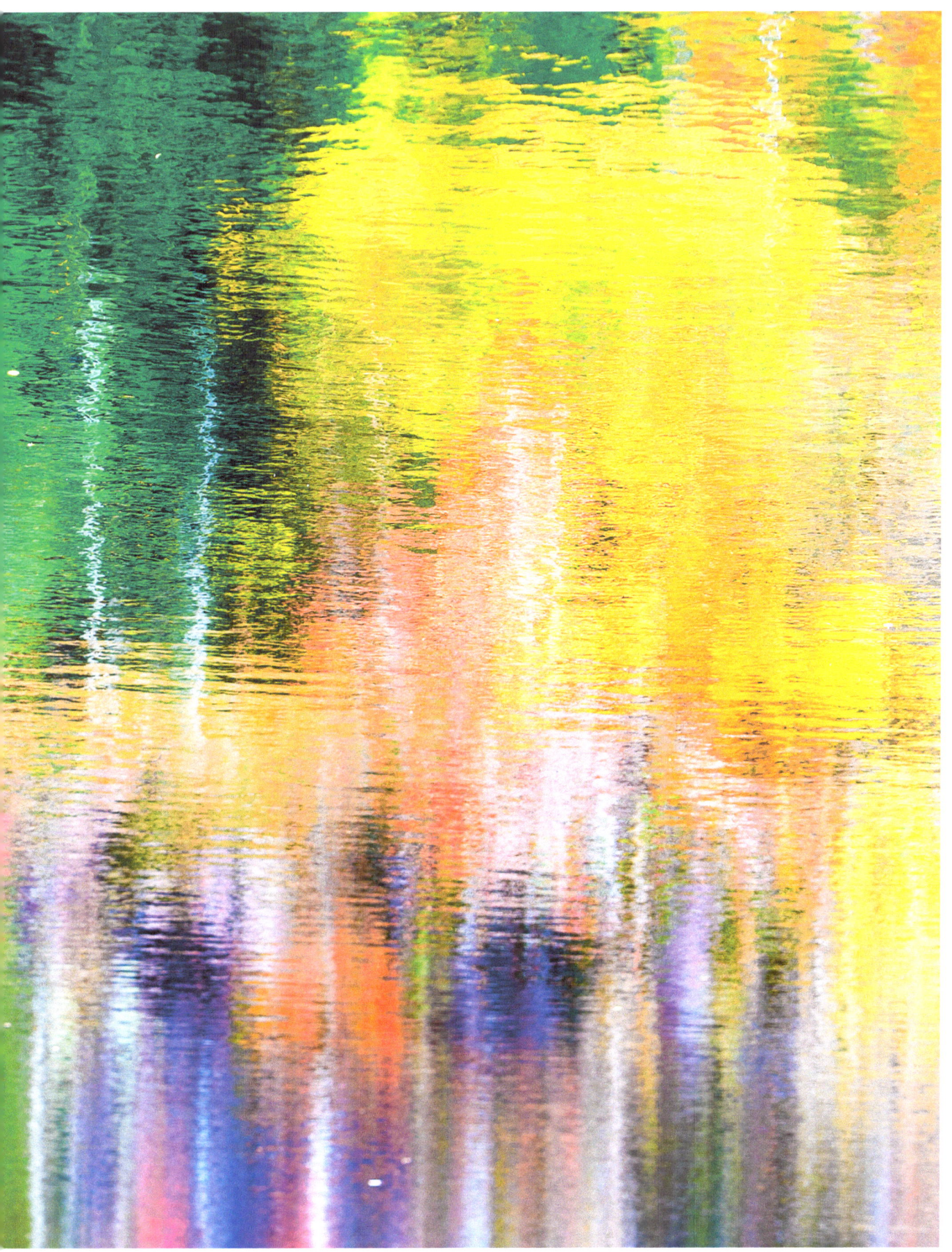

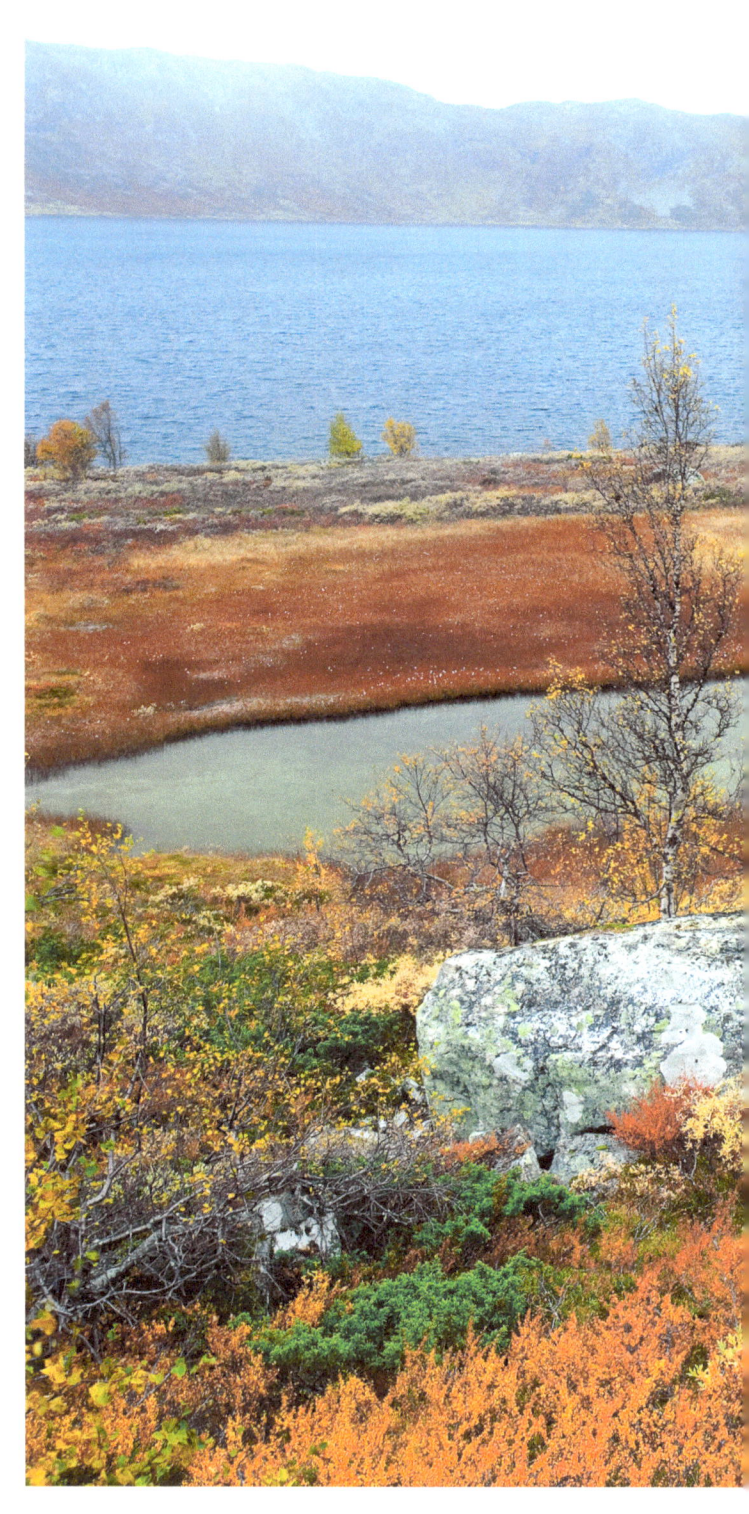

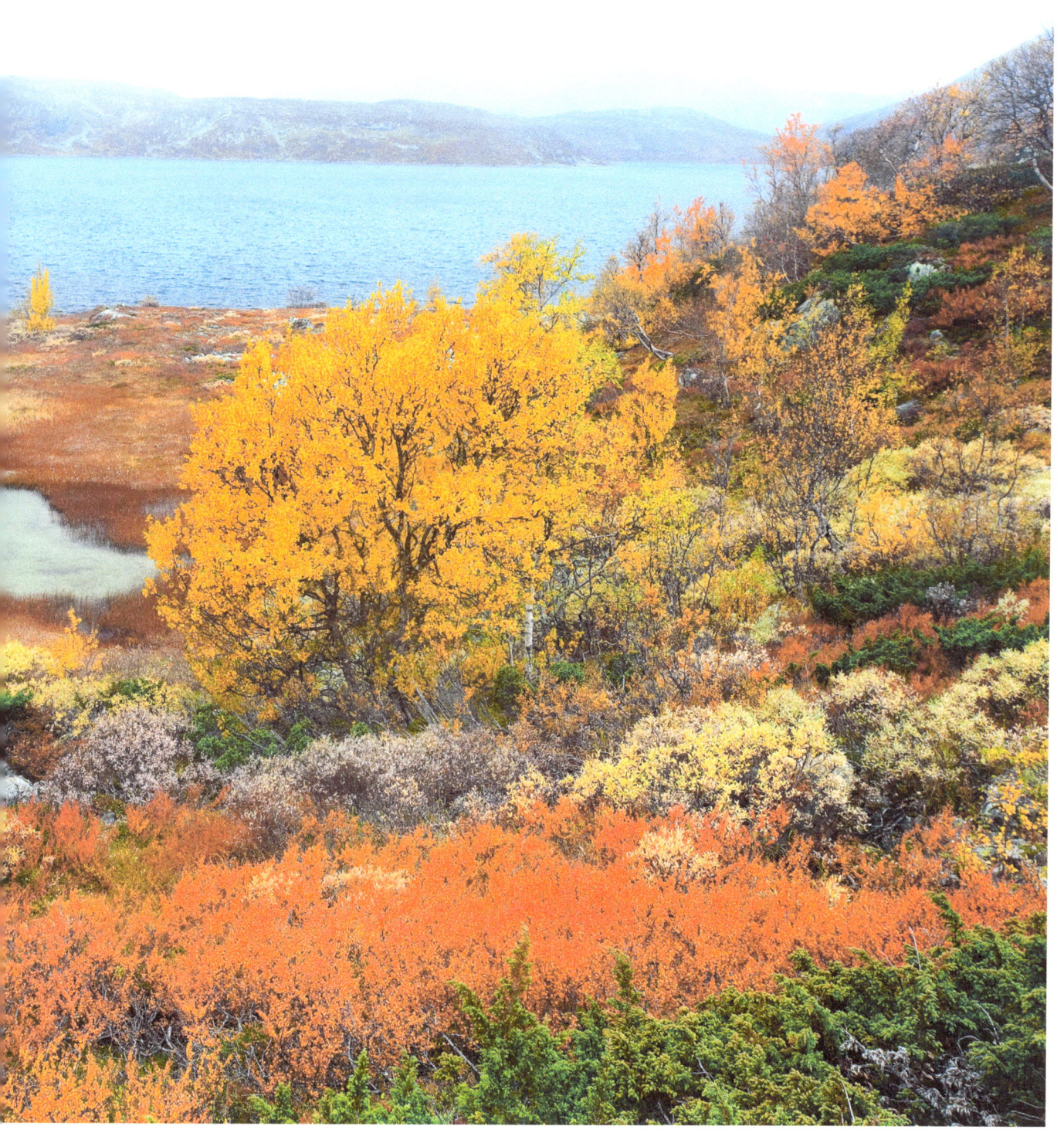

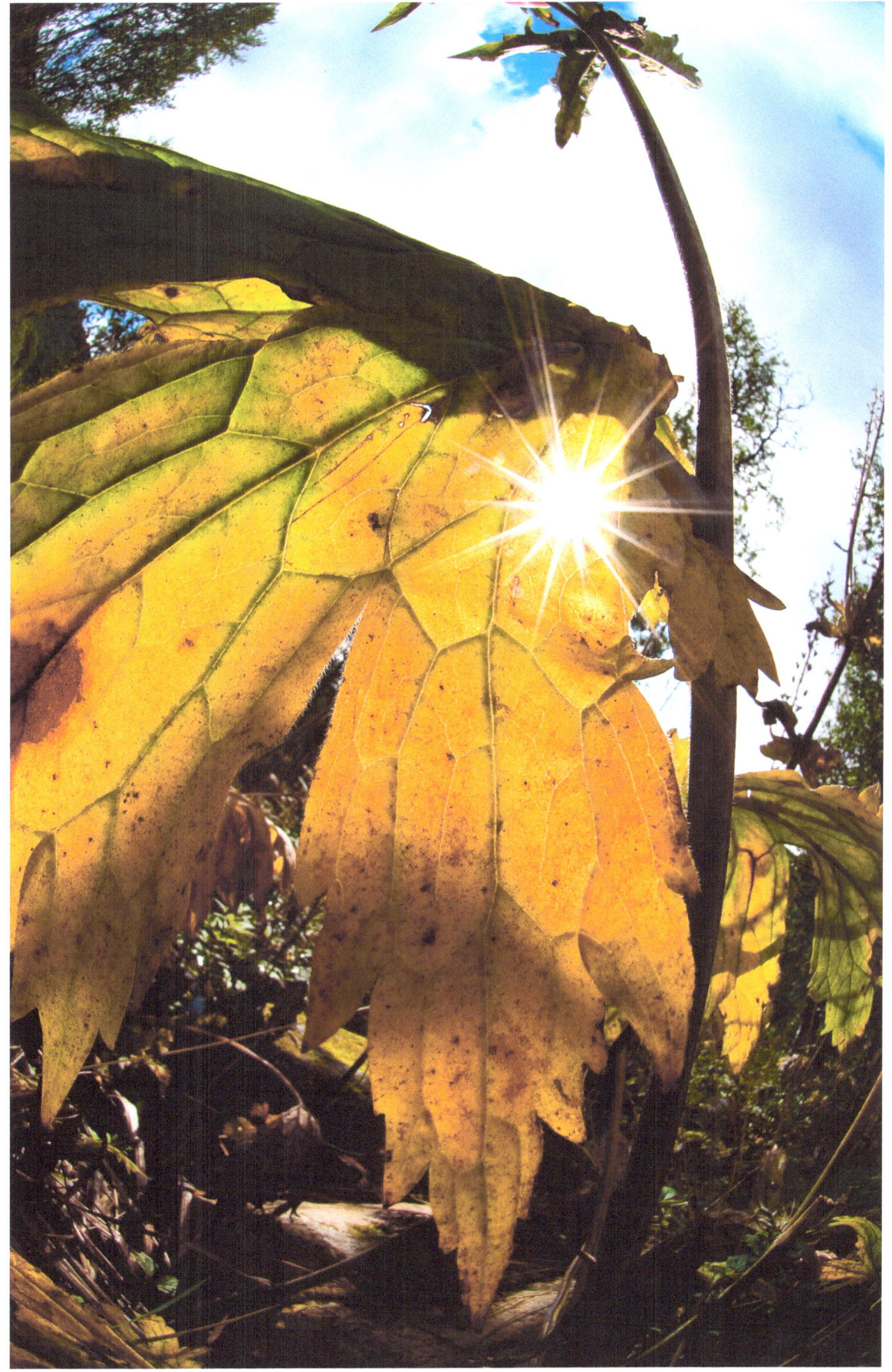

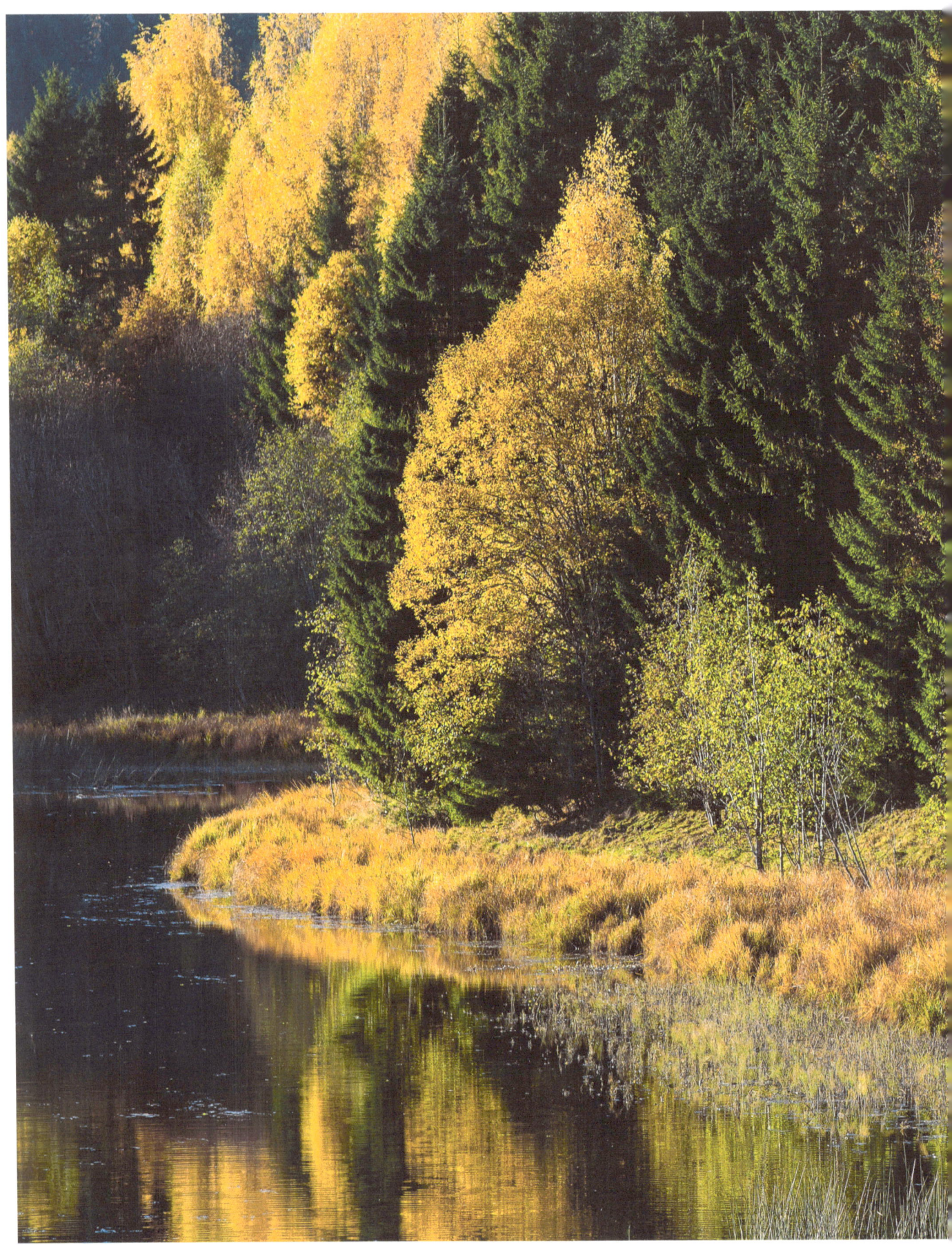

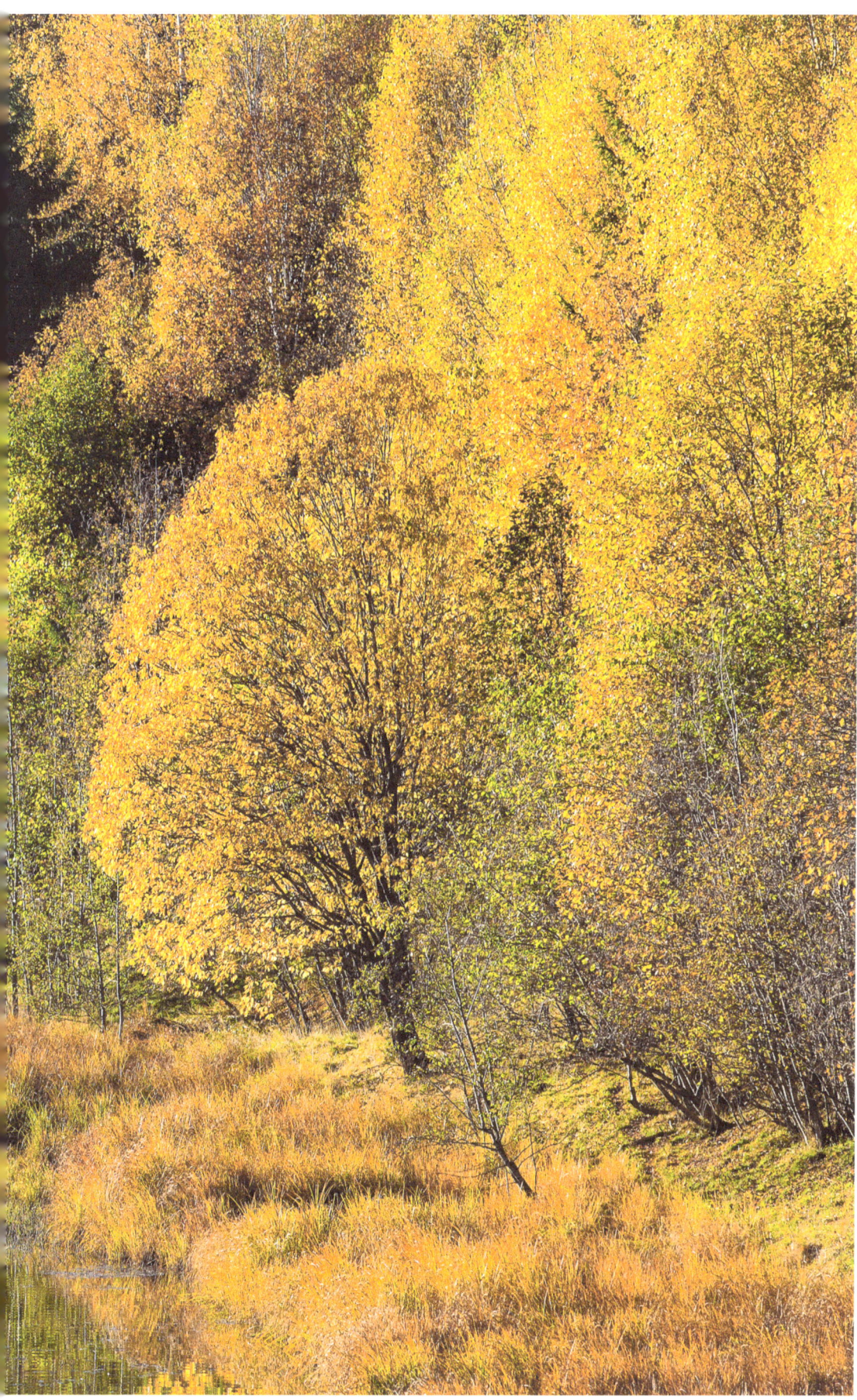

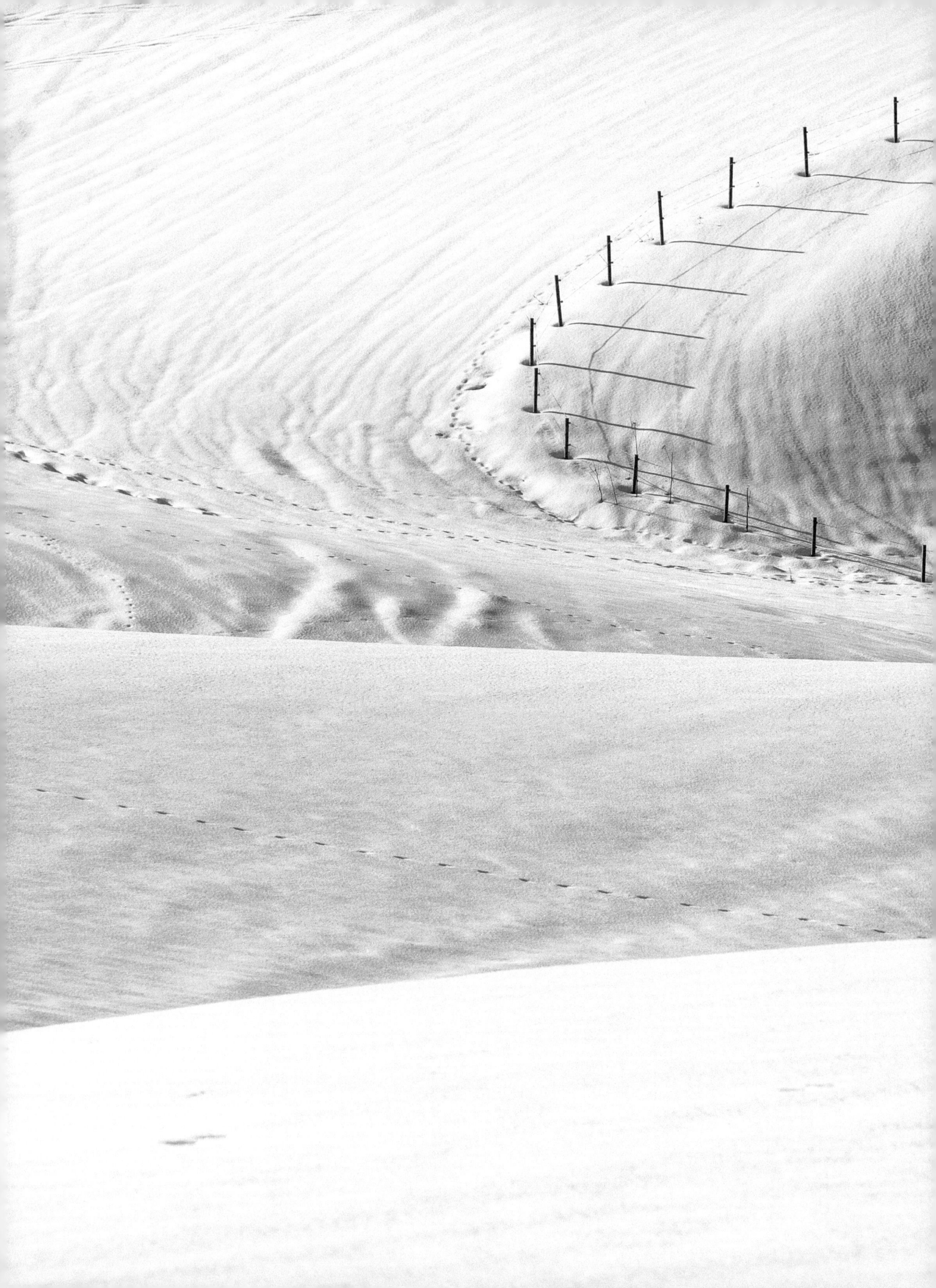

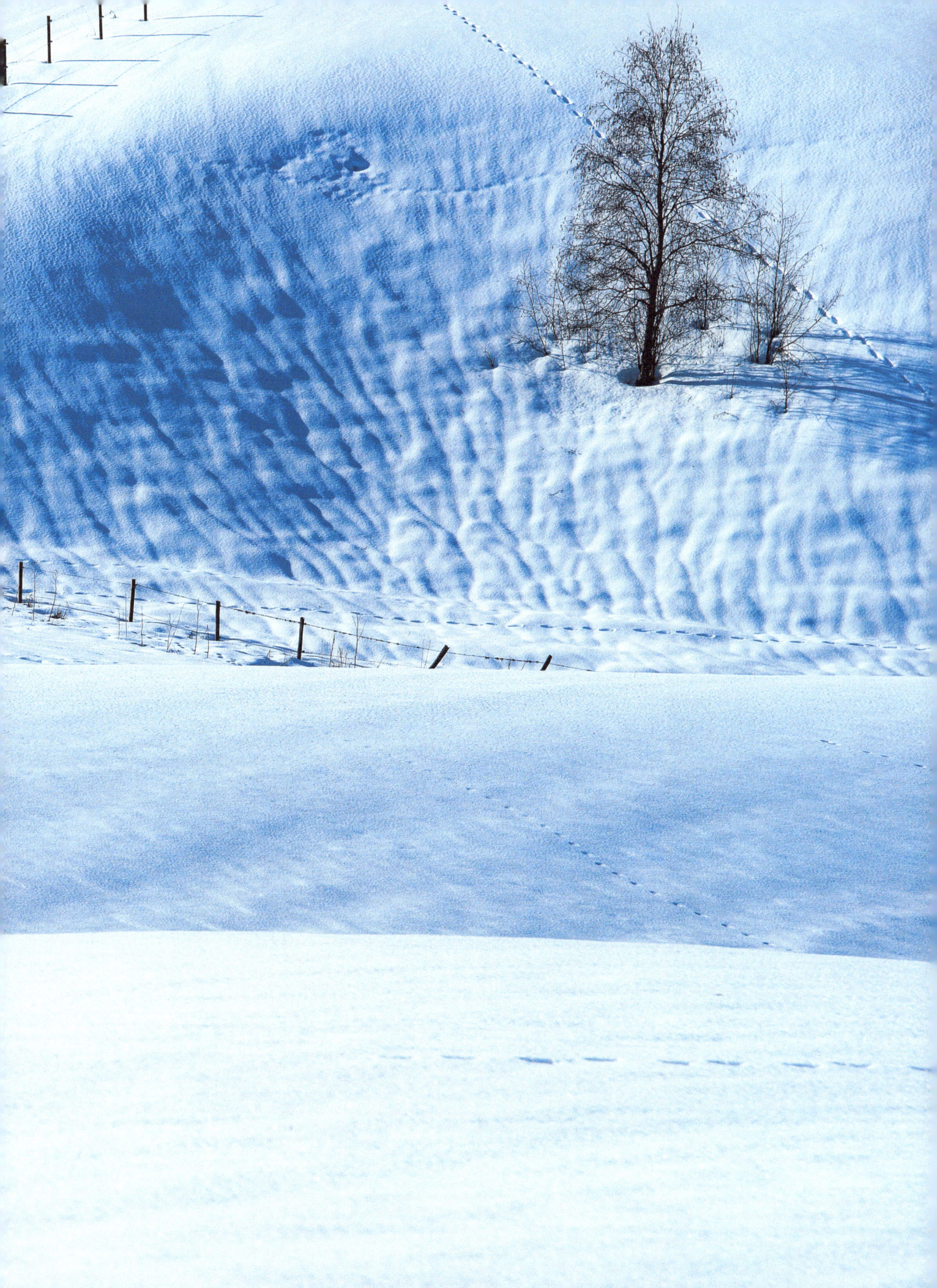

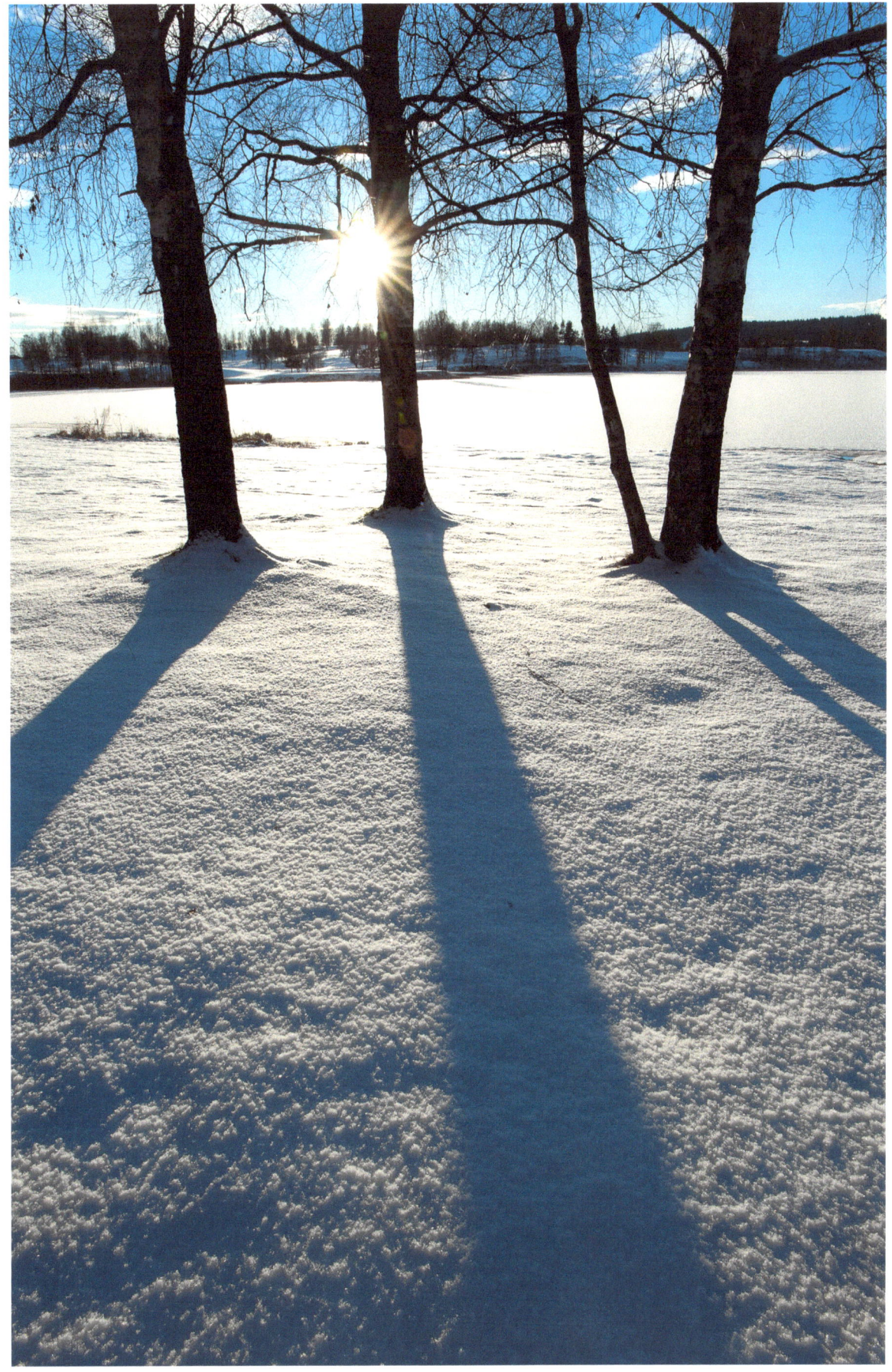

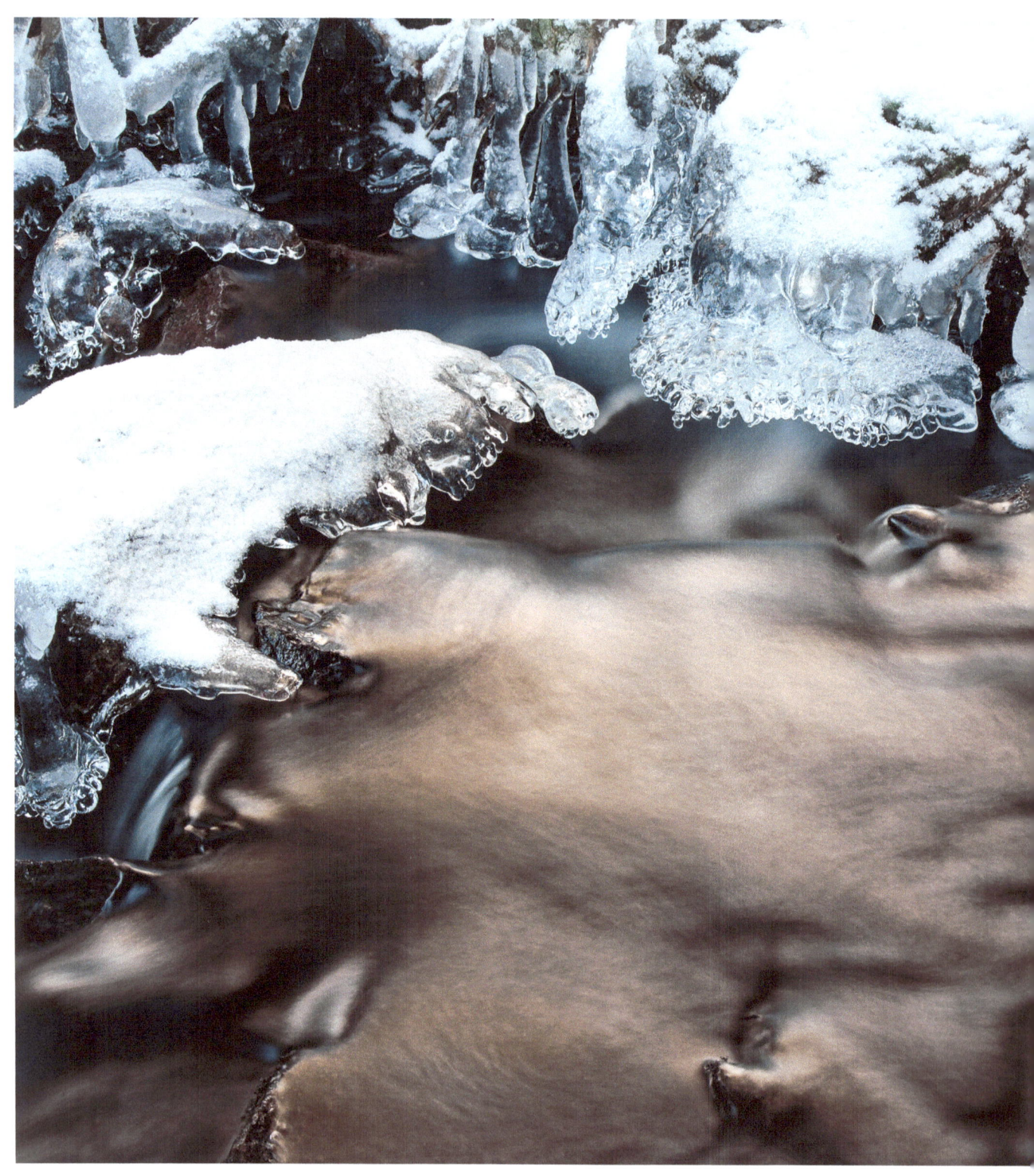

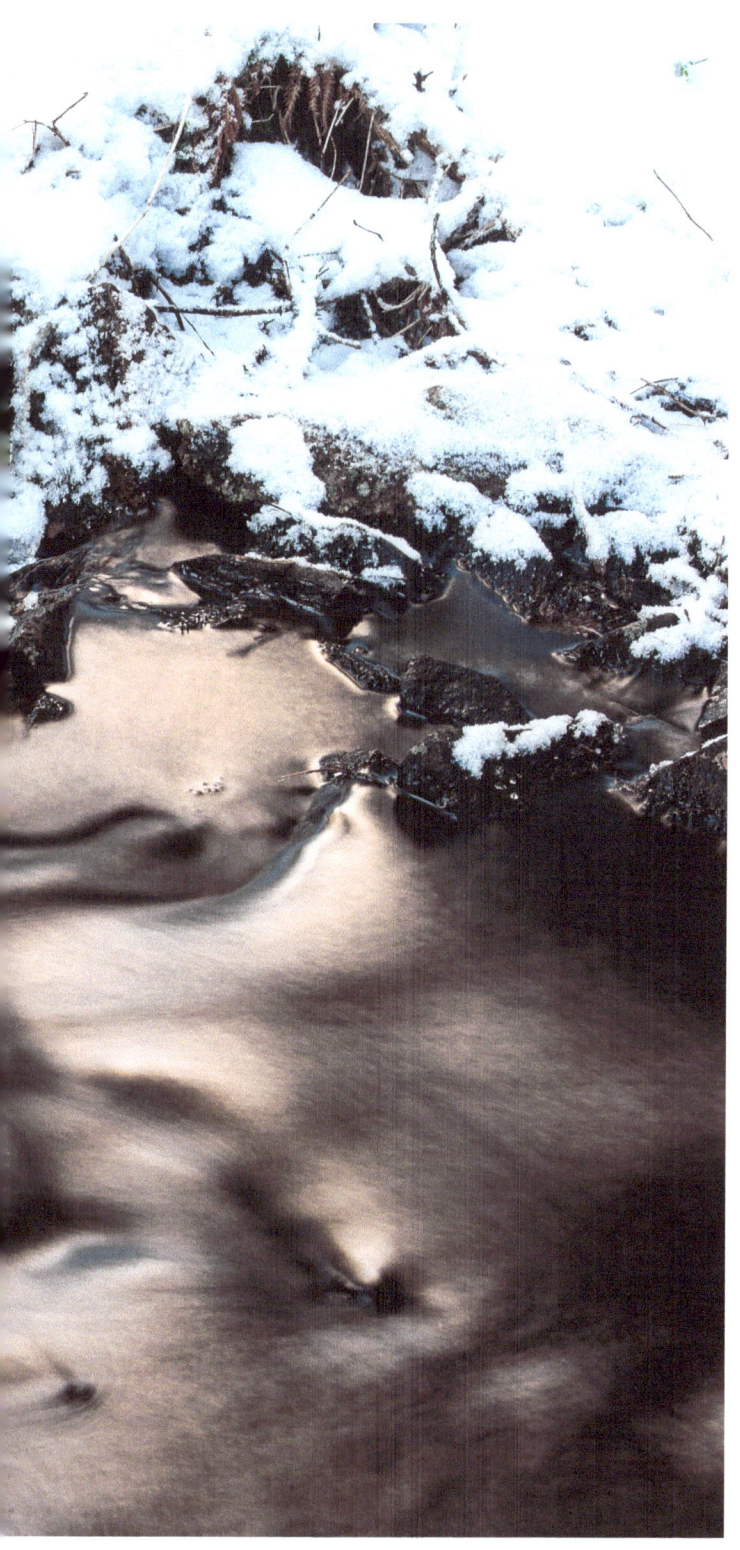

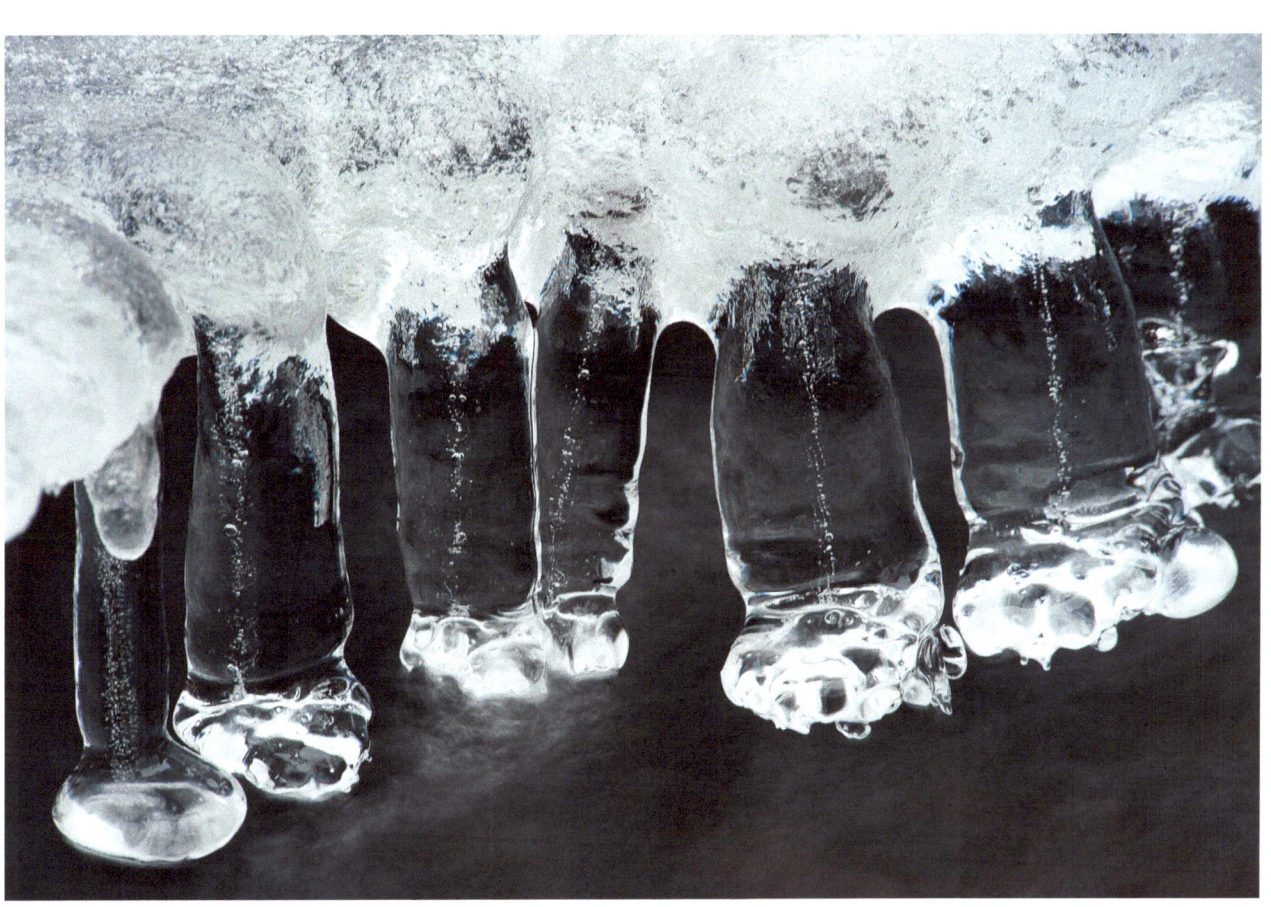

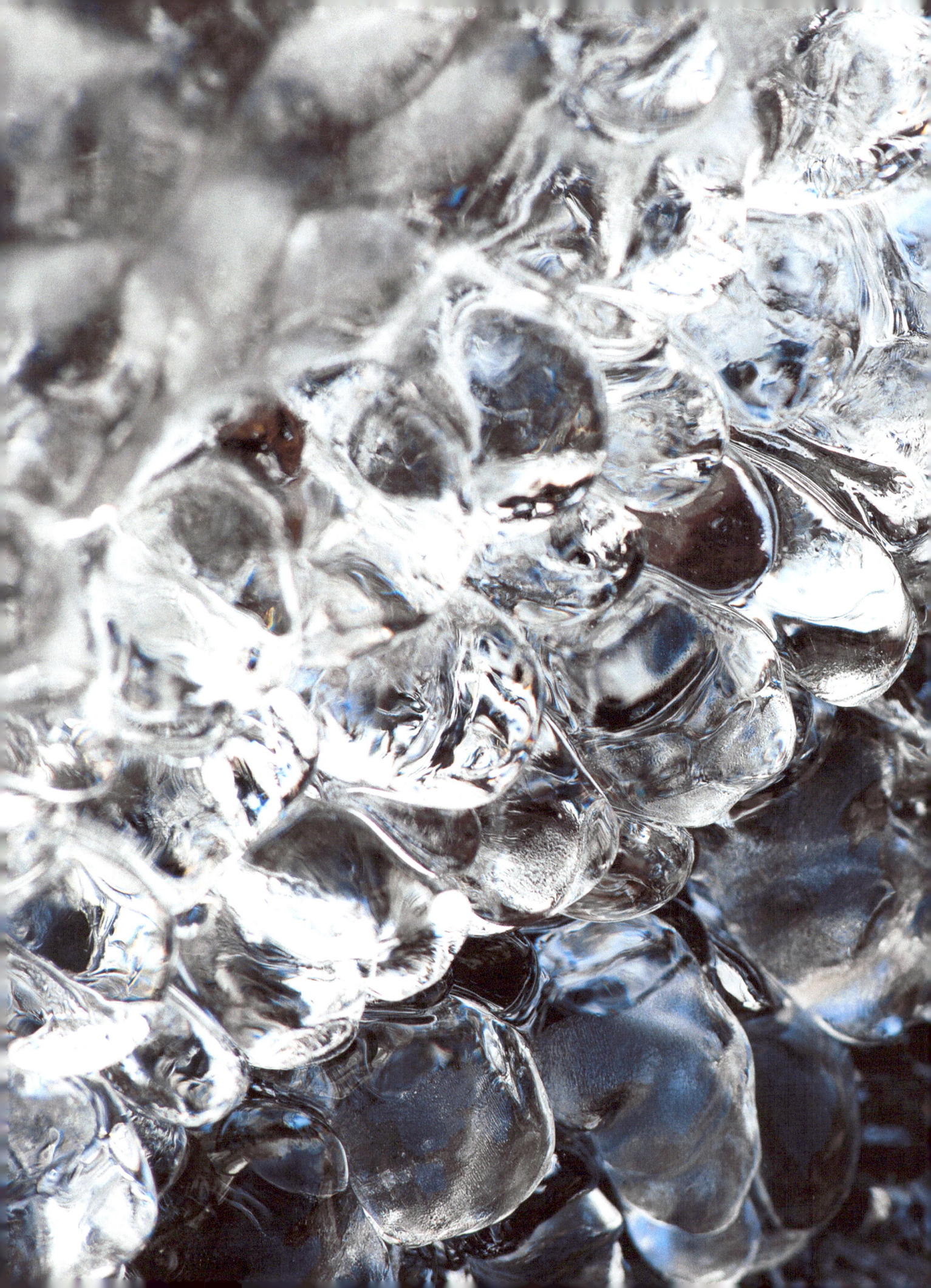

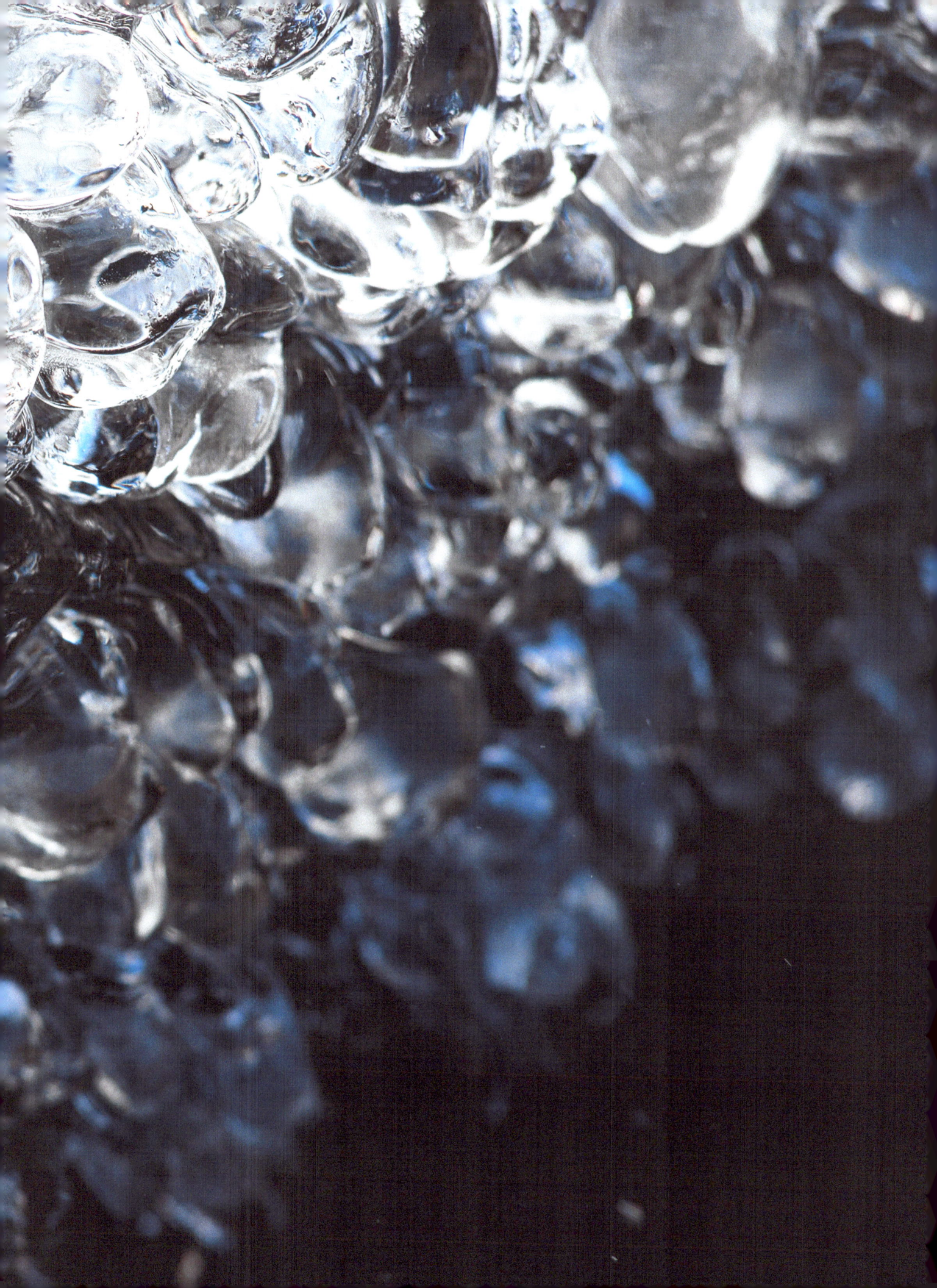

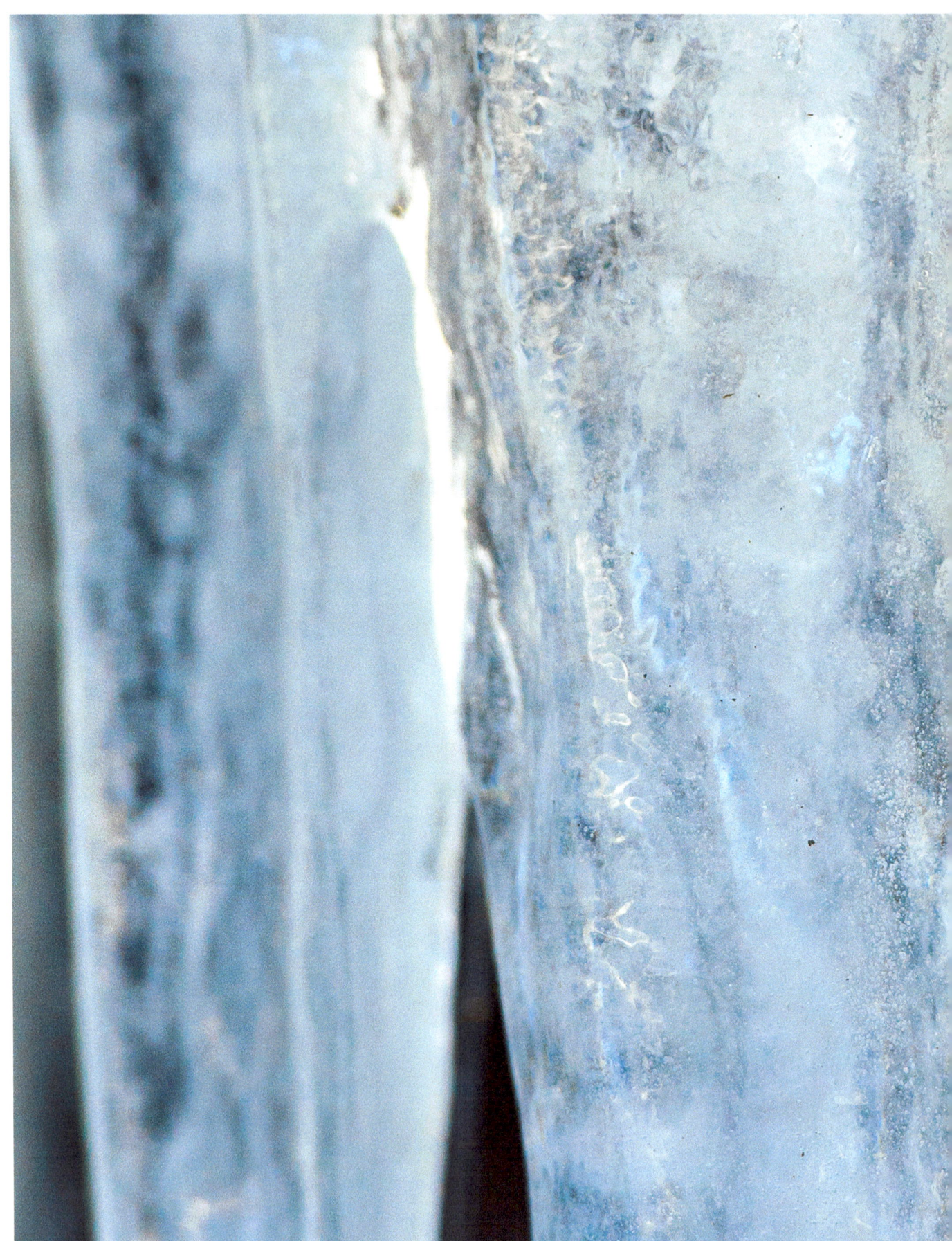

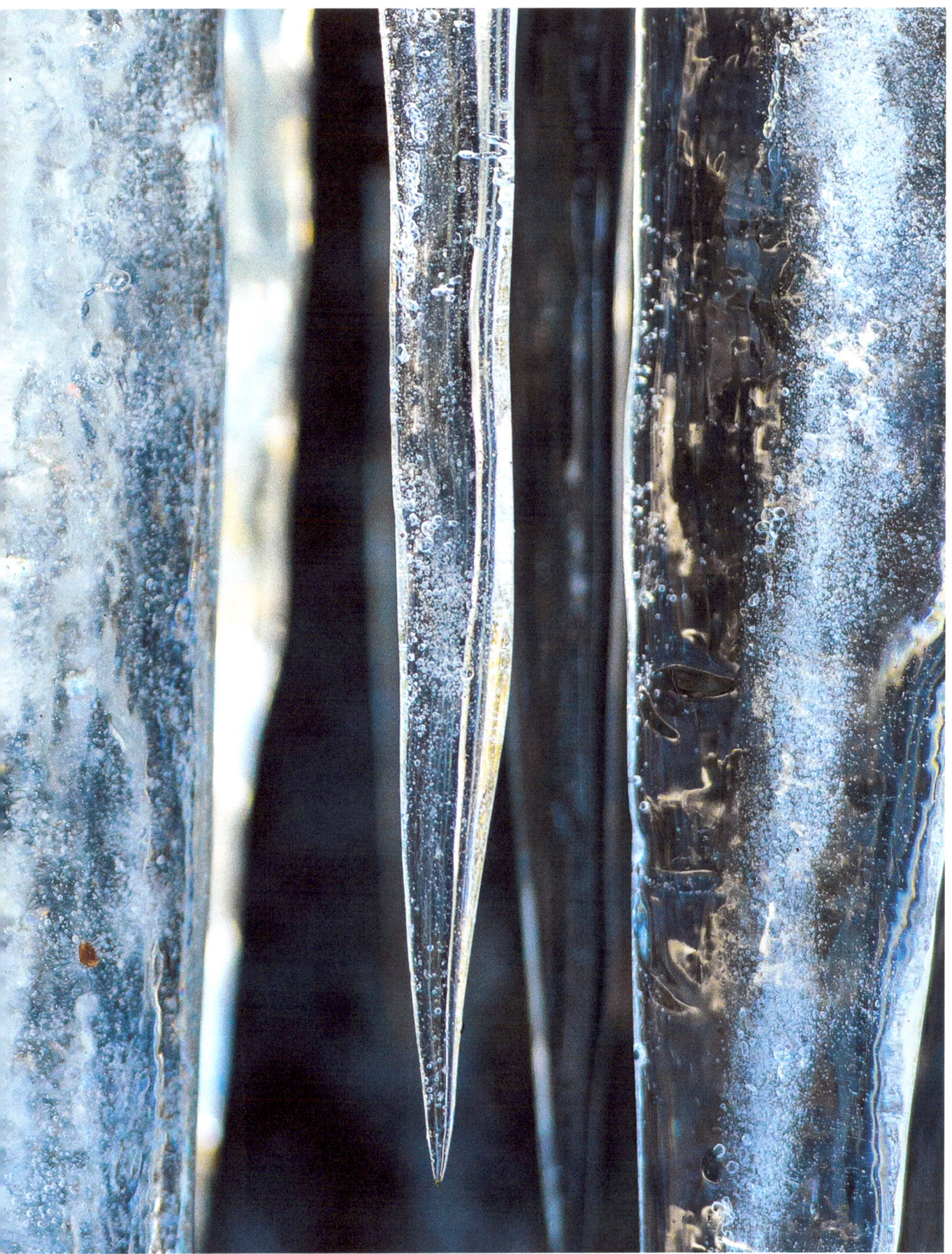

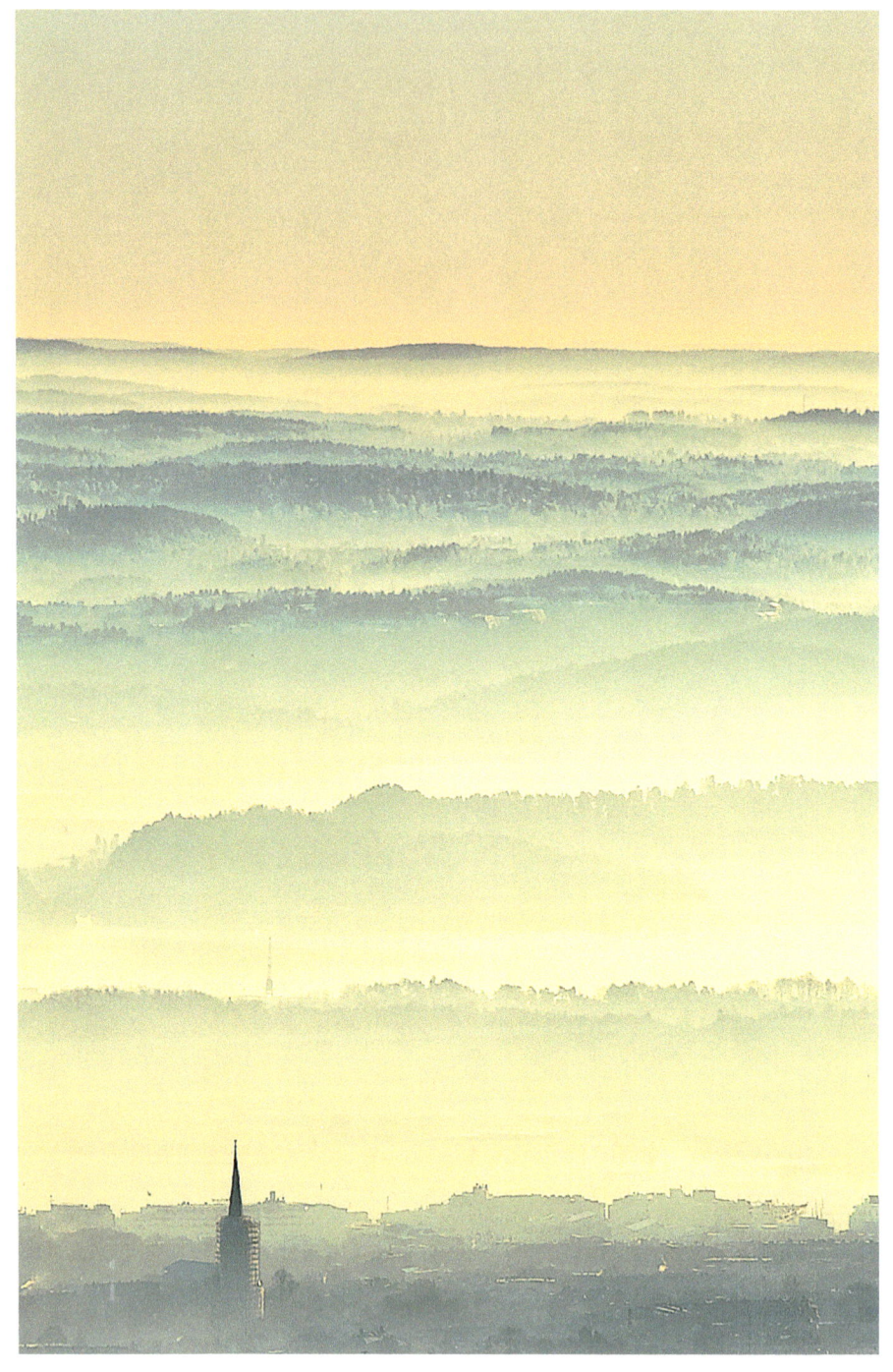

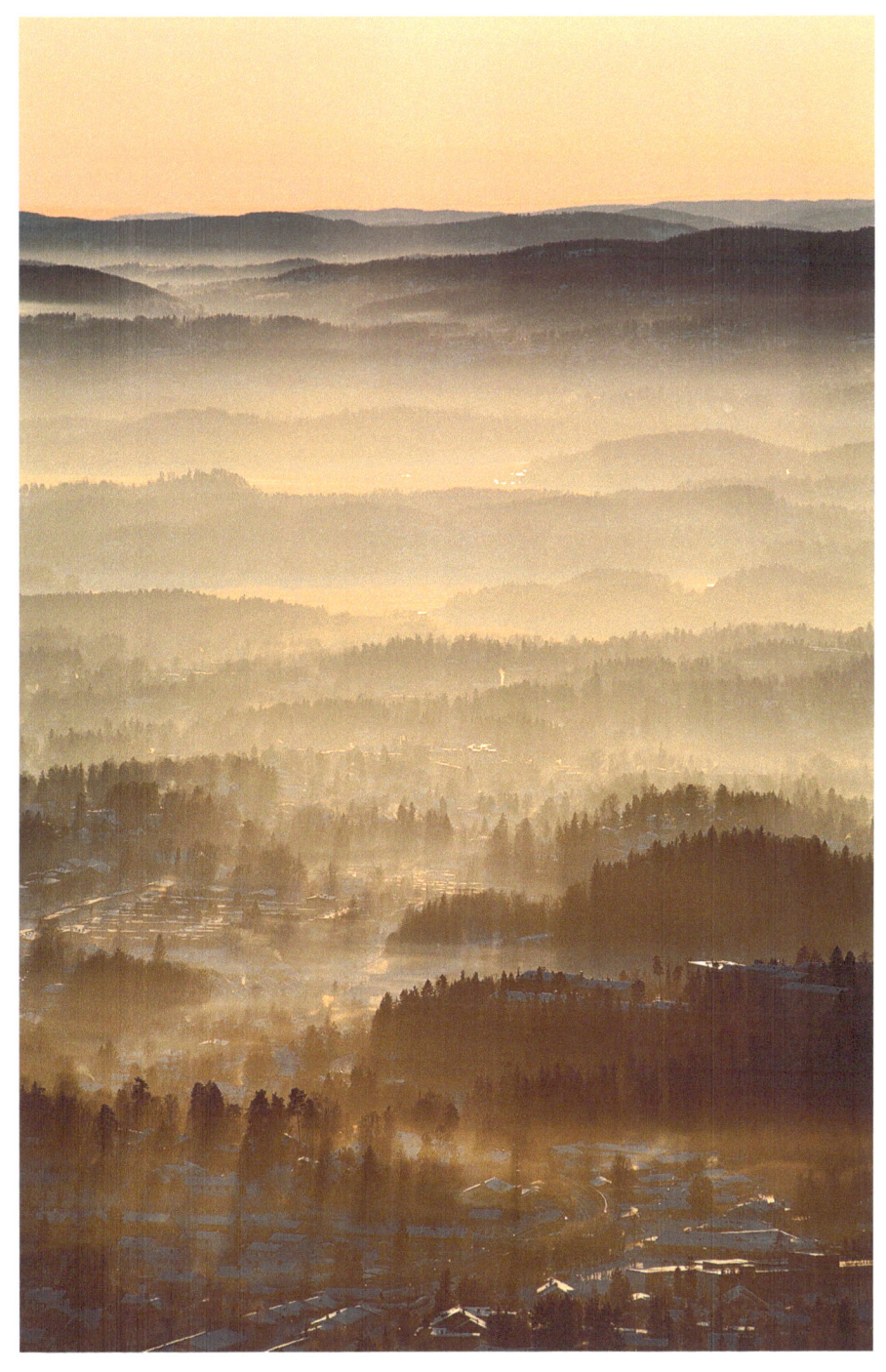

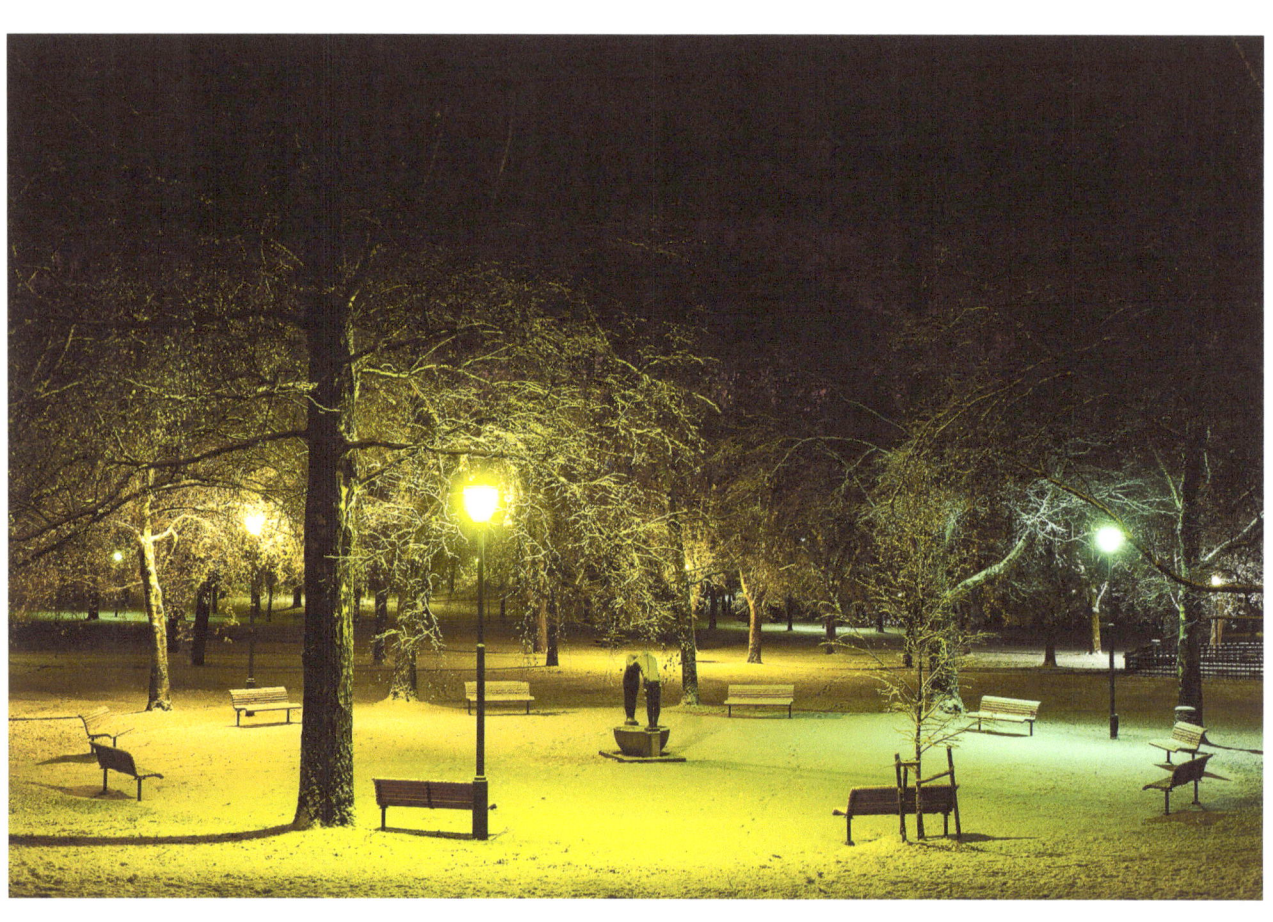

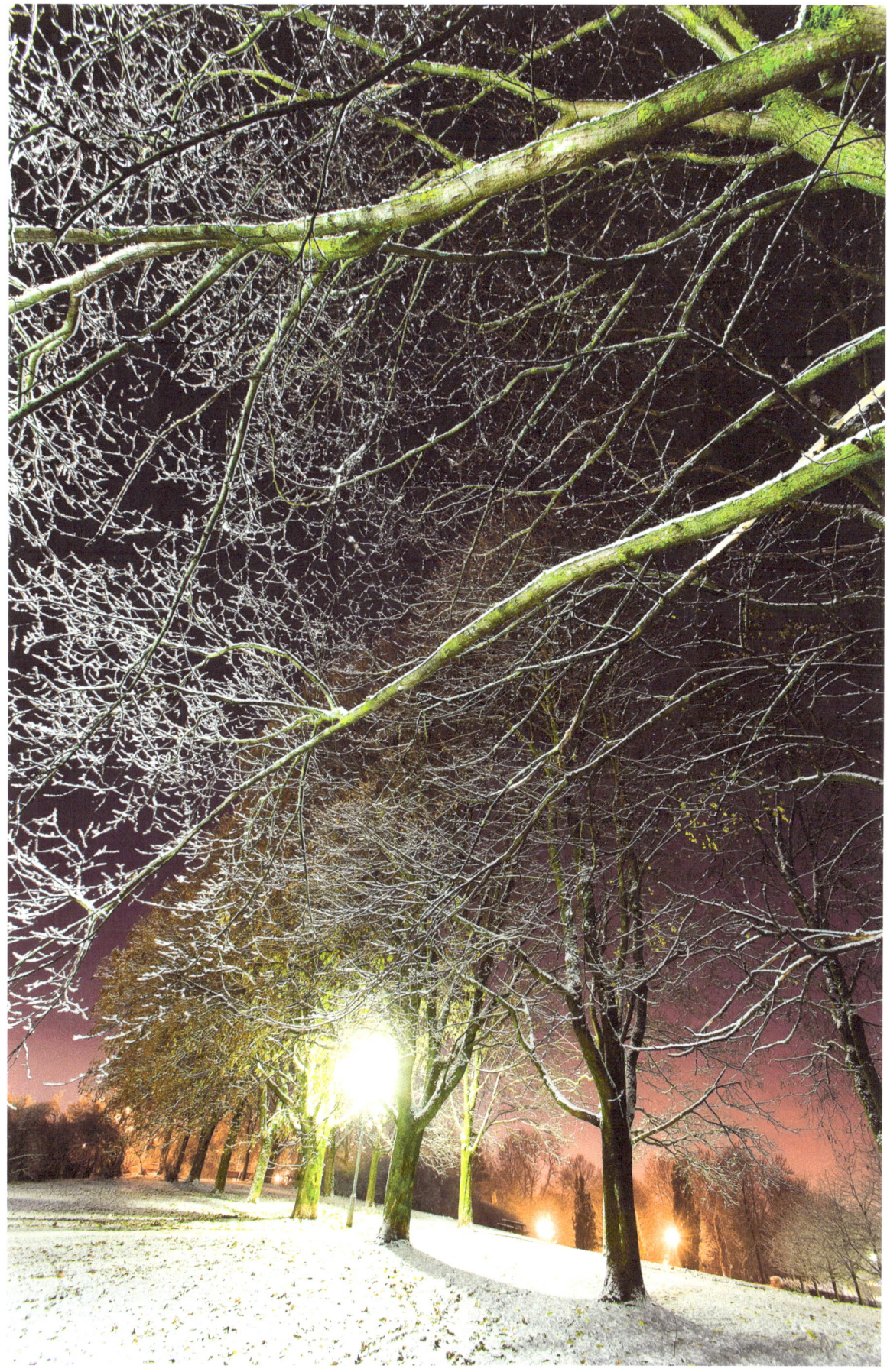

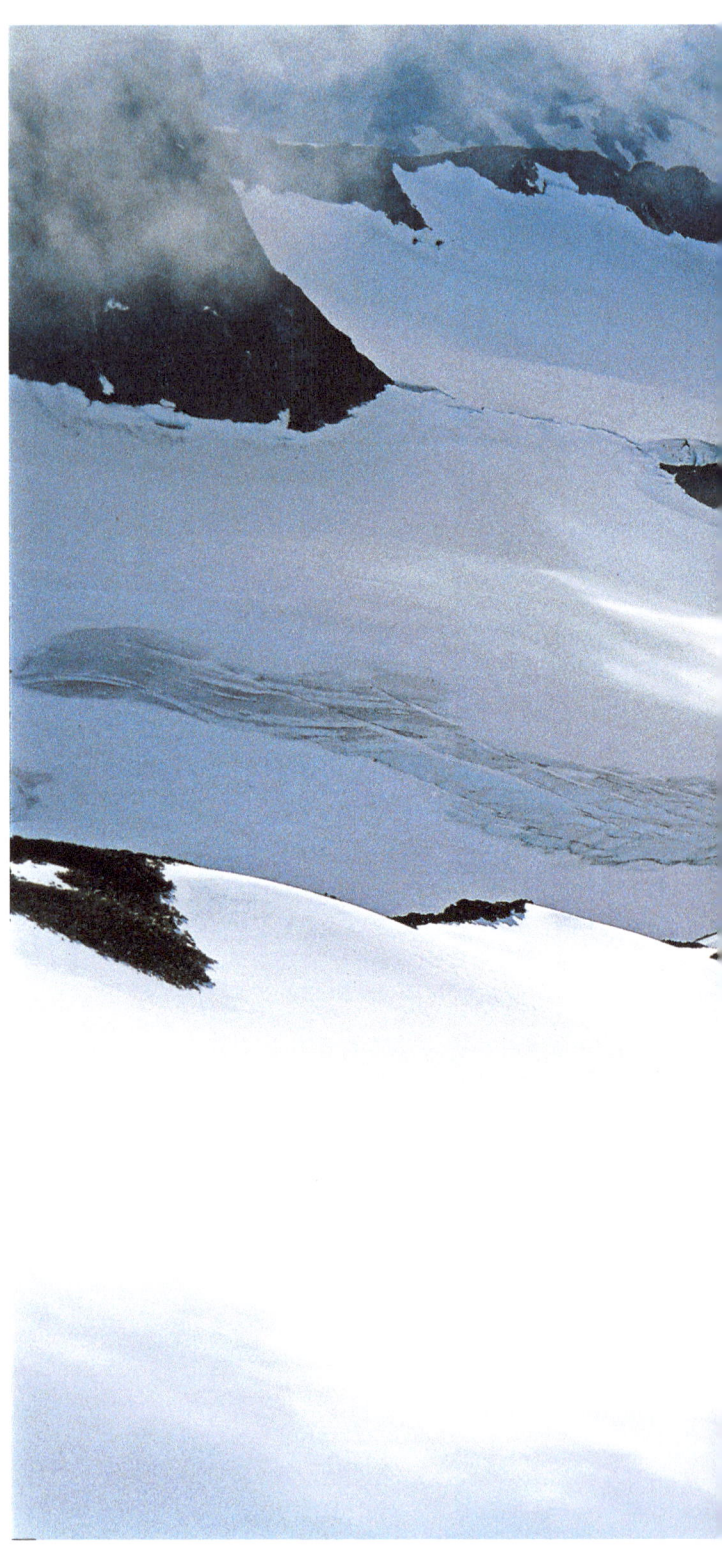

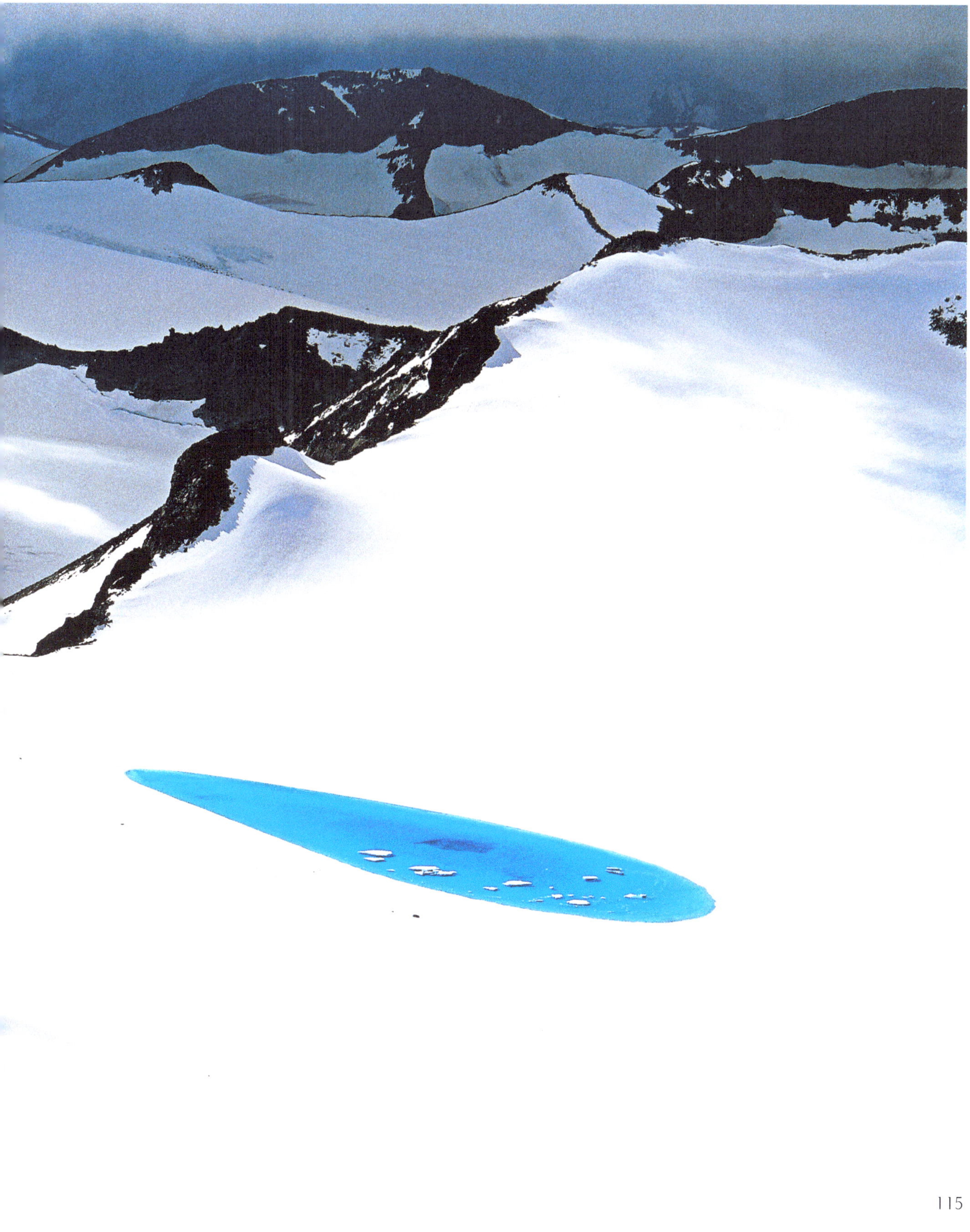

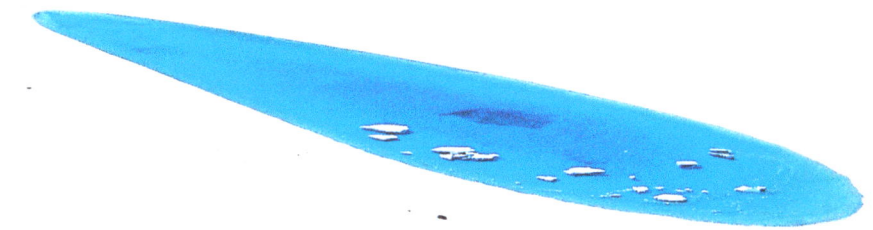

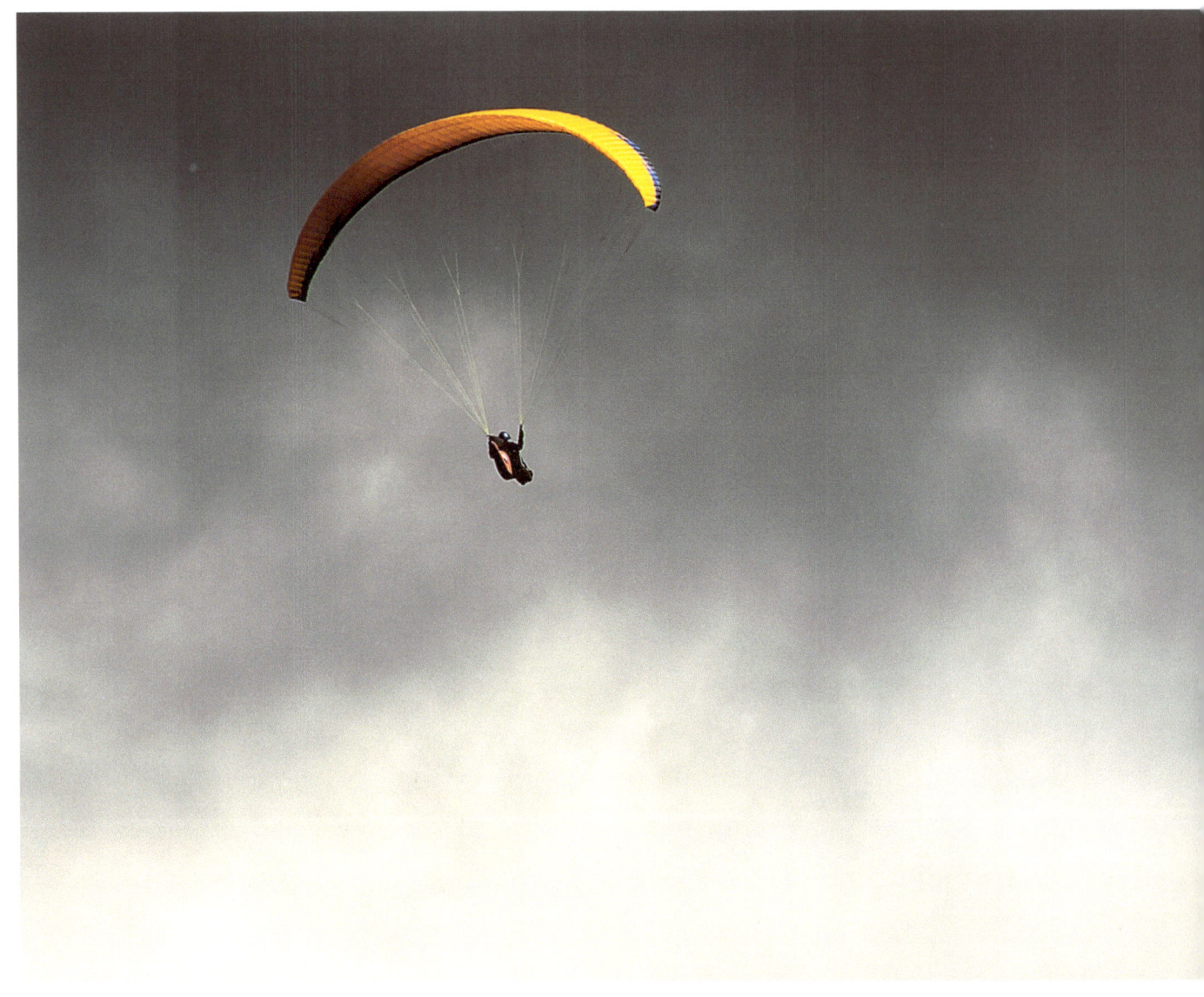

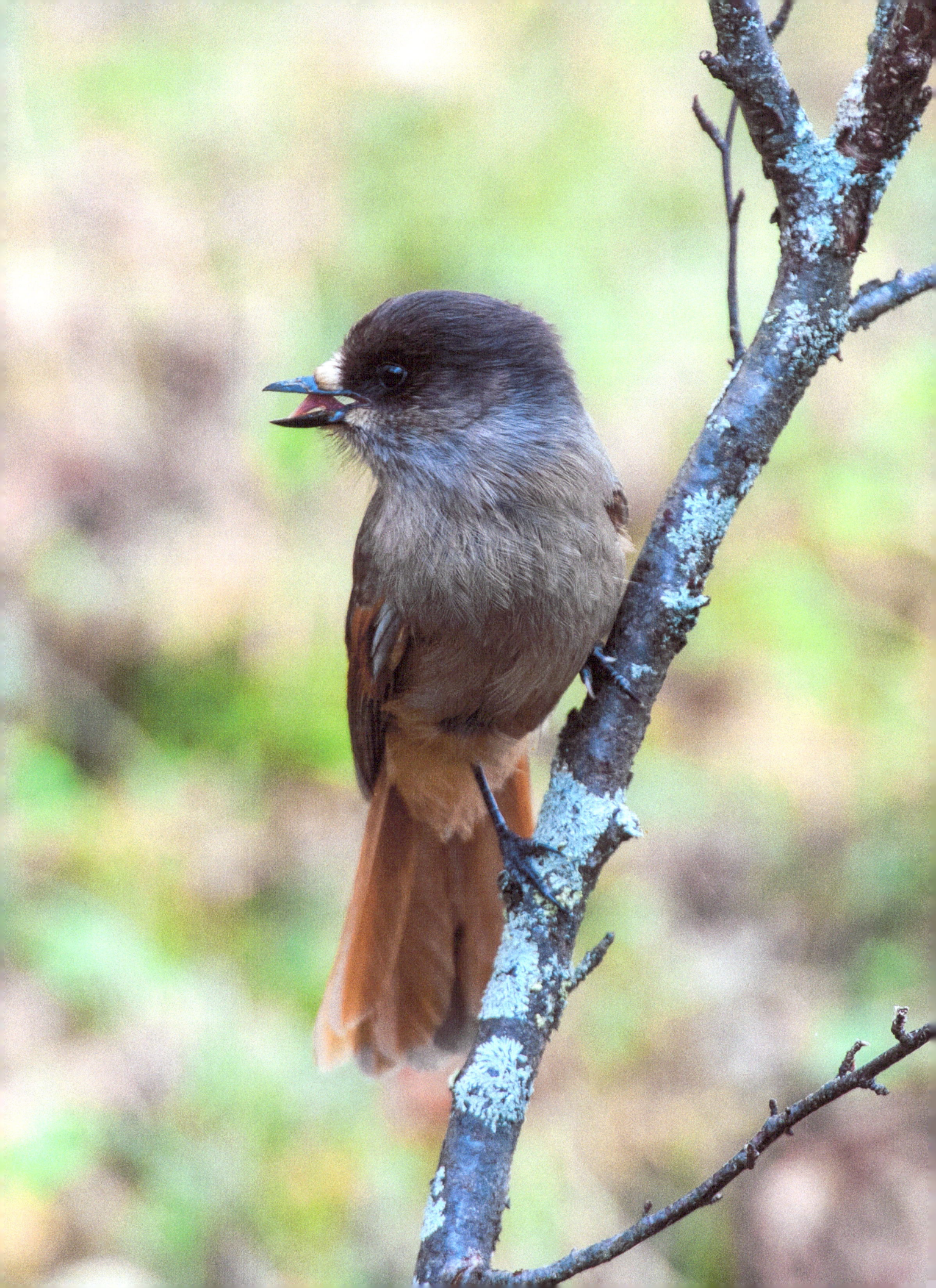

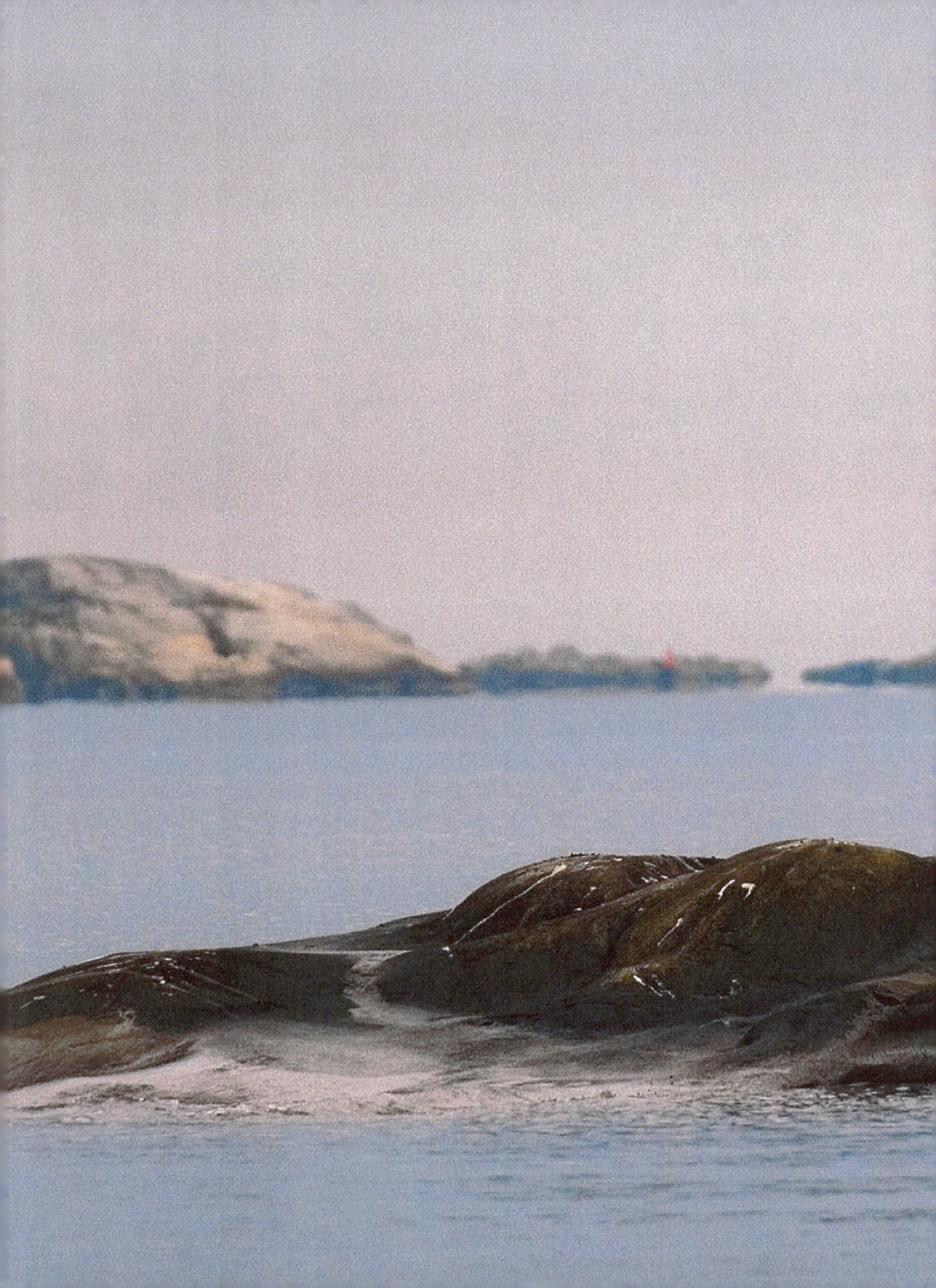

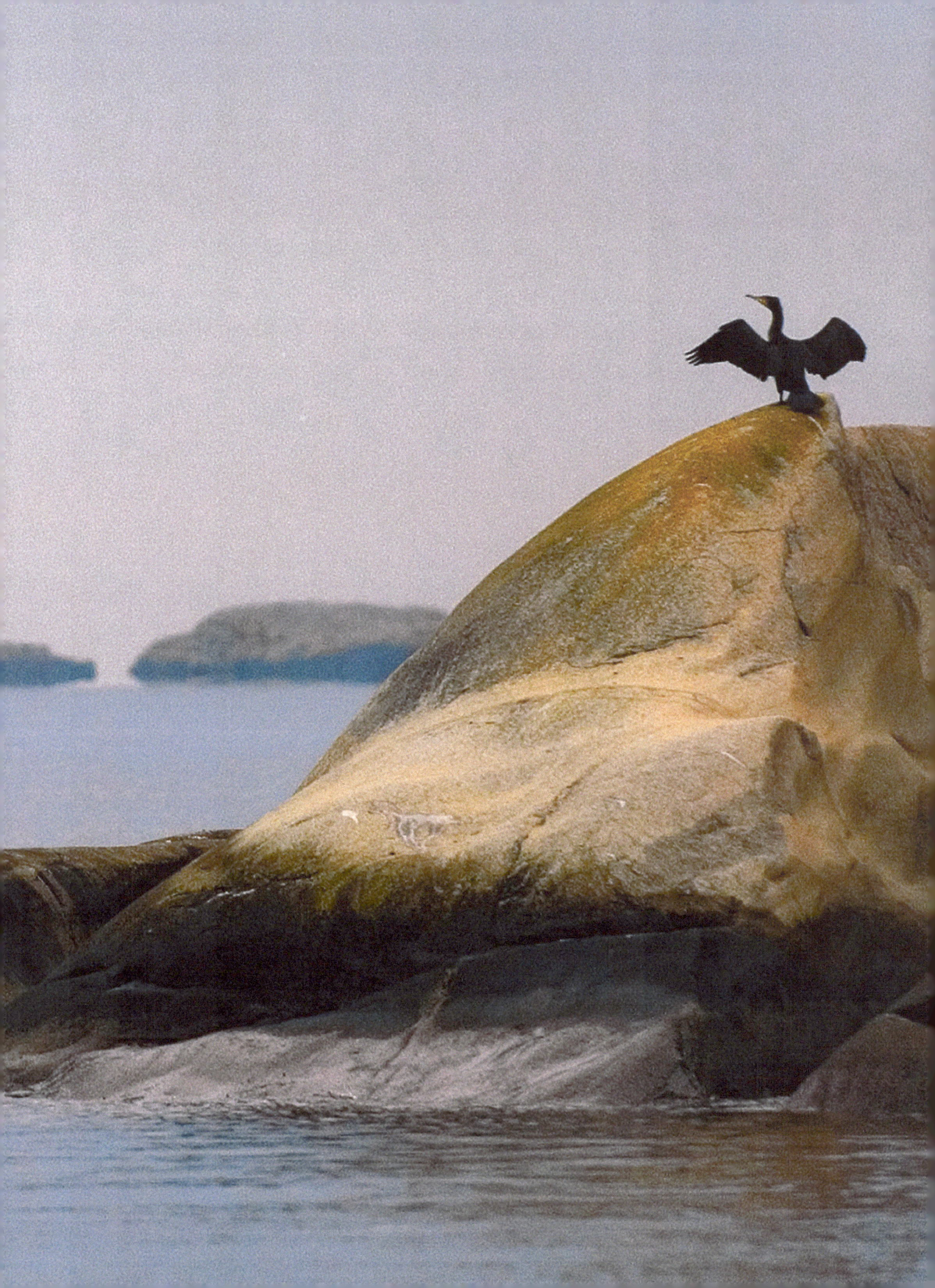

Index of photographs

2 – My Heart Belongs To You, Hemsedal
7 – Roarvika, Lofoten
8 – Bird View, Lofoten
10, 11 – Svenner Fyr (Lighthouse), Vestfold
12 – Kvalvika Beach, Lofoten
14 – Wooden Boat, Lofoten
15 – Boat At Bay, Lofoten
17 – Colourful Bow, Bergen
19 – Boat On Lake, Tyrifjorden
20, 21 – Leaving Norway, Sandefjord
22, 23 – Tree Boats, Stavern
24 – Reine, Lofoten
26 – Ormoeya, Oslo
28, 29 – Fishing Boat At Dock, Lofoten
30 – Boat And Mountains, Boede
32 – Traditional Rorbu, Reine
35 – Boathouse, Lofoten
36 – Boathouse By Sea, Lofoten
38 – Lonely House, Bergen
39 – Kalvanes Houses
40 – Barcode, Oslo
42 – Graffiti By Blaa Club, Oslo
43 – Colourful Doors, Stavanger
44 – Houses And Riverband, Lofoten
46 – Three Colours, Hemsedal
47 – Door In Hemsedal
49 – House Under Mountains, Sogndal
50 – Old House, Hemsedal
52 – Bryggen, Bergen
55 – Urasaetra
56 – Lonely House, Fargenes
57 – Boathouse And Mountains, Vesteraalen
58 – Courage, Svolvaer
60, 61 – Sunset Over Runde
62 – Naeroeyfjord Landscape
64 – Mountains And People, Kjerag
66 – Lysefjorden
67 – Lysefjorden
68 – Bessegen, Jotunheimen
71 – Ice On Bessvatnet, Jotunheimen
72 – Stone By Besseggen, Jotunheimen
74 – Green Mirror, Fargenes
76 – Rjukandefossen, Rjukan
78 – Trees And Lake, Drangedal
79 – Trees And River, Larvik
80 – Skomakertjern Lake, Nordmarka

82 – Trees In The Autumn, Sandvika
83 – Golden Trees, Oslo
84 – Lysebottaane, Hemsedal
86 – Autumn In Nittedal
88 – Tree By A Waterfall, Dammvann
89 – Path In The Woods, Oslo
91 – Colour Abstraction, Drammen
93 – Autumn By Vavatn, Hemsedal
95 – Sun In The Jungle, Hemsedal
96, 97 – Autumn Colours, Nittedal
98, 99 – Lonely Tree, Nittedal
101 – Bogstadvannet, Oslo
102, 103 – Stream Reflection, Nordmarka
105 – Icicles, Nordmarka
106, 107 – Frozen Kingdom, Blaafjell
108, 109 – Icicles, Lillomarka
110 – Church In The Morning Fog, Holmenkollen
111 – Mystic Sunset, Holmenkollen
112 – Mystic Vigeland Park, Oslo
113 – Winter Knocking, Oslo
114, 115 – Ice Lake, Jotunheimen
116, 117 – Paragliding In Hemsedal
119 – Siberian Jay, Hemsedal
120, 121 – Ha Det Bra, Sandefjord

www.ingramcontent.com/pod-product-compliance
Lightning Source LLC
Chambersburg PA
CBHW051151220526
45473CB00003B/730